URBAN REVOLT

URBAN REVOLT

Ethnic Politics in the Nineteenth-Century Chicago Labor Movement

ERIC L. HIRSCH

UNIVERSITY OF CALIFORNIA PRESS
BERKELEY   LOS ANGELES   OXFORD

University of California Press
Berkeley and Los Angeles, California

University of California Press, Ltd.
Oxford, England

© 1990 by
The Regents of the University of California

Library of Congress Cataloging-in-Publication Data

Hirsch, Eric L., 1952–
    Urban revolt: ethnic politics in the nineteenth-century
Chicago labor movement / Eric L. Hirsch.
        p.   cm.
    Bibliography: p.
    Includes index.
    ISBN 0-520-06585-9 (alk. paper)
    1. Working class—Illinois—Chicago—History—19th
century. 2. Labor movement—Illinois—Chicago—History—
19th century. I. Title.
HD8079.C4H57   1990
322'.2'0977311—dc20   89-4885
                                                                CIP

Printed in the United States of America
1   2   3   4   5   6   7   8   9

This book is dedicated with all my love to
Alex and Liza

Contents

Illustrations

Tables

Preface

I became interested in nineteenth-century Chicago labor history in an indirect way. I had begun a study of political mobilization in Chicago community organizing and felt that I could not understand the political process that led to such mobilization without also understanding the underlying political and economic forces that created issues for community groups. I undertook a study of disinvestment in an aging industrial city—investigating Chicago's loss of thousands of manufacturing jobs, the denial of mortgages and loans to black inner-city neighborhoods, and the flight of many middle-class residents to the suburbs. The political and economic consequences of these underlying trends resulted in the mobilization of community groups to fight job loss, crime, redlining, and housing abandonment.

I also became fascinated with the idea of comparing movements that arose as a result of decline and disinvestment with movements that responded to growth and investment in Chicago in its early history. I wanted to be able to answer the question how movements reacting to industrialization and urbanization in nineteenth-century Chicago differed from movements responding to deindustrialization and population loss. I also wanted to understand why the protest movements in the nineteenth century were generally labor oriented, but post–World War II, twentieth-century protests were more likely to be carried out by community organizations.

This interest led me to study the Chicago labor movement in the 1870s and 1880s, a period of industrialization and urban growth. I found an incredibly active movement that included strong craft unions, militant strikes by the less skilled, and highly mobilized, revolutionary socialist and anarchist tendencies. There was great diversity in political choice within the movement; it varied from passivity to mild reformism to anarchism.

The revolutionary tendency in Chicago in this period was not a marginal political sect; it may have been the most highly mobilized urban revolutionary movement in American history. Many workers believed that the economic and political system was the real source of their problems, and thousands participated in strikes, rallies, marches, and boycotts to try to change that system. Worker political actions in the 1870s included marches by tens of thousands of unemployed to protest an unfair and corrupt relief system; the formation of a political party—the Workingmen's Party of Illinois, which included in its platform such demands as an end to monopolies and the establishment of government ownership of several industries; a week-long general strike in 1877; and the formation of a socialist party that elected a number of legislators to city and state office.

In the 1880s, the revolutionary anarchist movement was founded. At its peak in the mid 1880s, the Chicago anarchist movement was the most highly mobilized in the country; it had seventeen political clubs with a total of one thousand members and five or six thousand sympathizers. A coalition of anarchist labor unions—the Central Labor Union—contained twenty-two unions, including the eleven largest in the city.

The platform at the anarchists' founding convention rejected the electoral system, argued that political institutions were agencies of the propertied class, and proposed that the only recourse was force. They advocated using whatever means necessary to destroy existing class rule, to establish a free society based on the cooperative organization of production, and to replace government with a system of contracts between autonomous communes and associations. The anarchists demanded total transformation of the economic and political systems, and they suggested guns and bombs to accomplish that aim.

But the movement was soon crushed. On May 4, 1886, several hundred Chicago workers gathered near Haymarket Square to hear speeches protesting the police killing of a striker the day before. When hundreds of police arrived to break up the peaceful meeting, someone threw a bomb into their ranks; the blast itself and the subsequent shooting by the police killed seven and wounded dozens of workers and officers. In the aftermath of the bombing, the authorities arrested hundreds of labor movement activists, shut down many labor-oriented newspapers, and banned all political meetings. There was little outcry a year and a half later when four anarchists blamed for the bombing—the Haymarket martyrs—were hanged, and one committed suicide to escape the hangman's noose.

In the following pages, I present an analysis of which workers joined various political segments of the Chicago labor movement and why. The time period covered is one of intensive industrialization and urban growth from the end of the Civil War until the Haymarket affair. The beginning point coincides with the onset of industrialization in the city; the end point was chosen because of the decline of the revolutionary anarchist movement following Haymarket.

At first I believed that a Marxist perspective would be best for interpreting the mobilization pattern in the Chicago labor movement. I expected to find that the periodic depressions and the constant tendency toward skill degradation in the crafts had created a politically united, class-conscious working class that had challenged the city's economic and political systems. Such was not the case. Instead I discovered a politically divided working class. Some workers were politically inactive, some worked to reform the existing system, and others worked actively to overthrow the economic and political order of the city. Recruitment to these various segments was based primarily on the workers' ethnic origins. The primary task then became to explain the reasons for these ethnically based political splits within the Chicago labor movement.

I also found that the existing theories of urban social and political movements could not adequately explain the mobilization pattern in the Chicago labor movement. *Marxist theory* overemphasizes the importance of economic class; ethnically based movements not built on the growth of working-class consciousness cannot be adequately analyzed within this tradition. The theory pays too much attention to analysis of macro-level, abstract class issues and neglects to adequately consider cultural factors and the importance of social networks in political mobilization efforts. Even revisionist Marxists, who have attempted to deal with the importance of cultural and social structural factors, often assume the development of working-class consciousness and movements based on such consciousness; this assumption is not always correct.

Classical urban social movement theory, growing out of the Chicago School of Sociology, considers important social and cultural factors. One might expect it to do a better job of analyzing ethnically based fragmentation in a labor movement; but its key propositions—that movements are a product of social disorganization and their participants are generally the socially marginal—are incorrect. In fact, movements are often built using social networks and cultural traditions found in close-knit urban communities, and participants in those movements are socially and culturally integrated.

Resource mobilization theory suggests that modern urban movements are likely to be bureaucratic, centralized, and hierarchical and to involve rationally calculating individuals who assess the costs and benefits of movement participation. This theory can explain some of the tendencies within the Chicago labor movement— notably the largely Anglo-American reform union tendency; but it cannot explain the revolutionary tendencies in the movement, tendencies that were nonbureaucratic and decentralized and that convinced participants to sacrifice their own self-interest to a group cause.

A fourth theoretical alternative, *solidarity theory*, better explains the mobilization of these revolutionary movements. The strengths and weaknesses of each of these theories are detailed in Chapter 6. However, the research concerns addressed here— especially the importance of class versus ethnicity in urban political mobilization and the reasons for reformist versus revolutionary responses to industrialization and urbanization—have grown out of the historical analysis. They have not been predetermined by allegiance to any of these theoretical traditions.

Although I try to explain the mobilization pattern in the Chicago labor movement for this period, the relevance of the findings for American workers in general or for theories of mobilization or revolution are subject to the reader's interpretation. Chicago was unusual in many ways, especially in the rapidity of its growth and industrialization and in its incredible ethnic diversity. An adequate explanation for the mobilization pattern in the Chicago labor movement in this period will not automatically be relevant to other movements in other places under different historical circumstances.

Chapter 1 describes the labor movement in Chicago from the end of the Civil War through the 1870s. Chapter 2 continues the history through 1886, the year of the Haymarket bombing. These first chapters give a historical account of events, but both also consider the ideologies, tactical choices, and social composition of the various reformist and revolutionary tendencies within the labor movement. I consider whether each tendency recruited different class sectors, trades, skill levels, ethnic groups, and genders. The evidence shows that the worker's ethnic origin was the best predictor of which tendency was chosen. Chapters 3, 4, and 5 discuss the reasons for these particular political choices for the three most important ethnic groups in the city—Anglo-Americans, Irish, and Germans. Chapter 6, which concludes the book, details theories of urban social and political movements.

A number of people were important in the completion of this book. I would especially like to thank certain authors whose work gave me important insights: Craig Calhoun, Manuel Castells, Sara Evans, John Foster, Jo Freeman, William Gamson, Bert Klandermans, Doug McAdam, John Mollenkopf, and E. P. Thompson. The work of two great Chicago historians—Bessie Pierce and Richard Schneirov—was simply indispensable, as was the assistance of the staff of the Chicago Historical Society, especially Archie Motley. The hard work of Naomi Schneider, Steve Rice, Amy Klatzkin, and Sylvia Stein at the University of California Press made this a much better book. A number of people read the manuscript at various stages of completion and made helpful suggestions. These include Sig Diamond, Roberta Garner, Ira Katznelson, Richard Taub, Bill Wilson, and three anonymous reviewers for the Press. Finally, I thank Andrea, Ann, Carol, Deborah, Don, Jane, Jeff, Lexi, Peg, and my father. Each was able to give me a different kind of support, all of which I appreciated.

Chapter One

Ethnic Segmentation in the Early Chicago Labor Movement

The setting for the rise of the Chicago labor movement was a rapidly growing industrial city. Although Chicago was founded in the mid nineteenth century as a commercial city, much of its economic growth in the post–Civil War period came in manufacturing. As the United States grew to the west, Chicago became the largest, most accessible city capable of transforming raw materials into finished manufactured goods and distributing them to consumers. The number of manufacturing establishments increased from 129 in 1860 to 730 in 1873 (Schoff 1873, 198). Those 730 establishments employed over fifty thousand workers, had over $50 million in invested capital, paid nearly $30 million in wages to employees, and created nearly $130 million in production value. By 1880, Chicago was the third most important manufacturing city in the country (Pierce 1957, 2: 147–75), with nearly four thousand manufacturing establishments, over eighty thousand employees, $85 million in invested capital, $40 million in payrolls, and $269 million in production value (Andreas 1884, 3: 715). Many of these manufacturing establishments clustered around the three branches of the Chicago River and the many railroad lines that met in the city's center (Hoyt 1933, 95–96; Schneirov 1975, 3–4).

But the industrialization of Chicago did not affect all city residents in the same way. Upper-class capitalists, such as Cyrus McCormick, George Pullman, and Philip Armour, realized huge profits and amassed large fortunes. Middle-class professionals and small businessmen cashed in on the need for services and the expansion of local markets. But the working class was not treated as kindly. Problems arose for the workers because of uneven economic growth and employers' incentives to reduce wages to the lowest possible level through mechanization.

Even in the most rapidly growing cities like Chicago, the business cycle—periodic booms followed by devastating busts—meant workers experienced long periods of unemployment and low wages. The business cycle was not the only problem. Mechanization introduced labor-saving devices into a variety of trades, reducing the skill level of many craft jobs. The use of labor-saving devices to degrade skills increased the number of potential workers available to perform particular jobs, thus allowing employers to reduce wages, resist union organizing, break strikes, and force workers to accept long hours and poor working conditions. Many craft workers consequently faced the prospect of higher unemployment, lower wages, and more alienating working conditions in this period; some of them fought back with the most powerful economic weapon at their disposal: the craft union.

The Craft Union Model of Economic Action

The ability of skilled workers in a particular trade to enjoy relative economic comfort was due largely to the ability or inability of those in the craft to organize a strong union. Some workers established unions that successfully fought both aggressive employers and the effects of the business cycle and mechanization. One of the most powerful unions and the first in the city was the Chicago Typographical Union no. 16 (Chicago Typographical Union, 1864–1887, 1880), founded in the early 1850s by fifty-four printers. Printers historically have been able to organize strong unions because their literacy and ability to print trade papers and newsletters allows for better communication between members of the trade.

The printers union was dramatically successful in its attempt to control the effects of the introduction of technology in the trade. The most important machine introduced into the printing trade in this period was the linotype, which allowed typesetting by keyboard rather than by hand. Even though a linotype machine is not much more difficult to operate than a typewriter, printers unions throughout the country were able to insist that linotype operators have three- or four-year apprenticeships and belong to the union (Barnett 1909). Their use of strikes, boycotts, and threats of mob actions allowed them to preserve a high degree of control over the labor supply in the trade, which in turn preserved high wages and employment security even during business slumps.

The union attempted to define the conditions under which its members were willing to work and then tried to impose these conditions on employers. Wage rates, for example, were not subject to negotiation in the early history of the union. Instead the Chicago Typographical Union simply published a list of prices and refused to allow its members to work below these rates. Employers who violated union rules faced strikes and boycotts, and the Chicago Typographical Union often fined, suspended, or expelled printers working at nonunion rates. Printers who refused to join the union were labeled "rats" and were socially scorned and morally condemned by union printers.

Non-membership [in a printers union], as a rule, arises from one of two causes—incompetency or moral cowardice—and no valid reason can be assigned why an honorable, qualified workman should refuse to identify with an organization which secures the highest remuneration for his services and whose primary and essential objects are his financial and material welfare. We insist the mechanic who refuses or neglects to identify himself with his trades organization is a libel on the human race, and unworthy of the name of protector, husband or father. (*Inland Printer* March 1884, 11)

By the end of the Civil War, other trades had followed the printers' lead and founded craft unions along a similar model. The Mechanics Union, founded in 1852, was followed by the Iron Molders in 1857, the Machinists and Blacksmiths in 1859, the Shipwrights and Caulkers in 1860, the Seamen and the Foundry Workers unions in 1861, the Painters and the Locomotive Engineers in 1863, and the Plasterers and Bricklayers and Stonemasons in 1864 (Pierce 1957, 2: 160–68).

Unfortunately, this solution to the problems faced by the city's working class was not available to all workers. Unlike industrial unions, which employ the *inclusive* strategy of attempting to organize all those hired by employers in a particular industry, craft unions such as the Chicago Typographical Union employed a conservative strategy of limiting the labor supply, of *excluding* groups from participating in the trade. Craft union power comes from its ability to control the labor supply through apprenticeship systems. Four-year apprenticeships were the rule, and the union required employers to hire only those who had completed such training. So everyone was not welcome to join the union; generally only friends and relatives of members were offered apprenticeships.

The use of the craft union organizing model meant that entire groups, such as immigrants, women, or prison inmates, often were excluded from the trade. This frequently relegated the excluded group to unskilled work or—in the case of women workers in the city—to low-paying sweatshop labor. This attitude is illustrated by the following quotes from Chicago's major printing trade journal, the *Inland Printer*. It is interesting that their argument used moral persuasion, not the assertion that excluding certain groups from the trade would have economic benefits for the largely Anglo-American male printers.

Probably the principal reason that there are so few lady compositors in our printing houses is the long time required to perfect anyone in the art. As a general thing, women do not engage in any kind of business except as a temporary employment, their ultimate goal being to preside over a household. (December 1883, 9)

[It is wrong to compel] her to earn her living by following a trade which requires three years of application to master, to which she is altogether unsuited by her taste and condition, while the tendency of that labor must inevitably lead to the lowering of the standard of workmanship . . . the tendency to force women . . . into indiscriminate competition with men must eventually prove disastrous to both, and is calculated to lower her in the social and moral scale. (September 1885, 534)

There is a vast difference between compelling the law-breaker to earn his living by the sweat of his brow and aggregating the crime of the state in two or three branches of industry, compelling those callings to bear the brunt of such crime, and leasing the labor of the convicts to unprincipled speculators for their own enrichment. (November 1884, 65)

Thus, the power of the craft union model was to define a limited group of eligibles and to exclude everyone else. In certain trades—especially printing, construction, machine, and iron and steel—workers were able to use this tactic to limit the adverse impact of depressions and mechanization; they managed to keep their wages fairly high and to mitigate the effects of unemployment with work-sharing schemes (Barnett 1909, 213). A smaller percentage of unions was able to successfully combat the effects of mechanization.

In business expansions, there was prosperity for workers in unions that had enough control over the labor supply to force up their wages in tight labor markets. These workers often made significant gains in wages, working conditions, employment security, and union strength. But most workers could not enjoy the benefits of work-sharing schemes during depressions and wage hikes during expansions because most workers did not belong to unions.

Labor Market Segmentation

The craft union or even a coalition of craft unions was not a very powerful weapon for the economic and political organization of the city's working class because it was an exclusive, not an inclusive, strategy. The organizing model excluded large sectors of the working class—especially the unskilled and women—from the organized group of workers. Even within the targeted group of skilled male workers, organizing efforts were not always successful. Those trades with strong unions that had been organized before the onset of industrialization had an advantage over those that had to scramble to respond with new organizing efforts once they began to be hurt by mechanization and business slumps. Certain trades (construction, for example) had stronger unions because their technical basis made it more difficult to substitute machines for workers.

Thus, some skilled workers—such as cigar makers, boot and shoemakers, and butchers—did not fare well in this period. They suffered skill degradation and eventually the total destruction of their trades with the move to factory production. Positions formerly occupied by skilled workers were taken by semiskilled or even unskilled workers. The crafts lost control over the labor supply available to the employer, wage levels went down, and craft workers were forced out of their crafts and into less skilled, lower paying work. The cigar makers union, for example, had great difficulty coping with the introduction of labor-saving devices into their trade; by the 1890s, most cigars were made totally by machine (Baer 1933).

Skill degradation could often be accomplished without mechanization. In many trades, labor-intensive production allowed use of the *putting-out* system. Employers set up sweatshop textile, clothing, or cigar-making operations in any tenement and found workers—usually women—from among those excluded from the discriminatory craft unions. Employers reduced wages and broke strikes by decentralizing the trade into hundreds of hard-to-locate, hard-to-organize workplaces.

Thus, workers in many low-status skilled trades fought a losing battle against the introduction of machinery and less skilled labor. Their inability to limit the labor supply meant that their economic condition was not nearly as secure as that of workers in the printing, construction, and metalworking trades. Their wages were always lower and their unemployment rates higher than those of workers in the elite trades. Their problems were especially severe during business slumps, when their unions often ceased to exist, and their economic condition sank to the level of the unskilled. Few low-status skilled unions survived the 1873–1879 depression; most were forced to reorganize when the business expansion of 1879 began.

Unskilled workers—such as laborers, servants, teamsters, draymen, and porters—faced even worse economic prospects. Their lack of skills and the consequent large size of the labor pool available to break their strikes rendered them unable to form unions. Because they were often searching for better jobs, they also experienced high residential and job mobility; that mobility made them difficult to organize and led to their being labeled tramps. With very low income per wage earner, entire families often had to work. Eventually, the less skilled were forced to enlist the support of those who did possess scarce skills or found it necessary to develop alternative *industrial union* models of organizing in order to gain any leverage over their employers. In this period, however, they rarely managed to gain such leverage.

Because of their inability to organize, unskilled laborers' wages were about half those typically paid to skilled workers, and unemployment rates were up to four times those characteristic of the best organized crafts. Unskilled workers were unable to take economic advantage of business expansions; depressions resulted in tremendous hardship as their wage levels fell, and unemployment rose dramatically.

TABLE 1. *Average Daily Wages in Chicago, 1870–1886*
(in dollars)

Occupation	1870	1872	1874	1876	1878	1880	1882	1884	1886
Blacksmith	2.07	2.65	2.47	2.22	2.56	2.67	2.88	2.80	2.90
Boilermaker	2.23	2.83	2.58	2.28	2.84	2.90	2.90	2.90	2.90
Bricklayer	2.29	4.20	2.01	2.36	2.92	3.50	3.50	3.50	4.00
Machinist	2.22	2.68	2.43	2.22	2.64	2.73	2.78	2.75	2.75
Printer	2.37	2.94	2.82	2.75	2.92	3.00	3.00	3.00	3.00
Hod carrier	1.02	1.26	0.82	0.82	1.46	1.50	1.50	1.75	1.75
Laborer	1.29	1.59	1.41	1.25	1.46	1.58	1.59	1.50	1.50
Teamster	1.43	1.75	1.62	1.59	1.99	2.05	2.04	2.04	2.04

Source. U.S. Department of Labor Bulletin no. 18, September 1898, pp. 665–82. This is the best source available on Chicago wage rates for the period. The data were compiled directly from establishments doing business continuously in the city from 1870. The department controlled for currency deflation in the 1870–1878 figures. These have been recalculated to reflect actual wage rates.

Thus, industrialization did not have a monolithic impact on the working class. The impact varied according to skill level; the unskilled suffered much lower wages and higher unemployment than the skilled crafts. Even among the skilled trades, there was much variation in economic status based on the history of organization in the trade and the union's ability or inability to resist skill degradation caused by mechanization or sweatshop production.

Table 1 indicates the tremendous differences in Chicago wage levels for a variety of trades between 1870 and 1886. Even the serious depression from 1873 to 1879 did not bring wage levels of the most highly skilled trades down to the level of the unskilled. The skilled were generally able to keep wages over $2 per day, while the unskilled sank to depths as low as $.82 a day. Perhaps just as important, various trades had different degrees of employment stability; the unskilled had much higher rates of both short- and long-term unemployment than the skilled. These differences in earning power and employment stability translated into dramatic disparities in economic consumption.

Differential ability to respond to economic problems must be reflected in the concepts used to analyze the working class. It will be useful to divide the class into three categories: the *labor aristoc-*

racy, low-status skilled, and the *unskilled.* Membership in the labor aristocracy is based on early craft union organization and relative invulnerability to skill degradation based on trade characteristics. Included in this category were printers, tinners, iron molders, machinists, blacksmiths, locomotive engineers, railroad conductors, and many of the construction trades (brick makers, bricklayers, stonemasons, carpenters, painters, plasterers, plumbers). These were the first trades to organize in the city, all of them having established trade unions prior to the Civil War (Pierce 1940, 1: 160, 165). Effective organization allowed their members higher wage levels, lower unemployment levels, and higher levels of economic consumption than others in the working class.

Low-status skilled trades included the cigar makers, tailors, bakers, tanners, harness makers, brewers and maltsters, boot and shoemakers, butchers, coopers, and cabinetmakers. Most of these trades organized unions, but not until after the Civil War. For convenience, various types of factory operatives making their first appearance on the Chicago economic scene are also included in this category; their economic situation was similar to that of workers in the less skilled crafts. But it is important to understand that there were few factory operatives in this period. For example, there were only 688 mill and factory operatives listed in the 1880 Census out of about 40,000 workers in the low-status skilled category (U.S. Census of Population 1880, Table 36). The typical worker in this category was not a semiskilled operative in an automated factory but rather a skilled craftworker experiencing skill degradation due to the introduction of simple labor-saving devices and/or the increasing division of labor within the trade.

The unskilled were represented by the laborers, freight handlers, hod carriers, teamsters, servants, launderers and laundresses, messengers, packers, porters, and lumbermen. These workers, unable to create strong unions, faced low wages, high unemployment and job turnover, economic insecurity, and poverty.

The distribution of these three economic subgroups in the working class can be seen in Table 2. The unskilled are the largest category, accounting for about a third of the city's entire occupational structure in all three years. The low-status skilled represent a little less than one-fifth in 1870, one-quarter in 1880, and one-fifth in 1890. The labor aristocrats are about one-fifth of the distribution in all three census years.

TABLE 2. *Chicago's Occupational Structure, 1870, 1880, 1890*
(in percentages)

Class	1870	1880	1890
Upper middle and upper	12.7	12.2	11.5
Lower middle	16.5	17.7	20.1
Labor aristocracy	18.3	18.3	20.0
Low-status skilled	17.9	24.0	19.1
Unskilled	34.5	27.8	29.3
Total	99.9	100.0	100.0
N	97,725	166,498	393,069

Sources. 1870 Census of Population, Table 32, p. 782; 1880 Census of Population, Table 35, p. 566; 1890 Census of Population, Table 118, p. 650.

The relative stability of the percentages in different class groups should not lead to the conclusion that there was little individual mobility from one class to another. These group figures say nothing about individual mobility from group to group. In a period of rapid job growth, as was occurring in the Chicago labor market during this time, stable percentage figures may conceal significant individual mobility.

One striking fact is the tremendous size of the Chicago working class in this period. It represents around 70 percent of the occupational structure in all three census years. There was certainly the potential for the working class to be a major political force in the city based on sheer numbers alone. But that potential may have been reduced by the important economic differences between working-class segments, differences that might be expected to be reflected in political disparities within the class.

Earnings within the working class varied significantly according to sector. Table 3 shows that the mean earnings of the labor aristocrats were approximately $710 per year, compared to $487 for low-status skilled and $376 for the unskilled. Similar but smaller differences occur with regard to family income and savings. The aristocrats managed $752 versus $592 for the low-status skilled and $484 for the unskilled. The family income differences are narrower because those families with lower earnings from the primary wage earner were more likely to seek employment for spouses and children. As far as potential savings—the amount family income ex-

TABLE 3.   *Earnings of Head of Household, Family Income,*
and Savings for 1884, by Working-Class Sector
(in dollars)

Working-Class Sector	Earnings	Family Income	Savings
Labor aristocrats	710.49	752.44	34.68
Low-status skilled	487.41	592.05	−1.60
Unskilled	375.81	484.42	10.10

Source. 1884 Bureau of Labor Statistics Report.

ceeds expenses—the aristocrats saved around $35 per year, the low-status skilled had an average debt of $1.60, and the unskilled saved around $10. The aristocrats had greater earning power and a better life-style than the low-status skilled and the unskilled.

This three-category variable is an excellent predictor of earnings in the Chicago labor market. For 1884, it had a correlation of .68 with annual earnings (t-statistic of coefficient = 15.42, significant at the .001 level). This result can be interpreted as indicating the crucial role of strong craft unions in elevating the wages of Chicago workers.

Perhaps if industrialization had had a similar or characteristic effect on all or nearly all of the Chicago working class, there might have been a unified working-class response to the problems created by industrialization. But "what if" questions are difficult to answer. In fact, the differences in impact meant that the Chicago working class was economically segmented; different parts of it experienced different kinds of economic problems and had different capacities to respond to them. These disparities limited the possibility of a unified political response to industrialization and made working-class political fragmentation more likely.

The Beginning of the Labor Movement

There was no unified response by Chicago's working class to the problems caused by industrialization. Many workers never became active in labor politics at all. Among workers who did become active in the movement, there were important variations in approach. Some argued for *reform,* saying that the city's economic and political systems could meet the needs of the working class with some minor adjustments; others suggested that only a *revolution*, a new system, could meet those needs. These differences created severe factionalism that made unified working-class political action difficult at first and later impossible.

The reform tendency was founded in 1864 when a printers' strike led to the formation of the city's first trades assembly. The *Morning Post* had attempted to hire and train forty women compositors to work at cut rates. Using the exclusive strategy typical of elite craft unions, the Chicago Typographical Union no. 16 decided to strike and boycott the paper; the idea of including the women in the union was never considered (Chicago Typographical Union minutes 1864).

Boycotts require mass support, so the Chicago Typographical Union strikers tried to secure the cooperation of other unions; they called a meeting of all the union members in the city, paying the expenses of hall rent and brass band. Not wishing to alienate their friends in high places, the Chicago Typographical Union invited the mayor of Chicago to preside over the meeting and the editor of the *Evening Journal* to be the principal speaker (*Inland Printer* June 1886, 287–88). By the next year, the coalition that was formed as a result of this strike, the Chicago General Trades Assembly, had eighty-five hundred members in twenty-four unions (Pierce 1957, 3: 168).

Also founded in 1864 by the Chicago Typographical Union was the *Workingman's Advocate,* the first significant labor journal in the city.* Edited by a leader of the printers union, A. C. Cameron, the *Advocate* was the primary voice of the Chicago labor movement until it ceased publication in the mid 1870s.

The Trades Assembly and the *Advocate* did not attempt to challenge the underlying basis of Chicago's economic and political systems. Both had relatively privileged constituencies—the city's best organized, best paid, most stably employed labor aristocrats. The paper and the General Trades Assembly fought for candidates

---

*The *man* in the title of the paper and in the name of many of the period's workers associations indicates the discriminatory nature of the movement. There were few attempts to organize women workers but many successful attempts to exclude them from the crafts.

and for legislation to ameliorate the plight of the workingman in Chicago and not for the revolutionary overthrow of capitalism or representative democracy. Variation in economic conditions meant that the trades assembly was sometimes strong, sometimes weak, and sometimes nonexistent; but throughout the 1860s, 1870s, and 1880s, the assembly was *the* crucial advocate of labor reform in the city.

Labor movement factionalism was based on ethnic group membership, not only on economic factors. Many of the city's early unions, the Trades Assembly, and the reform tendency itself were dominated by the native born (Schneirov 1984, 18). Apprenticeships were given primarily to the sons of members or to the sons of members' friends and relatives; women, convicts, children, and non-Anglo immigrants were largely excluded from union membership. An exception was made for those of English, Welsh, and Scottish birth, who were often included in craft unions due to their skilled backgrounds, union organizing experience, and cultural similarity to the native born.

One response by non-Anglo immigrants to their exclusion from the elite native-born unions was to form ethnically based unions in each trade. These ethnic unions remained a crucial part of the labor movement throughout the period, providing an organizing base for an alternative to the Anglo-American labor reform tendency.

The first group to form such unions was the Germans, one of the biggest ethnic groups in the city with large numbers in the skilled working class and a tradition of guild organization. As early as the 1850s, Germans formed unions of the coach makers, carpenters, tailors, and cabinetmakers; and the German Trades Assembly actually was founded seven years before the largely Anglo General Trades Assembly. The German assembly had a membership of one thousand in 1865 (Pierce 1957, 2: 166–67), and two thousand members and a weekly paper by the spring of 1869 (Schneirov 1984, 37).

Certainly, there were some German advocates of labor reform. But from early on, many Germans were sympathetic to ideologies that asserted the need for more basic changes in the economic and political systems. Marxist ideas gained popularity because a number of political refugees of the German workers revolt of 1848 settled in Chicago. Among these "forty-eighters" was Josef Weydemeyer, a friend and correspondent of Karl Marx. These Germans published a Marxist paper called *Der Proletarier* as early as 1853 (Pierce 1957, 2: 186). The German Trades Assembly became an important forum for these revolutionary pronouncements, as did the German Social Democratic Turnverein, which were German nationalist gymnastic societies.

In 1858, representatives of German workers in the city appeared at the first congress of the International Workingmen's Association, which had been organized in New York the year before. The platform passed at the conference held that the right of revolution was guaranteed by the Declaration of Independence and that scientific, technical, commercial, and industrial progress had reached a stage that necessitated a change in the American form of government. They demanded the right to organize unions, protested against the treatment of labor by capital, and attacked political party platforms and private charity programs as offering no remedies for the working class (Pierce 1957, 2: 186). As early as the 1860s, there were important political differences between organized Anglo-American and German workers.

Also in the sixties, a new ideology, called Lassalleanism, began to compete with Marxism for the allegiance of the city's German workers. Lassalle stressed political action as the key to the emancipation of the working class and scorned trade unions as impotent, even irrelevant. Political action was seen as crucial because it could force the government to grant aid to workers' producer cooperatives, making these worker-owned institutions competitive with existing capitalist-owned firms. Eventually, Lassalle proposed, workers would control entire industries and markets, especially if the government could be forced to break up the monopolies that were beginning to dominate some industries (Foner 1955, 2: 414).

Marxists rejected this analysis, arguing that a workers party should not be formed until it could successfully influence elections and that the party would not be able to do that until it was based in a strong trade union movement. So there was a running, seesaw battle from the sixties until the eighties in the Chicago labor movement between Lassalleans and Marxists, that is, between political action advocates and economic action advocates. Which group dominated depended on the business cycle. During expansion periods, trade unions had many members and were strong because of the greater demand for labor; this led to the domination of the

Marxist position. During depressions, Lassallean ideas were dominant because weak unions rapidly disintegrated, economic action was precluded, and political action was viewed as the only viable remedy.

Certainly, the primary appeal of Lassalleanism was to German workers. But some of the native born, most notably A. C. Cameron, of the printers union, flirted with Lassallean ideas (Pierce 1957, 2: 188). Marxism, however, with its much more critical view of the capitalist economic and political system, *never* achieved significant allegiance from the native born.

Thus, the organizational and ideological context of the labor movement in the early seventies was as follows. Anglo-American skilled workers, that is, the native and British born, were organized in a trades assembly that advocated mild legislative reform as a response to the plight of the working class. Some progressive Anglo reformers advocated stronger measures such as cooperation to deal with the workers' plight. German workers were organized into the German Trades Assembly; Marxist, Lassallean, and reform ideologies and organizations competed for the allegiance of these German workers. The unskilled, including many of the city's third most numerous ethnic group, the Irish, were largely unorganized.

Early Response to the Depression: The Unemployed Marches and the International

Debates between advocates of reform versus revolution, between Anglo-American and German workers, were abstract until the mid 1870s, when a serious depression created severe economic problems for the working class. The depression, lasting from 1873 to 1879, resulted in a large number of business failures, and each new victim took with it many working-class jobs. As Pierce (1957, 3: 240–41) describes it:

Skilled and unskilled alike were thrown out of work, and where employees were retained, reductions in wages ensued. The growth of industry, which had been stimulated by the city's rebuilding [after the 1871 Chicago fire], stopped dead in its tracks. Closing banks swept away the savings of thrifty thousands, and even the rich were touched by the palsying depression.

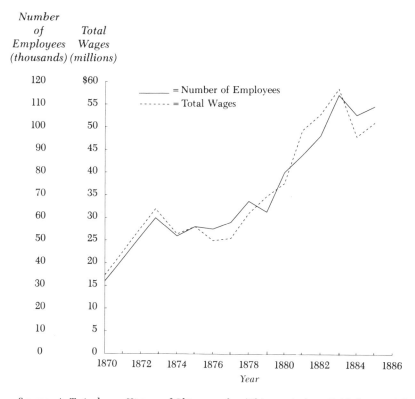

Source. A. T. Andreas, *History of Chicago*, vol. 3 (Chicago: Andreas Publishing, 1884), pp. 714–16.

Figure 1. Chicago business cycle, 1870–1885: Number of employees and total wages in manufacturing.

The trends in business activity can be seen clearly in Figure 1, which shows the number of employees and total wages in manufacturing establishments in the city for 1870 to 1885. Booms affected the city from 1870 to 1873 and from 1879 to 1884. A depression from 1873 to 1879 is clearly shown, as is the recession that began in 1884.

Prices were unstable as well. As can be seen in Figure 2, the effect of the depression was partially mitigated by falling prices from 1873 through 1878. But inflation often ate into any wage gains that the working class made during business expansions, such as during a boom beginning in 1879. From 1879 to 1882, wages re-

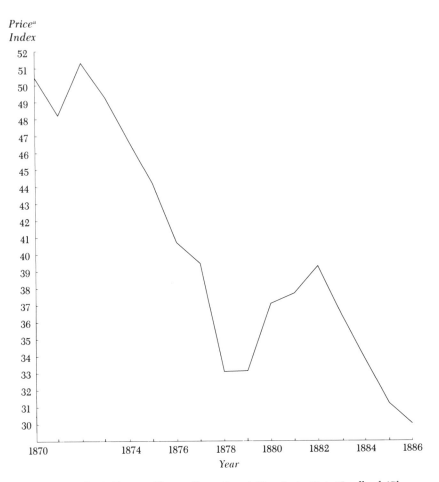

Price[a]
Index

Year

Source. Wesley J. Skogan, *Chicago Since 1840: A Time Series Data Handbook* (Champaign, Ill.: Institute of Government and Public Affairs, 1976), Table 2, p. 21.
[a]1959 = 100

Figure 2. United States price index, 1870–1886.

mained fairly stable while food prices and overall living costs increased at a rate of up to 33 percent a year (Pierce 1957, 3: 239).

The 1873 depression clearly threw many out of work; a study by the Relief and Aid Society in early 1874 found a 37 percent unemployment rate among the non–building trades. This means that the actual unemployment rate was probably even higher because the construction trades were recognized to have had the highest rate of joblessness (Schneirov 1975, 184). The most important result of this was to destroy many of the city's unions; unemployed workers do not pay union dues. By January 1874, there were only eleven mostly Anglo-American unions left in the city (Schneirov 1984, 43–44).

Only one union affiliated with the Marxist International Workingmen's Association, the German Carpenters and Joiners Union, was still in existence by this time. But some of the Marxists had formed a political club, the Social Political Workingmen's Union, in 1870; and it began to respond to the economic crisis with political action. Apparently this club had no Anglo-American members; it originally had four hundred members in three sections: one German, one French, and one Scandinavian (Schneirov 1975). By 1873, it had five hundred members in six sections: three German, one French, one Scandinavian, and one Polish.

On the advice of the leaders of the International in New York, the Chicago section organized a movement for the relief of the unemployed. They called for a meeting at a German *Turner hall* on West Twelfth Street on December 21, 1873 (Hillquit 1977, 183; Pierce 1957, 3: 241). But even this large hall was not large enough; five to seven thousand largely foreign-born workers packed it, and many were forced to wait outside. Speeches were made in German, Swedish, Polish, French, and English, but the first speaker was German, perhaps reflecting the high proportion of Germans in the audience. He expressed militant sentiments, maintaining that charity was inadequate and that it was high time a laborer became something other than a machine. "Our aristocratic rulers and manufacturers do not care whether laborers in the city die of starvation," he continued. "We must stand together and show the bloated aristocracy that laborers have some rights that must be respected" (*Chicago Tribune* December 22, 1873, 11). A Frenchman argued that it was not the workers' fault that they had nothing and the capitalists had everything. The laws were made for the aristocrats, not for the laborers. Workers must demand their rights. They were strangled by the biased press, by the bourgeoisie, and by the priests, all of whom did everything in their power to prevent the emancipation of the working classes (*Chicago Tribune* December 22, 1873).

Following a model provided by the national office of the International, the provisional committee formed by the workers resolved to demand "(1) work for all that are out of employment and able to work, on an eight hour per day basis; (2) advances to those able to support themselves; (3) a working class committee to be appointed to oversee the relief effort in order to insure that aid go only to those in real need; and (4) the use of city credit to obtain relief funds" (Foner 1955, 1: 445). There was loud applause and cheers for these resolutions; many of the workers approved of them.

Finally, there was a proposal to assemble the next night to march to the city council to pressure the council members to meet these demands. The Social Political Workingmen's Union planned to present six thousand signatures of unemployed workers—what they claimed was one-quarter of the unemployed in the city at this time—to the mayor and city council (*Chicago Tribune* December 23, 1873).

The procession took place as scheduled. The *Tribune* reported that there were twenty thousand marchers. Several dozen locked arms and led their fellow workers; two had flags; one had a drum. As Currey (1912, 2: 364–65) puts it, "The whole working class population seemed magically to have been drawn together; there appeared to be no leaders but the men fell into orderly lines; and they marched sometimes hand in hand as quietly as a funeral procession to City Hall." Workers carried placards with such sentiments as "Work or Bread!" "War to Idleness!" "Death to Destitution!" "One for All and All for One!" "United We Stand, Divided We Fall!" "Unity Gives Strength!"

The orderly crowd was unable to get close to city hall because three hundred police had many of the streets leading to it barricaded, but the demands were presented to the council nevertheless. The mayor and council assured the workers' representatives that they would respond to their grievances and resolutions; they appointed a committee to discuss the disbursement of funds to the destitute with the main organization responsible for poor relief in the city, the privately sponsored Relief and Aid Society.

The workers' view of the Relief and Aid Society was not a positive one. They charged that the society had taken many of the contributions for the relief of fire sufferers and had distributed them among its own members or to those with connections in high places (Flinn 1973, 147). Over $1 million had been contributed to the society, but as of late 1873, $700,000 had not been publicly distributed (Foner 1955, 1: 447). The workers committee demanded a meeting with society officials; the audience was at first denied, but the appearance of one thousand workers outside their offices changed their minds (Foner 1955, 1: 447). Following the meeting, the Relief and Aid Society announced that it would provide relief for the families of unemployed workers; 9,719 families were eventually provided with aid. But because no public jobs were ever offered by the mayor or city council, this was viewed as only a minor victory for those who had marched to protest unemployment (Pierce, 1957, 3: 242; Schneirov 1975, 184).

This first major militant demonstration by the Chicago working class was not an indication of class unity; it did not include significant numbers of native or British-born workers. The organizational work and hundreds of the participants came from the Workingmen's Union, which did not have an American section. The *Tribune* reported that the native-born workers were shocked by the demonstration, that it "fell upon the American portion of the population like lightning from a clear sky" (December 23, 1873, cited in Pierce 1957, 3: 241). The political differences between the Anglo-American and other foreign-born workers continued as the latter organized the city's first labor party.

The Workingmen's Party of Illinois

The unemployed marches continued throughout January. But many of the workers were dissatisfied with their inability to influence city officials through direct action. Naturally, they began to discuss the possibility of replacing those elected officials with others more sympathetic to their interests. Many suggested forming a political party to represent the interests of the rapidly growing working class in the city. On Sunday, January 11, 1874, two mass meetings were held by Chicago's workers to establish the Workingmen's Party of Illinois (WPI) (*Chicago Tribune* January 12, 1874).

The party represented a turn toward Lassalleanism and away from trade union action and organizing in the International. By March 1874, the WPI had twenty-two sections and seven thousand members. These sections generally consisted of workers of one nationality or language group. The party was overwhelmingly German; fifteen of the twenty-two sections were German, three were Bohemian,* three were Polish, and only one was American. There were no Irish or Scandinavian sections.

Not only the rank and file was overwhelmingly foreign born; the executive committee was foreign born, with only one exception. Moderate Anglo-American labor reformers were hostile to the WPI proposal that the government ought to provide employment to Chicago workers. As A. C. Cameron argued when the WPI was formed:

In a republican government, the State is not bound to find employment for the citizen. Here we have all the incentives to industry, frugality, and perseverance. If we were to admit the correctness of the theory that the State is bound to find employment for the citizen, we would destroy the noblest ambition in man, that of independence and he would become a simple pensioner. (*Workingman's Advocate* January 17, 1874, cited in Schneirov 1984, 63)

In an atmosphere of great hope, the party nominated several candidates for city council in north side, predominantly German wards. In the spring elections of 1874, the ticket got fewer than a thousand votes; in the fall of 1874, it received 785 votes, not even close to the twenty-five hundred party members were certain they had cast (Commons et al. 1918, 2: 229–30). The *Vorbote* claimed vote fraud (not the last time it would do so), and many in the party became disillusioned with electoral efforts. Eight sections of the party dissolved in the next four months, and there was no further participation in elections until spring 1877, when the party polled around six hundred fifty votes (Schneirov 1975, 13).

Typically, when political action failed, the pendulum moved back in the direction of the Marxists, with the workers again devoting themselves to trade union action in order to provide the foundation upon which political action could be based. This time was no exception. The Lassallean editor of the *Vorbote* was soon replaced with a Marxist, and the two remaining sections of the International were fused with the remnants of the WPI (Commons et al. 1918, 2: 230). This happened nationally as well; on July 15, 1876, delegates from the International met in Philadelphia and dissolved their or-

---

*Bohemians were immigrants from that part of Europe now known as Czechoslovakia.

ganization. They then joined the Workingmen's Party of the United States (WPUS), which was established several days later. The WPUS adopted a trade union emphasis consistent with Marxism, and Chicago—with 593 party members and the four thousand circulation German-language weekly *Vorbote*—became a center of WPUS activity (Foner 1976, 18).

The Marxists found plenty of economic action to support as strikes in 1875 and 1876 became increasingly militant. Violent strikes by outdoor laborers—mainly Irish coal heavers and brickyard workers and Bohemian lumberyard workers (called *lumber shovers*)—were opportunities for organizational work. The unskilled laborers had no scarce skills and no strong craft unions; the only alternative was to gather in large crowds to verbally and physically intimidate strikebreakers, to try to prevent scabs from replacing them on the job. Such *mass strikes* (Schneirov 1984, 147) had limited aims (usually higher wages) and were conducted by weak temporary economic organizations.

The common pattern was for workers in one company to collectively agree to strike. Those workers would form a band, arm themselves with clubs and other primitive weapons, and proceed to other unskilled workplaces—brickyards, lumberyards, coalyards—where they would convince workers to quit work and persuade employers to shut down their operations. Because the unskilled lived near their jobs, these mass strikes often mobilized community residents as well as workers; women, who did not necessarily work in the yards, often joined in crowd actions designed to enforce the strikes.

Skilled workers, especially Anglo-American trade unionists, showed little interest in these strikes. But the largely German WPI tried to support the unskilled strikers. Speaking at a strike rally of several thousand at a Bohemian Turner hall, a WPI leader suggested that the workers ought to drill with wooden rifles if they could not get real ones; when the time came, they would be able to acquire muskets and cartridges (Schneirov 1975, 11). Another suggested that a proletarian revolution would come "within a few decades if the ruling classes threatened to suffocate the labor movement" (Pierce 1957, 3: 243).

Physical intimidation played an important role in the mass strike model of economic action, giving both employers and the police an easy excuse to retaliate in kind. Confrontations between police and crowds of foreign-born workers were frequent by the mid 1870s. In 1876, a lumberyard owner shot and killed a striker and wounded three others attempting to prevent crowds of as many as fifteen hundred workers from enforcing a strike by Bohemian lumber shovers. When seven strike leaders were arrested, a contingent of four hundred marched to a police station to secure their release. The mayor was forced to close all gun shops when a committee of workers attempted to secure weapons. That same year striking brick makers gathered in Bridgeport to march to the North Side to tear down a prison where convicts were making bricks under contract. The police arrested twenty-five to prevent this march: eight Irish, five Germans, four native born, and the rest Scandinavians, Bohemians, and Poles (Schneirov 1975).

Some German workers responded to police repression by forming armed worker resistance groups called the *Lehr und Wehr Verein* (Educational and Resistance Societies) (David 1958, 57). Bohemian workers soon followed the lead of the Germans, forming their own society, called the *Lincoln Guards*. These militia units drilled regularly, practiced bayoneting, picket duty, deployment, skirmishing, and shooting in formation. The native born did not participate in these associations, and few of the city's Irish residents did either. These working-class units were more significant for the anxiety they caused the city's middle and upper classes than as actual military units; they represented little threat to the authorities because they had a peak strength of three hundred (Illinois State House of Representatives 1879, 39).

Although the strikes of the unskilled provided a few opportunities for political agitation by the mainly German members and leadership of the WPUS, the party did not have any real influence on the mass of Chicago workers until 1877, the year of the great railroad strike. As George Schilling, a party leader at the time, put it:

The daily press paid little or no attention to us in those days [before 1877]. We called public meetings in all parts of the city, but the masses were slow to move. Oft-times, after posting bills and paying for advertising, we were also compelled to contribute our last nickel for hall rent, and walk home instead of ride. At all these meetings A. R. Parsons was the only English speaker.

Our influence as a party, however, both in Chicago and elsewhere, was very limited until the great railroad strike of 1877. Before this the labor question was of little or no importance to the average citizen. The large mass of our people contented themselves with the belief that in this great and free Republic there was not room for real complaint. The idea that all Americans were on an equal footing seemed to be recognized as an incontrovertible fact in the halls of legislation, in the press, and the pulpit. (Parsons 1889, xvi–xvii)

July 1877:
Railroad Strike and General Strike

The strikes of the mid 1870s were but harbingers of much more serious events in 1877.* The depression had not abated, and the railroads decided to try to recoup some of their losses by cutting workers' wages. By 1877, most railroad workers had already suffered wage cuts of from 21 to 37 percent; still, late in May, several railroads announced that they would cut wages and salaries another 10 percent (Foner 1977, 28). On June 2, railroad workers formed the secret Trainmen's Union, an organization that aimed to organize all railroad workers for the sole purpose of carrying out a national railroad strike. The union successfully recruited all but the elite engineers and conductors along the entire Pennsylvania Railroad as well as other lines (Pennsylvania State Senate and House of Representatives 1878).

When the Baltimore and Ohio Railroad announced a 10 percent wage cut on July 16, 1877, the local section of the Trainmen's Union in Martinsburg, West Virginia, struck. The strike soon spread along the B & O line and then to other lines through Cumberland, Maryland, Newark, Ohio, and then to Pittsburgh and Chicago. Attempts to suppress the strike were unsuccessful because the local militia often threw down their arms or, as in the case of the Philadelphia militia, were driven from the city. Federal troops were called out in both Maryland and Pennsylvania to try to end the strike in those states (Foner 1977; Schneirov 1975, 14).

---

*The following account of the 1877 strike is based on a number of sources including Foner (1977) and a reading of the city's daily papers for the period. But I am most indebted to Richard Schneirov (1975), who has provided the most detailed account of the events that took place in Chicago during the strike.

Railroad workers in Chicago were discussing the strike two days after strike activity had begun in the east; most wanted higher wages (*Chicago Tribune* July 19 and 22, 1877). As the *Tribune* reported, "All hands felt hard towards the railroad company because they had reduced the poorest paid workingmen and left the President, Managers, superintendents and foremen alone" (July 22, 1877, 6). But the strike was mobilized primarily by the unskilled and semiskilled, predominantly Irish track laborers, switchmen, firemen, and brakemen. The more conservative engineers and conductors brotherhoods—dominated by the native born—spoke against the strike and never joined it (*Chicago Tribune* July 23, 1877).

The WPUS was quick to jump on the strike bandwagon. The party's national executive committee met and issued a directive to all local sections to support the railroad strike and to demand both government ownership of the railroads and telegraph companies and the eight-hour day (Schneirov 1975, 16). The Chicago section began agitation immediately, talking to railroaders on Friday, July 20, advocating a strike, and assuring the workers of their full support.

On Saturday night, the WPUS held a rally in a vacant lot at Twelfth and Halsted attended by over one thousand workers. Huge banners were displayed reading "Down with the Wages of Slavery!" "Why Does Our Production Cause Starvation!" "We Want Work, Not Charity!" WPUS leader Albert Parsons—the best known native-born socialist in the city—asked the crowd, "If the proprietor has a right to fix wages and say what labor is worth, then aren't we bound hand and foot—as slaves? We should be perfectly content with a bowl of rice and a rat a week!" He told them, "if the laboring man agrees to work 12 to 15 hours for the bosses and allows them to take five-sixths of the profit, then the laboringmen are themselves to blame" (*Chicago Tribune* July 23, 1877, 17). Parsons closed with the Lassallean demand for worker cooperatives and exhorted the working class to organize. They must "strike while the anvil is hot"; they must follow the example of the eastern strikers. Parsons, a veteran of the movement to free the slaves, often used the slavery analogy to describe the plight of Chicago's working class. An inspiring orator, he was cheered and applauded on this and on many future occasions.

The strike began as expected on Monday, July 23, when many of the city's semiskilled switchmen walked off their jobs. The city's business class and the mayor reacted instantaneously. Many of the railroad lines serving the city rescinded the wage cut to avoid a strike. Many others stopped all freight runs, thus locking out their employees to avoid strikes and property damage (*Chicago Tribune* July 24, 1877).

These actions were effective in preventing a militant strike by railroad workers in Chicago. When the wage cuts were rescinded, the railroaders saw no reason to continue the job action; by the middle of the week, most said they wished to return to work so they could support their families (*Chicago Tribune* July 25 and July 27, 1877).

But railroaders who wished to return to work were unable to do so. Crowds of less skilled foreign-born workers prevented the railroads from operating and had closed down most of the workplaces along the Chicago River as well. Railroad workers reported to the *Tribune* that two-thirds of those who had intimidated them into quitting work were not railroad workers and that there were no attempts on any day by railroad workers to induce non–railroad workers to quit work (*Chicago Tribune* July 25, 1877). The railroaders maintained that they would "protect the corporations' property with sword and gun if it became necessary," publicly deprecated all attempts at violation of the law, and said that they could not see what interest the "rabble" had in their affairs. One switchman said: "We are afraid to work. The mob has intimidated us. They have sent word that we must quit work or suffer. But we want to work if we can only be protected" (*Chicago Tribune* July 27, 1877, 3).

This was no longer a railroad strike at all, but rather a near general strike against the low wages and massive unemployment suffered by unskilled workers in foreign-born enclaves near the Chicago River. Through the efforts of crowds of less skilled foreign-born workers—mainly the outdoor laborers who had been active in the 1875 and 1876 strikes such as the lumber shovers, brickyard workers, and coal heavers—the strike had spread well beyond the railroad yards to the industrial areas of the city.

The WPUS, believing that perhaps the revolution was at hand, lost no time in trying to expand the strike; it held a mass meeting as early as Monday night. The leaflet announcing the meeting ended: "Every day, every hour that we remain disunited only helps our oppressors to bind more firmly the chains around us. Throughout the entire land our brothers are calling upon us to rise and protect our labor. For the sake of our wives and children and our own self-respect, LET US WAIT NO LONGER! ORGANIZE AT ONCE!" (*Chicago Tribune* July 23, 1877, 9). The meeting was massive; estimates of the crowd ranged from fifteen to forty thousand. Six speaker stands were erected because a single speaker could not be heard by so many. Workers from all over the city carried torches and signs in various languages, including German, Scandinavian, and French. The banners read "Life by Labor or Death by Fight!" "United We Stand, Divided We Fall!" The crowd was militant, and those who suggested moderation were shouted off the speaker stands (*Chicago Tribune* July 24, 1877; Schneirov 1975, 19).

Again Albert Parsons spoke, denouncing the actions of the monopolies and Jay Gould, W. H. Vanderbilt, and other capitalists. He asked how the workers could feed and clothe their families on $.90 a day and suggested the workers act in a determined way to maintain their rights (*Chicago Tribune* July 24, 1877). He concluded:

It rests upon you to say whether we shall allow the capitalist to go on exploiting us, or whether we shall organize ourselves. Will you organize? (Cries of "WE WILL!") Well, then enroll your names in the grand army of labor, and if the capitalist engages in warfare against our rights, then we shall resist him with all the means that God has given us. (Loud and prolonged applause!) (*Chicago Daily News* July 24, 1877; cited in Foner 1977, 143–44)

In the most militant statement of the night, WPUS activist John McAuliffe suggested that low wages, strikes, poverty, and greed were all effects of the capitalist system. The solution was to take control of the government, by force if necessary. Workers from the crowd also spoke from the stands. One Irish Civil War veteran said: "We fought for the Negro and brought him up to the level of the white man, why not do something for the workingman? We fought for the big bugs, but what have the capitalists done for us? We must bring the capitalists down to our level with powder and ball!" (Schneirov 1975, 19–20). The crowd cheered wildly, and someone yelled, "We are the boys to give it to them!" (Schneirov 1975, 19–20).

A reading of the WPUS strike platform, which included nationalization of key industries, organization of unions, and the eight-hour day, was enthusiastically received. The meeting ended with three cheers for shorter hours and better pay, three cheers for the strikers, and the singing of the "Marseillaise" (*Chicago Tribune* July 24, 1877).

On Tuesday, committees of workers began to roam the streets, closing all rail lines to freight service, then spreading the strike to other industries. Onlookers in foreign-born neighborhoods near the city's industrial center cheered these committees. Many workers visited by the committees agreed to join the strike; railroad officials or the managers of other firms often closed their places of business as the crowds approached to avoid property damage (Schneirov 1975, 23).

Schneirov estimates that a minimum of five to six thousand workers participated in the crowd actions in and around the railroad yards and the city's West Side industrial district by the end of Tuesday. Thousands more were out on strike or had been locked out by their employers. By evening, most of the West Side factories and lumberyards and nearly all the railroad freight runs in the city were shut down (Foner 1977, 145; Schneirov 1975, 26).

On Tuesday afternoon, the WPUS executive committee met to discuss its response to the strikes and crowd actions. Desperately trying to organize the strike under its banner, the party called for a meeting at which striker delegates would plan further action. But such organization was difficult to attain because those active in the strike—the unskilled—did not have preexisting economic organizations, and those workers who had organizational resources—the skilled—were not active in the strike. Only fifty-two delegates came to the WPUS meeting, and few delegates attended subsequent gatherings. The WPUS never had control of the strike.

The workplace closings had been accomplished by loosely organized groups of unskilled workers supported by a few WPI socialists but not by the craft unions. The lack of action by the predominantly Anglo-American Chicago Typographical Union no. 16 was typical. The printers, with the sole exception of Albert Parsons, did not participate in crowd actions, offered no money for strike support, and passed no resolution of solidarity (Chicago Typographical Union minutes 1877). Labor reformers in the city never endorsed the general strike or engaged in any actions to support it.

On Tuesday, a meeting of labor reformers endorsed the railroad strike but withheld support for the general strike (Schneirov 1984, 67). Not until Thursday did a small number of German skilled unions begin to discuss the strike, the eight-hour day, and the possibility of demanding pay increases.

This movement was mobilized by unskilled residents of the city's foreign-born neighborhoods; it was *not* a class-conscious movement by Chicago's entire working class. Anglo-American workers gave the strike little support. Schneirov (1975) found that of the 132 arrested during the strike, the majority of crowd members were foreign born: Only 15 percent had English names, 37–45 percent had German or Bohemian names, 34–42 percent had Irish names, 3 percent were Polish, and 2 percent were Scandinavian.

Schneirov also considered which wards spawned crowds: The fifth through the eighth and the fourteenth through the seventeenth predominated; those were the most heavily foreign-born wards in the city at this time. Finally, newspapers listed the addresses of those killed Wednesday night and Thursday. Twenty-seven percent of those addresses were in the seventh and eighth wards, near the Bohemian community where the Halsted viaduct conflicts occurred. Sixty-seven percent came from the fifth and sixth wards, which were predominantly German, Irish, and Bohemian (Schneirov 1975, 54).

The fact that this was a movement by only one part of Chicago's working class made it easier for the city's well-organized political and economic elite to crush the strike. An unnamed business leader paid for eight hundred special police, and the militia was ordered to its armories. The mayor met with businessmen, police, and militia commanders and issued a statement calling for neighborhood patrols to preserve order. He also required that all saloons be closed, ostensibly to prevent drunken rioting; but another reason may have been to prevent striking workers from utilizing the saloons as meeting places. He ordered all gun dealers to remove firearms from their shops, and all armories were placed under guard to prevent workers from obtaining firearms (Foner 1977, 142; Schneirov 1975, 17–18).

The authorities had found the strategy that would end the strike by the middle of the week. Three to five thousand workers had gathered for a rally at Market and Madison on Wednesday evening. During the first speeches, a group of police arrived and began to club the workers indiscriminately, forcing the crowd to disperse. There followed numerous assaults on peaceful meetings. As the *Inter-Ocean* reported, "When the mob was attacked, except in one or two instances, they were attacked for assembling in crowds and not for any unlawful acts they were committing" (July 28, 1877; cited in Schneirov 1975, 51). From this point on, the conflict deteriorated into a violent battle with police, a battle the unarmed workers could not win. The continuing pattern of police violence intimidated the socialists as well as the strikers; the WPUS was never able to hold another mass meeting.

The authorities did not even tolerate indoor discussions. A meeting of three hundred and fifty cigar makers concerning a strike for the eight-hour day was broken up, the coopers narrowly escaped the same kind of attack, and thirteen tailors were arrested for simply discussing the strike (Schneirov 1975, 45).

At the Twelfth and Halsted Streets Turner hall, two to three hundred journeymen German cabinetmakers were meeting to consider the eight-hour day question and some of their other grievances. A group of police, both regulars and specially appointed, attacked this meeting without provocation. They entered the hall and began firing and clubbing everyone in sight, killing one and wounding several others. The *Chicago Tribune* reported that the workers "ran hither and yon like rats in a pit" (Foner 1977, 153). Two policemen then took turns beating a man pinned to a table while a sergeant took potshots at passersby in the street.

When the police left, the National Guard arrived and, with drawn bayonets, drove everyone in the neighborhood into their homes (Foner 1977, 153). The police involved in the incident were later tried, convicted of inciting a criminal riot, and fined six cents each (Schneirov 1975, 45). Both this event and the subsequent trial of the perpetrators in 1879 were covered extensively in the German press (*Illinois Staats Zeitung* April 26, 1879). The Lehr und

Wehr Verein gained recruits as a result of such unprovoked attacks by the authorities.

By the middle of the week, the conflict had moved into the residential neighborhoods of the foreign born, and they began to fight back more aggressively. As the strike moved into the community, women—many of whom worked in less skilled jobs at home or in neighborhood workplaces—became more prominent in the crowd actions. The conservative *Inter-Ocean* blamed women for many of the most militant worker actions during the course of the strike (Foner 1977, 154–55).

On Thursday, three thousand women and teenagers from the surrounding neighborhoods gathered along Halsted Street and began cutting telegraph wires and damaging streetcar lines. The police soon arrived and attempted to break up the crowd by charging and clubbing everyone in sight. But the crowd soon grew to five thousand and refused to disperse. Angered by the police actions of the previous days, the crowd met the police with a volley of stones. The police began to fire at will and dropped many, but they were outnumbered and forced to retreat. A squad of reinforcements arrived, and the police attacked again, killing several crowd members (Schneirov 1975, 41).

Ten thousand packed the same area the next day, but the workers and residents had few guns and could not confront the police directly. They resorted instead to guerilla warfare; when police or cavalry approached, the crowd would briefly disperse and then close in behind them, throwing stones and pieces of wood. When the police charged, the crowd would run into alleyways. Small groups of workers used the rooftops to shower the police and troops with missiles. Neighborhood residents helped the injured and refused to tell the authorities where the wounded were hiding. Police and troops were routinely denied food and water. Crowd members also attempted to liberate captured workers, sometimes successfully.

By this time, the police actions had had very serious consequences. Between twenty-eight and thirty-five workers had been killed and approximately two hundred wounded seriously. The lopsided nature of the conflict can be seen in the fact that no police or troops were killed during the week, and only eighteen were injured, none seriously (Schneirov 1975, 46). The workers and neighborhood residents, unable to acquire guns, finally gave up their attempts to confront the police; the cost in killed and maimed was too high, and they had no prospect of victory.

The great strike was essentially over by Friday, when most of the railroad workers went back to work (Schneirov 1975, 75). The daily papers and employers showed that they understood that this had not been a railroad strike. The *Tribune* praised the railroad workers for their loyalty to the companies (July 28, 1877), Illinois Central management allowed full pay for the time lost by its employees, and other railroads followed their lead (Lightner 1977, 201).

Socialist Electoral Campaigns

Finding again that elected officials had failed to take their side in a conflict, the socialists moved back into the electoral arena. The WPUS nominated a full slate of county officers in the November 1877 elections and did quite well. The continuing depression and the memory of police repression of workers just a few months before undoubtedly helped the party's candidate for treasurer Frank Stauber net 6,592 votes, 13.7 percent of the total votes cast. He received over 20 percent of the vote in the seventh, fifteenth, and sixteenth wards, over 30 percent in the fifth and fourteenth, and over 40 percent in the sixth (see Table 4). This success again led to the strengthening of the political action viewpoint within the party.

At the next national WPUS convention, the party name was changed to the Socialist Labor party (SLP). It was determined that all sections should form state organizations and hold conventions before each election; the SLP was to be an electoral machine. One crumb was thrown to the trade unionists: A resolution was passed suggesting that the party "should maintain friendly relations with the trade unions and should promote their formation upon socialist principles" (WPUS Proceedings 1877; cited in Commons et al. 1918, 2: 278–79).

Party reorganization allowed the English-speaking section and other political action advocates in the Chicago SLP to wage a strong campaign in the spring 1878 election. Prospects seemed so bright that even the largely German Marxists and the *Vorbote* accepted that political action would be the SLP direction in the near future (Commons et al. 1918, 2: 279). The city's trade unions also

TABLE 4.   *Socialist Vote for County Treasurer, Fall 1877, by Ward*

Ward	Number of Votes	Percentage
1	37	1.8
2	212	10.2
3	78	3.9
4	101	3.3
5	1,020	30.2
6	1,071	41.6
7	685	21.0
8	286	7.5
9	74	3.6
10	223	14.1
11	65	2.6
12	21	0.6
13	52	2.6
14	1,096	30.1
15	663	24.0
16	652	27.3
17	166	6.9
18	90	2.8
Total	6,592	13.7

Source. Chicago Tribune, November 7, 1877.

were optimistic about political action; over twenty endorsed the SLP for the April elections, and more than one hundred trade unionists distributed ballots for the party on election day.

The party again did well, receiving approximately eight thousand votes, one-seventh of the total vote cast. Frank Stauber was elected alderman in the fourteenth ward, and the party suggested that its candidates would have been elected in the fifteenth and sixteenth wards had there not been a recurrence of vote fraud. The socialists also received more than 20 percent of the vote in the fifth and sixth wards (see Table 5).

The socialists followed this modest success with victories in the November 1878 elections. They elected three representatives to

TABLE 5. *Socialist Vote for Alderman, Spring 1878, by Ward*

Ward	Number of Votes	Percentage
1	30	1.9
2	67	3.0
3	4	0.2
4	108	4.9
5	733	21.4
6	616	21.0
7	674	16.2
8	592	15.6
9	27	1.2
10	153	10.3
11	no candidate fielded	
12	no candidate fielded	
13	41	1.9
14	1,416 Stauber elected	41.3
15	744	29.9
16	762	21.9
17	191	8.0
18	no candidate fielded	

Source. Chicago Tribune, April 4, 1878.

the Illinois House (out of twenty-one for the city) and one state senator out of seven. Their candidate for sheriff received a majority of the vote in the fifth, sixth, and fourteenth wards and close to a majority in the fifteenth and sixteenth. In the congressional races, they received a majority in the sixth, fourteenth, and sixteenth wards and close to a majority in the fifteenth (*Chicago Tribune* November 7, 1878).

But the height of the socialists' electoral strength was reached in the April 1879 election for city officers. Their candidate for mayor, a German doctor named Ernst Schmidt, garnered 20.4 percent of the vote, 11,807 total votes. He received over 25 percent of the vote in the seventh ward; over 30 percent in the fifth, fourteenth, and fifteenth; 45 percent in the sixth; and 51 percent in the six-

teenth. The party also received 20 percent of the vote for city attorney and city clerk and elected three aldermen in the sixth, fourteenth, and sixteenth wards (see Tables 6 and 7).

The party's strength in the late 1870s was in the foreign-born
wards, especially in those dominated by Germans. They received
their highest vote percentages in the fifth, sixth, seventh, eighth,
fourteenth, fifteenth, sixteenth, and seventeenth wards. Table 8,
which shows the ethnic composition of Chicago's wards, indicates
that the wards with the highest proportion of Germans were the
sixteenth (72.7 percent), the fifteenth (70.4 percent), the seventh
(44.0 percent), the sixth (38.7 percent), and the fifth (33.8 percent).
The sixth and eighth wards also have a high percentage of Bohemians (32.1 percent and 11.3 percent, respectively).

TABLE 6.   *Socialist Vote for Mayor, Spring 1879, by Ward*

Ward	Number of Votes	Percentage
1	155	6.1
2	305	11.2
3	152	6.6
4	241	7.0
5	1,611	33.9
6	1,528	44.8
7	1,070	27.5
8	698	15.2
9	166	6.0
10	393	20.3
11	131	4.4
12	57	1.6
13	179	7.1
14	1,312	34.2
15	1,112	36.0
16	1,368	51.0
17	469	17.0
18	362	10.5
Total	11,807	20.4

Source. Chicago Tribune, April 3, 1879.

TABLE 7. *Socialist Vote for Alderman, Spring 1879, by Ward*

Ward	Number of Votes	Percentage
1	115	4.4
2	222	8.4
3	93	4.1
4	154	5.1
5	1,688	35.6
6	1,532	45.3*
7	786	24.5
8	552	12.0
9	97	3.5
10	361	18.7
11	116	3.8
12	38	1.2
13	149	5.9
14	1,718	39.6*
15	903	29.4
16	1,520	57.8*
17	322	12.1
18	235	6.9

Source. Chicago Tribune, April 3, 1879.
*Candidate elected.

Schneirov (1975, 66) calculates that the eight wards with the highest percentage of foreign born in the city contributed 76 percent, 92 percent, 82 percent, and 77 percent of the socialist vote total in the fall 1877 to spring 1879 elections. None of these results conclusively indicates who voted socialist. For example, it is possible that the 27 percent of non-Germans in the sixteenth ward voted socialist and that Germans actually voted for mainstream parties. This phenomenon, known as the *ecological fallacy*, means that it is not possible to know actual ethnic voting patterns because only the *percentage* foreign born and *percentage* voting socialist are known.

But the high correlation between foreign-born, German, and Bohemian wards with high socialist voting is not the only indication that Germans and Bohemians provided most of the votes for the

TABLE 8.   *Percentage Native and Foreign Born
in Chicago's Wards, 1884*

Ward	Native Born	Bohe-mian	En-glish	Ger-man	Irish	Norwe-gian	Polish	Swed-ish
1	51.0	0.2	4.2	20.0	16.8	0.6	0.6	1.7
2	39.2	0.2	5.6	24.7	12.5	0.1	2.4	0.5
3	55.0	0.2	5.2	23.7	12.1	0.2	0.4	1.2
4	51.5	0.1	5.6	25.0	11.0	0.2	0.2	0.6
5	8.8	2.6	3.4	33.8	39.5	0.5	2.6	4.1
6	4.7	32.1	1.2	38.7	12.6	0.5	5.6	1.7
7	9.0	5.5	2.2	44.0	27.7	0.2	1.6	0.5
8	17.8	11.3	3.0	19.9	36.5	0.2	0.8	0.6
9	44.1	0.1	5.6	17.9	20.8	0.4	0.2	0.4
10	14.5	0.6	3.9	25.1	25.7	15.5	0.6	3.8
11	48.6	0.1	5.1	14.6	13.7	8.2	0.2	3.6
12	68.2	0.1	6.5	9.1	9.2	0.3	0.0	0.4
13	33.7	0.3	6.8	21.6	24.2	3.5	0.0	2.2
14	4.6	1.6	1.9	45.1	7.2	11.8	18.9	2.8
15	15.1	0.4	1.6	70.4	5.8	0.6	2.3	2.0
16	13.6	0.1	1.4	72.7	5.5	1.1	0.5	3.6
17	6.4	0.2	2.2	19.5	27.7	3.1	1.7	34.8
18	44.4	0.0	3.0	28.1	15.9	0.9	0.1	4.6
Total for city*	23.2	4.6	3.3	34.0	18.5	3.0	3.8	3.8

Source. Chicago Board of Education, Report on School Census, 1884.

*Percentages do not add up to 100 because minor nationalities have been deleted. Those nationalities combined total less than 6 percent of the Chicago population, and no one deleted group represents more than 1.5 percent of the total population.

SLP. First, it is known that many of those in the party were Germans on the north side in the fourteenth through sixteenth wards. Second, several of the wards that voted socialist were the location of the 1877 strikes and crowd actions, mobilized by the foreign born. The socialists had never run candidates in the fifth and sixth wards before the strikes; their voting strength there came from those dissatisfied with the official response to the July 1877 events (Schneirov 1975, 67).

Third, Schneirov examined precinct voting patterns in an effort to reduce the seriousness of the ecological fallacy. He found that the precincts where many of the crowd actions had occurred had voted socialist to a greater degree than other precincts. The fourth precinct of the sixth ward was a largely Bohemian area that included that part of the city where most of the crowd actions had occurred. It ranked first in the city in the percentage voting socialist: From 55 to 67 percent voted socialist in each election. Two conclusions seem warranted: Socialists did particularly well in the German and Bohemian communities, and they did well in areas affected by the events of July 1877. Of course, the two propositions overlap because there were many Germans and Bohemians living in strike-affected areas.

By early 1879, Chicago was the unquestioned center of the U.S. socialist movement. The SLP was publishing four socialist papers: the *Arbeiter Zeitung* and the *Vorbote* in German, the *Socialist* in English, and the *Nye Tid* in Norwegian (Commons et al. 1918, 2: 282). Although the party had fewer than a thousand dues-paying members (Schneirov 1984, 110), it had been successful in the electoral sphere. Also, many of the city's largest German unions—including the cabinetmakers, cigar makers, shoemakers, coopers, upholsterers, silver guilders, clothing cutters, and wood carvers— were officially affiliated with the SLP and/or met at SLP headquarters (Schneirov 1984, 110). Other unions, many of them predominantly German, such as the machinists and blacksmiths, bakers, carpenters, iron molders, boxmakers, German Typographical Union no. 9, shoemakers, stonemasons, and tailors, participated in an 1878 picnic and parade organized by the SLP (Schneirov 1984, 111). Thus, although the party had few official members, it had many supporters, primarily in the German trade union movement.

Socialist legislators even managed to bring about the appointment of a committee to investigate the causes of the continuing depression in Illinois in 1879. Half a dozen SLP members appeared before the committee, and their testimony documents their beliefs about the economic and political system at the time of their greatest strength. The socialist analysis of the causes of working-class problems goes well beyond the moderate early WPI platforms. Their statement suggested that labor-saving machinery never helped working people and that it increased the comforts of the middle and upper classes at the cost of creating a life of drudgery and imprisonment for those in the working class (Illinois State House of Representatives 1879, 8). They argued that the fundamental causes of labor difficulties were problems within the existing industrial system of private capitalist production, that free competition was directly opposed to the common welfare of the working class, that the means of labor ought to be placed in the hands of all the people, and that the present system of wage labor ought to be abolished. Other SLP speakers suggested that the country faced a revolution that would come inevitably, either peacefully or forcefully (Illinois State House of Representatives 1879, 39–40).

The SLP speakers also stated that the involuntary idleness of workers, the insufficient wages of those employed, the general depression of business, the unsatisfactory condition of the public treasuries, and the existence of a large criminal class were all due to one cause: unrestricted competition within the planless mode of capitalist production. The solution was to liberate the laborer from the yoke of capitalist exploitation and replace the present system with a cooperative system of production organized by the government, thus guaranteeing workers adequate remuneration for their labor. The statement ends with a call for the state to guarantee employment for all workers (Illinois State House of Representatives 1879, 42–45). These were revolutionary sentiments, clearly calling for replacing the current economic and political systems with something radically different. However, support for the SLP demands and proposed solutions soon dropped precipitously when relative prosperity returned in the middle of 1879.

The Decline of the Socialist Labor Party

By the fall of 1879, the six-year depression was ending. The result of prosperity was declining support for the SLP and their subsequent defeat at the polls. In the fall of 1879, the socialists managed only 3,939 votes for county treasurer versus 22,514 for the Republican candidate and 18,777 for the Democrat. In the spring of 1880, the party did manage to reelect Stauber to the city council, but by a slim thirty-one-vote majority. Stauber's opponent refused to accept his defeat, challenged the result, and several election judges stuffed a ballot box during a recount. It took Stauber a year and the party $2,000 to regain the fraudulently denied seat. The SLP was never again an important factor in Chicago elections.

A party member, George Schilling, suggested, "This circumstance did more, perhaps, than all other things combined to destroy the faith of the Socialists in Chicago in the efficiency of the ballot" (Parsons 1889, xviii). Their alternative was the use of force; Schilling reported that the Lehr und Wehr Verein gained many new recruits after such instances of vote fraud, just as they had after the 1877 police repression of meetings.

Another indication of SLP weakness was increasing political conflict between German and (less numerous) Anglo-American activists in the party. The two groups had had an uneasy truce during the successful electoral campaigns. But there had always been suspicions on both sides. As one socialist leader put it, "the German Socialists were suspicious of the English Section and oft-times gave them to understand that the damned Yankees needed watching" (Parsons 1889, xv).

In the SLP, the problems had surfaced in 1878, when the issue of armed worker defense groups had become divisive. The German socialists planned a procession in April 1878 to include mainly the Lehr und Wehr Verein (with a strength of over two hundred German workers) and two Bohemian defense groups—the Bohemian Sharpshooters and the Jaeger Verein (with a hundred members each) (Schneirov 1975, 70). The German-language *Vorbote* also supported the procession, suggesting the defense groups were necessary if the ruling class should again dare to restrict the rights of free speech and public assembly (Commons et al. 1918, 2: 281). On June 13, just before the procession was to begin, the national executive committee, along with most of the Anglo-American members of the Chicago SLP, repudiated the armed groups because of their worry about alienating potential voters.

The two factions found another issue to be divisive in 1879. The yearly SLP convention met in December of that year and decided to endorse the Greenback presidential candidate. Greenbackism was a monetary reform strategy that suggested all would be well for workers if more currency were put in circulation. The German trade unionists immediately condemned the "Greenback compromise" as reformist. Both the *Vorbote* and the *Nye Tid*, the party's Norwegian organ, spoke of the move as a sellout of party principles. The American faction accepted the Greenback compromise and proceeded to expel the editors of the *Vorbote* and the *Nye Tid* from the party.

Amid chaos, the SLP put the Greenback compromise to a vote. It carried nationally, but the Chicago rebels would not submit. The German and Scandinavian sections gained control over the local central committee one week after the vote and elected a new executive committee. The foreign-born faction gained credibility when the Greenbackers received only three hundred thousand votes nationally.

As a result of these factional fights, as well as the declining electoral fortunes of the party, the SLP split into two groups; most of the German trade unionists remained with a socialist faction including the furniture workers, carpenters, tanners and curriers, silver guilders, and socialist shoemakers. They continued to push for the principles of socialism.

Most Anglo-American members, including some printers, painters, shoemakers, sailors, and butchers, returned to more conservative labor reform principles (Schneirov 1984, 126). One of the American printers suggested in his resignation speech that many of the Germans demanded immediate revolution yet refused to learn English and were ignorant of American institutions. He referred to the need to "Americanize socialism" (Schneirov 1984, 127). The *Socialist*, the sole English-language paper of the party, folded at this time after only one year of publication. From 1880 on, the socialist movement in the city separated into two clear factions: the English-speaking reformers versus the largely German (and some Bohemian) revolutionaries.

Conclusions

There were clear differences in the political activities of the skilled and the less skilled. Highly skilled workers, particularly those in the best organized unions, were the first to organize craft unions, and they used those unions as a basis for the first trades assemblies. The Trades and Labor Council, founded by Chicago printers, became a forceful voice for legislative reform to benefit the working class, for the eight-hour day, and for the election of city officials who would be more sympathetic to the plight of the working class.

Because they had no scarce skills and so usually had no unions, the unskilled faced more serious economic problems. Their high unemployment rates and low wages made it hard for them to support themselves and their families, especially during the 1873–1879 depression. The struggles of these less skilled workers and their families were less ideological, more pragmatic, yet more militant than those of the skilled. They demanded public jobs during the unemployed marches and wage increases during the 1877 strikes. Their tactics were much more likely to be outside normal institutional channels: mass marches, mass protest rallies, and the general strike. The mass strike model, whose strength came from the ability of crowds of strikers to intimidate easily obtainable, unskilled strikebreakers, was developed to compensate for the inability of the unskilled to found strong craft unions.

It is not possible to account for the pattern of political mobilization in the Chicago labor movement by examining only workers' economic positions. Another factor, *ethnicity*, also played a crucial role in determining political choice in the movement. There was a clear ethnic basis for an important political split between Anglo-American reformers and German revolutionaries, a split that occurs even among native-born and German workers in the same trades at the same skill levels.

The Anglo-American elite craft unions were the moving force behind the Trades and Labor Council and its program of mild legislative reform combined with electoral work. These Anglo unions were trade conscious rather than class conscious, and they did not participate in the more militant actions of the unskilled. With a few notable exceptions, such as Albert Parsons, Anglo-American skilled workers were inactive during both the 1873 marches and the 1877 strikes.

By contrast, the Germans were the main constituency for the Marxist International, the Lassallean Workingmen's Party of the United States, and the Socialist Labor party. Most of the votes the SLP garnered were cast by Germans and Bohemians, and election fraud was often directed against socialist German candidates. Skilled Germans in the International and in the Workingmen's party exhibited their class consciousness by attempting to provide organized leadership in both the 1873 unemployed marches and the 1877 general strike.

The most militant actions by the unskilled in the 1870s (protest rallies, militant strikes, the general strike, and mass marches) were carried out largely by the foreign born, particularly by German, Bohemian, and Irish lumber shovers, coal heavers, and brickyard workers. These workers developed the mass strike model in Bohemian, Irish, and German communities, largely without Anglo-American participation. It was in these foreign-born communities near the river industrial district that laborers experienced the wrath of the Chicago police during the 1877 events.

There were a few limited political coalitions between the Anglo-American workers and the Germans. During the 1873–1879 depression, German Lassalleans and a few Anglo labor reformers agreed on the need to found producer cooperatives. The Socialist Labor party and Trades Assembly included a significant number of both Anglo-Americans and Germans in the late 1870s, but this shaky coalition lasted only until the return of prosperity as the 1880s began. There was a severe ethnically based split in the movement between reformers and revolutionaries, a split that was to become more severe as the 1880s began.

Chapter Two

Anarchism and the Eight-Hour Movement

The end of the 1870s depression deepened the ethnic split in the labor movement. The Anglo-Americans returned to a strategy of strikes in the elite trades to induce employers to raise wages and continued their political lobbying and electoral work. The city's foreign-born workers were less able to take advantage of returning prosperity because they were excluded from most of the high-status trade unions; and even peaceful strikes by the foreign born were often met with police repression. Without significant wage increases, workers saw their real incomes fall as prices rose in the recovery. Another means of responding to this plight, such as electing sympathetic candidates to office, was also unavailable to the foreign born; fraud that denied them fair representation, especially to the Germans, was common.

Many city workers felt that the only solution was revolution. In 1880, the SLP's German, Bohemian, and Norwegian members held meetings at which it was resolved to merge with the armed resistance groups. They repudiated the continuing use of an electoral strategy by the Anglo-Americans in the nearly dead SLP and in the Trades and Labor Assembly. They issued a call asking all revolutionaries in the country to "get ready to offer an armed resistance to the invasions by the capitalist class and capitalist legislatures" (*Vorbote* December 4, 1880; cited in Commons et. al. 1918, 2: 290). The English-speaking faction responded by condemning the proposed use of violence and suggesting again that more moderate political action was the worker's only reliable weapon (Commons et al. 1918, 2: 291).

In October 1881, an *anarchist* movement was organized in the city based on a model provided by the International Working People's Association—the *Black International*—which had convened in London in July of that year. Anarchism was in conflict with Marxist-inspired state socialism. The anarchist ideology rejected both state authority and the state's claim to a monopoly over the legitimate use of physical coercion. Anarchists such as Proudhon argued that the power of capital and the power of the state were synonymous; thus, the proletariat could not emancipate itself through the use of state power. Others such as Bakunin proposed spontaneous worker uprisings to abolish the state and replace it with a system of self-regulated, federally linked, autonomous communes that would be like the Paris Commune of 1871 (Bottomore 1983, 18).

Despite the differences in ideology, the anarchist movement in Chicago mobilized many former socialist activists from the German trade union wing of the SLP. They continued to call for the abolition of private property because they saw it as a major cause of social inequality; they believed that equality was a necessary condition for the successful realization of an anarchist society. They had changed only in that they no longer believed they could reach their goals by working within the existing political system. That view came not from the uncritical borrowing of Black International ideology but from mainly German and Bohemian workers' frustration with the disruption of peaceful meetings in the July 1877 strike and with electoral fraud in the late 1870s. Anarchism, with its goal of abolishing the existing state, offered the obvious solution to the problem of German and Bohemian workers' exclusion from political influence in Chicago.

Albert Parsons, the German upholsterer August Spies, and representatives of the Lehr und Wehr Verein, the Jaeger Verein, and other workers' armed defense groups were among the thirteen delegates at the first U.S. anarchist convention held at a Chicago North Side Turner hall (David 1958, 73). Members in any part of the city could organize an autonomous group with not fewer than ten members; unions could also be granted membership. The groups were to be united only by a nearly powerless central committee whose decisions were to have binding force only if not objected to by any given group at its next meeting. The central committee was also forbidden to spend more than $20 without authorization from all the clubs. Chicago was instructed to establish a national information bureau for the movement, but it did not do so until April 1883 (Commons et al. 1918, 2: 293). Two Chicago papers, the *Vorbote* and the *Nye Tid*, were recognized as party organs.

Chicago did not have a strong anarchist movement until at least 1882, when the most prominent national leader of the anarchists, Johann Most, visited the city and gave a series of fiery speeches. The well-attended gatherings drew German support away from what was left of the SLP, and Most's extreme radicalism moved city anarchists to more revolutionary positions (David 1958, 87–88).

The national movement, now called the Social Revolutionary movement, was given real form at the October 1883 Pittsburgh convention, at which Chicago was represented by delegates from five political groups. Twenty-four of the twenty-six delegates at the convention were German, Parsons being one of only two English speakers. Johann Most was the dominant force, calling for "propaganda of the deed" (acts of violence against capitalists and state and church officials) and arguing eloquently for the execution of all reactionaries, for the confiscation of capital by the people, and against electoral work.

The Chicago anarchists fought Most in an effort to gain support for a more formal relationship between the anarchist political cells and the union movement; they did manage to get a resolution sponsored by August Spies passed. It stated that trade unions fighting for the abolition of the wage system would be the foundation of the future anarchist society. But when the convention wrote the theoretical basis of American anarchism—the Pittsburgh Manifesto—it was clearly inspired by the ideas of Johann Most (Commons et al. 1918, 2: 294–95):

We could show by scores of illustrations that all attempts in the past to reform this monstrous system by peaceable means, such as by the ballot, have been futile, and all such efforts in the future must necessarily be so. . . . The political institutions of our time are the agencies of the propertied class; their mission is the upholding of the privileges of their masters; any reform in our own behalf would curtail these privileges. . . .

That they will not resign these privileges voluntarily we know . . . since we must then rely upon the kindness of our masters for whatever redress we have, and knowing that from them no good may be expected, there remains but one recourse—FORCE!

What we would achieve is therefore, plainly and simply:

First:—Destruction of the existing class rule, by all means, i.e., by energetic, relentless, revolutionary, and international action.

Second:—Establishment of a free society based upon cooperative organization of production.

Third:—Free exchange of equivalent products by and between the productive organizations without commerce and profit-mongering.

Fourth:—Organization of education on a secular, scientific, and equal basis for both sexes.

Fifth:—Equal rights for all without distinction of sex or race.

Sixth:—Regulation of all public affairs by free contracts between the autonomous (independent) communes and associations, resting on a federalistic basis.

Recommendations for arming the working class were presented, and reaction was favorable. The Chicago Jaeger Verein urged that the proletariat be armed with the most recent scientific knowledge in the field of chemistry in order that it have the ability to assemble dynamite bombs.

Shortly after the congress, the SLP offered to affiliate with the Chicago Social Revolutionary clubs, but Spies prevented unification by suggesting that the SLP break up into autonomous groups prior to joining the anarchist group. The now largely Anglo SLP was soon dead. George Schilling withdrew as a candidate and then left the party altogether in 1882; the rest of the leadership left the SLP in 1883. From this point on, the Social Revolutionary clubs were the only major organizations for labor radicals in the city (Ashbaugh 1976, 52–53).

Yet in the early 1880s, the anarchists remained politically marginal, with a membership of a few hundred (Nelson 1981). Despite their commitment to union work, the Chicago anarchists had no official trade union representation on their central committee prior to 1884. In August 1883, a demonstration by the Social Revolutionaries had been attended by just three German trade unions: the printers, cabinetmakers, and house carpenters. Most of the Anglo-dominated unions, including the printers, stonecutters, seamen, bricklayers and stonemasons, carpenters and joiners, and iron molders, belonged to the Trades and Labor Assembly.

The city's Anglo workers had little reason to join an anarchist movement; many of their unions had been waging successful strikes for higher wages in the inflationary early 1880s (Bogart and Thompson 1920, 452). Political action in their trades assembly was confined to lobbying for legislation favorable to workers (such as laws prohibiting contract, convict, and child labor; mandating factory inspections; and establishing a labor bureau).

But as the recovery began to lag in 1883, the advocates of revolution gained support and began to become more of a political threat to the reformers in the Trades and Labor Assembly. Partly because they worked in one of the first trades to be hurt by the downturn, cigar makers provided many early recruits for the anarchist movement. The resultant political split between reformers and revolutionaries in the city's cigar makers union anticipated the similar fragmentation of the labor movement as a whole.

Labor Politics in the Chicago Cigar Makers Union

When founded in 1864, the Chicago Cigar Makers Union no. 11 did not accept the revolutionary ideology that would characterize its pronouncements in the 1880s; rather, it exhibited the reformist politics characteristic of the Chicago Typographical Union no. 16 and the citywide labor coalitions that the Chicago Typographical Union helped found (*Workingman's Advocate* June 15 and August 25, 1866; August 3 and 17, 1867; April 11 and May 22, 1869).

But the cigar makers chose a more radical political path as the 1870s depression wore on. Despite the death of their union after the onset of the depression, cigar makers were one of the few skilled trades to be involved in the July 1877 strikes. Three hundred fifty cigar makers met to discuss the feasibility of striking for the eight-hour day and for a wage increase, perhaps the first indication of socialist influence in the trade because the eight-hour day was a WPI demand during these events. Their peaceful meeting was broken up by club-swinging police, an experience that may have radicalized a few of those present.

There were definitely some socialist cigar makers. One of the most prominent, Frank Hirth—soon to be a SLP candidate for city council—proposed at the 1877 cigar makers international convention, "Whereas, trades unions are utterly incompetent to remove the pressure resting upon them, caused by the above mental and social infirmities, the delegates in convention hereby recommend to and urge upon all local unions to form themselves into labor bodies upon the basis and platform of the Workingman's Party of the United States" (*Cigar Makers Official Journal* 15th Session Proceedings, 1883). The convention tabled this resolution, and it was not reconsidered. By 1878, the socialist influence among the cigar makers was even more obvious. Three hundred cigar makers participated as a group in the June 16, 1878, Socialist Labor party picnic (*Chicago Tribune* June 17, 1878). The cigar makers' participation at this and other SLP events implies they were active in the late 1870s socialist electoral campaigns.

But the socialist influence was among German and not Anglo-American cigar makers. The city had about equal numbers of each throughout the period; the 1880 Census reports that there were 599 U.S.–born and 667 German-born cigar makers out of a total of 1,599 cigar makers in the city (U.S. Census of Population 1880, Table 36). By 1879, a serious split had developed between largely German socialists and largely native-born reformers. The latter felt that the revival of trade signaled the need to return to the reformist politics of the 1860s; the Germans disagreed. The result was the secession of the Anglo-Americans. As the *Tribune* reported on March 29, 1879 (p. 29): "The Cigarmakers Union, having been turned into a Socialistic and political organization by the leaders, some of the members became dissatisfied, and, with other cigar-makers, have organized a new union and procured a charter. It is known as No. 14."

The problems between the two factions were only beginning. At the International convention in September 1879, a leader of the socialist union no. 11 sent from Chicago caused a great stir.

His propositions were so extreme, and of so high-flown a character that the Convention resolved to strike them entirely off the minutes. Six months prior to this convention, Union 11, Chicago, had been split into two divisions; the trades union men quitting No. 11, which was evidently neither more nor less than a socialistic club, and organizing Union 14, which is at present one of our most flourishing unions. Scarcely had the delegates returned to Chicago when a general uproar took place.

Union 11 denounced the International Union in a public meeting as being of no benefit to the craft. Thereupon the officers of Union 14 preferred charges against them. The executive Board promptly revoked their [no. 11's] charter, and thus weeded out those professional kickers from the ranks of the International Union. (*Cigar Makers Official Journal* 15th Session Proceedings, October 1883, 21)

Political splits remained in the union despite the union's engaging in a successful strike in 1879. As the *Tribune* noted:

Many of the cigarmakers claim that the dissension in their ranks is caused by the Socialist Union #11 which they allege is run in the interests of Mr. Sam Goldwater and his political friends. Union #14 claims to be run solely in the interests of the trade and its members *defy anyone to point out any instance of their participation in politics.* The great objection raised by the trade to the organization of one local union is the fear that it will be used as the tool of some party. (*Chicago Tribune* October 10, 1879, 17, emphasis added)

Clearly, the "party" the moderates were concerned about was the SLP; the tendency they were worried about was that of the German cigar makers to form socialist "political societies."

As long as prosperity reigned, such political differences could usually be handled. But by the fall of 1883, the developing recession was hurting the cigar trade; workers in trades that produced luxury goods such as cigars were particularly hurt by the business cycle because consumers cut back on purchases of such goods first. Cigar makers were also under severe pressure from tenement and sweatshop cigar manufacturing and the mechanization of the trade. These conditions aided the organizing of an anarchist cigar makers union in Chicago; such an organization had already been formed in New York City as early as 1881 under the name the Progressive Cigarmakers Union.

The trouble in New York had begun when the International Union attempted to secure the passage of a bill abolishing tenement house cigar manufacturing, an action consistent with the usual exclusionary craft union practices. However, largely German anarchists felt that the tenement house workers ought to be organized into rather than excluded from the union. The president of the International reacted to the political attacks by the German anarchists with an attack of his own in his report to the union in 1883:

I deem it my duty to make you fully acquainted with the history of the troubles in New York City, and the causes which have created the same. These causes derive importance from the fact that they are directly traceable to a method of political agitation prevailing in Europe. This method may be useful there, aiming as it does at the establishment of a republican form of government. The working classes of this country are striving for an improvement of their condition, and their line of policy is sufficiently indicated by the trade union movement. Hence, any attempt to force upon them methods which are not consonant with actual conditions will fail, and moreover, retard the practical labor movement.

Within the last three years a number of so-called socialists have arrived from Europe. Their object in joining the union, according to their own statements, frequently repeated, was to propagate the principles of socialism—i.e., to turn the same into a socialistic political club. True, these elements already existed in the union, creating a certain amount of trouble, but being few in number they could do but little mischief. They not only created trouble among cigar makers, but also among other trades. Full many a trade organization in the large cities has been wrecked by them. They have a small following in almost every large city, which compelled me to watch their movements for years, knowing that a few fanatics can do more mischief than a hundred can do good.

The socialistic members of the union, especially those among them who had not been longer than from six months to a year in the United States, believed that the special mission of the International Union was to be the tail of the Socialistic kite. (Supplement to the *Cigar Makers Official Journal* 15th Session Proceedings, 1883, 23–24)

These pronouncements ought to be interpreted with caution because they are written in the heat of a political battle; it is in the president's interest to suggest that the socialists have little support and that they are mainly recent arrivals who do not understand American conditions. The statement does show clearly the nature of the political split within the union as well as its ethnic basis.

Unhappy with the reformism of the International, the New York Progressives seceded in 1881, vowing to organize and not to exclude the tenement house cigar workers. As the *Cigar Makers Official Journal* (April 1884, 6) put it, "Their members [the Progressives] are now employed in every tenement house factory in New York, and they even boast that that is the way to educate them to trades unionism." The president of the International made the political differences clear when he described tenement house organizing as "nothing less than open war against the fundamental principles of trades unionism. The primary object of trades unionism is to maintain a fair rate of wages, sufficient to secure for the workers the necessary means whereby to maintain reasonable comfort and a respectable standing in society" (Supplement to the *Cigar Makers Official Journal* 15th Session Proceedings, 1883, 25).

The factionalism soon spread west in the fall of 1883 when a number of cigar makers announced their intention to form a Progressive Cigarmakers Union in Chicago. Five hundred attended a recruitment meeting called by the New York Progressives. One of their leaders spoke in both German and English, tearing the International Union to pieces, contrasting the corrupt International with the Progressive Cigarmakers Union, which he said was founded on democratic and anarchist principles and had no president at all. He asked those present to found a progressive union in Chicago (*Chicago Tribune* September 24, 1883).

There was apparently a great uproar; the *Chicago Times* reported that the meeting was animated and confused and that the police had to be called to restore order. Supporters of neither the Progressives nor the International had a clear majority at the meeting (*Chicago Times* September 24, 1883). Those favoring the Progressives were largely German, undoubtedly from union no. 11; fifteen to twenty "mostly Germans" expressed their willingness to join the anarchists at the meeting. Many more joined later that night when an official branch of the Progressive Cigarmakers Union was founded in the city (*Chicago Daily News* October 24, 1883).

Opposition to the Progressives came from the reformers of union no. 14. The union's president appealed to those present to remain loyal to the International; the president of the International Typographical Union appeared at the meeting to argue the same thing. As the printer put it, "It would be folly to espouse the cause of a few designing men," thereby jeopardizing one's own interests (*Inter-Ocean* September 24, 1883, 6). After the meeting, the financial secretary of union no. 14 stated:

There is not real trouble and what appears to be such is caused by a few socialists [*sic*] who have been unceremoniously bounced from the union because they are fomentors of trouble and of no advantage to us. These men are not satisfied with the effort of the working classes to improve their condition and are attempting to force themselves to the front and retard the practical labor movement. (*Chicago Times* September 24, 1883, 11)

He also claimed that the Progressive membership consisted of a small group of socialists recently arrived from Europe, of the "poorer class of workmen, who can scarcely hold a situation or earn a good living and are all inclined to socialism." He suggested, following his International president, that the purpose of the Progressives was to "propagate the principles of socialism and to turn the union into a socialist political club" (*Chicago Times* September 24, 1883, 11).

The factionalism between anarchists and reformers occurring largely along ethnic lines resulted in a trade split right down the middle because there were approximately equal numbers of native-born and German cigar makers in the city. Nativist sentiments soon began to surface in the attacks on the Progressives. The *Cigar Makers Official Journal* (November 1883, 43) said of the Chicago meeting: "Then Mr. Walther commenced one of his long-winded German socialistic speeches. . . . the whole meeting was a concocted socialistic gathering consisting of the editor of the German socialistic press, his reporters, and hangers on who were not cigar makers, but came for the sole purpose of creating confusion."

The moderates claimed the new union would recruit very few. No. 14's financial secretary said: "I do not anticipate any trouble [with the Progressives] as our union is too strong to be much disturbed by anything they might try to do, and there is no possibility that the new organization will gain a very strong foothold because its principles are absolutely bad and not in accordance with American institutions" (*Chicago Times* September 24, 1883, 12). The Trades and Labor Assembly was apparently more alarmed; the forty delegates to it, half of whom were printers, denounced the attempt to organize a Progressive union, calling it "a piece of socialistic legislation which could only result in harm to the laboring man!" (*Chicago Tribune* October 1, 1883, 7; Chicago Typographical Union minutes May 30, 1880; April 26, 1885).

The predictions of union no. 14 and of the International Union concerning the potential success of the Progressive recruitment efforts did not prove accurate. By December 1883, the Progressives had one hundred fifty members, far more than the twelve the reformers had suggested they would enroll. The reformist cigar makers were forced to try to crush the upstart organization by refusing to work with its members (*Chicago Tribune* December 14, 1883).

But the Progressive Cigarmakers Union continued to grow, soon making very clear its sympathy with anarchist principles. On Sunday, February 17, 1884, the Progressives called for a meeting to consider the eight-hour day. Many of the speeches were in German and were quite militant. At this meeting, the Progressives adopted—word for word—the Pittsburgh Manifesto as a statement of their principles. They called for the destruction of class rule by revolutionary action, cooperative organization of production, free education for both sexes, equal rights for all sexes and races, and the regulation of all public affairs by contracts between autonomous communes and associations (*Chicago Tribune* February 18, 1884). The anarchists went on to resolve:

That labor legislation, having for its presupposition class rule, will not and cannot lead to the abolition of class domination and the establishment of a free society, we consider it a device by which the oppressed are being led astray by designing politicians, and that the only means through which our aims, the emancipation of all mankind can be accomplished is open rebellion of the despoiled of all nations against the existing social, economic, and political institutions. (*Chicago Tribune* February 18, 1884, 25)

The Trades and Labor Assembly held a meeting attended by union no. 14 the same day the Progressives were making these revolutionary pronouncements. The assembly heard a report from a committee appointed to study the "Relations Between Labor and Capital." But this committee did not espouse revolution; on the contrary, it suggested only that some branches of industry were being monopolized by a few employers to the detriment of workers and that child and female labor were being used at half wages, especially in cigar factories. Several resolutions were passed at this meeting; one praised the city council for refusing to give city printing to nonunion shops and for not allowing convict labor on city hall construction. Another recommended that Chicago increase the number of tenement and factory inspectors to ten. Another suggested that the city stop burning manure in its buildings (*Chicago*

Tribune February 18, 1884). The contrast with the resolutions passed by the Progressive cigar makers could not have been more striking.

The inadequacy of a purely economic explanation of labor politics in Chicago is shown by these dramatic differences between the politics of the German Progressives and the native born in union no. 14. Although both unions were in the same trade, in the same city, facing the same devastating economic conditions, the Germans advocated abolishing the economic and political systems, and the Anglo-Americans advocated minor legislative reform.

Workers' Coalitions in the 1880s:
The Knights of Labor, the Trades and Labor Assembly,
and the Central Labor Union

Soon an alternative to both the reformism of the Trades and Labor Assembly and the revolutionary sentiments of the anarchists was defined. The Knights of Labor had begun organizing workers as early as 1877 in Chicago, but they did not achieve real influence in the labor movement until the mid 1880s. The significance of the Knights lies mainly in their attempt to create economic organizations, called assemblies, that mixed both skilled and unskilled workers. The idea was to draw on the organizational and financial resources of the skilled in order to support organizing the unskilled. Thus, although some Knights were in particular trades, others belonged to mixed assemblies based on ethnic or geographical criteria. The Knights also often gathered together previously unattached unions or revived failing locals (Commons et al. 1918, 2: 345).

Their emphasis on organizing the unskilled meant the Knights were ethnically heterogeneous. They also included groups that craft unions generally excluded; women were included in Knights assemblies as early as 1879. Women held some of the most powerful Knights' positions in the mid 1880s; Elizabeth Rodgers, for example, was the Master Workman (*sic*) of District Council 24.

On more general political questions, however, the Knights followed the lead of the reformist Trades and Labor Assembly and rejected the revolutionary militancy of the anarchists. The Knights accepted the basic capitalist economy and the existing political system. They emphasized the importance of forming cooperatives and mutual aid societies in ameliorating the plight of the worker. They called for reforms such as the breakup of monopolies that were robbing workers of their opportunity to found and own successful businesses. The Knights were a backward-looking organization, wishing to return to a competitive system of small producers and farm owners. As the Chicago *Knights of Labor* suggested (March 1886, 1):

We do not war upon capital, our aims are not to put the grip of an iron hand upon its neck and strangle it, but on the contrary we desire to assist capital in building up of the great industries of the country and to enlarge to the utmost the sphere of their usefulness. All we ask of capital is to give us what is justly our portion of the proceeds of our toil and to ameliorate to the greatest possible extent the condition of the toiling millions of earth, give us more time at home with our families, more time to improve our minds and to cultivate our social relations. We are censured for striking for our rights, it is true that sometimes we do that, but it is after all other means have failed, for one of the great fundamental principles of the order is that every endeavor in our power must be made to arbitrate our differences and only as a last resort, when all moral suasion has failed do we make a virtue of necessity and strike for our rights.

The Knights sometimes did engage in militant strikes, despite the conservatism of the organization's official ideology. But these often were mobilized by the unskilled against the wishes of Knights leaders, who were generally skilled craftsmen.

Many of Chicago's SLP members, including Albert Parsons and George Schilling, joined the first Chicago Knights assembly when it was established in August 1877. The Knights grew slowly and had little influence in these early years, in part because they were a secret, oath-bound organization. Catholic church opposition to such "heathen," secret practices kept many unskilled Irish Catholics from joining the organization. By 1878, there were only eight local assemblies organized in the first district assembly, no. 24. In 1881, an organizer came to the city, hired eight additional organizers, and established fourteen local assemblies among the skilled and unskilled (Bogart and Thompson 1920, 456).

By 1882, the district assembly had opened a headquarters and a labor bureau and begun to publish a paper, the *Progressive Age*.

Membership increased from 1,464 in 1879 to 1,518 in 1880, 1,766 in 1881, and 2,192 in 1882. After the 1881 decision to become a nonsecret, public organization, the Knights assemblies began to recruit large numbers of unskilled Irish; by the mid 1880s, a third of the Knights leadership was Irish (Nelson 1986b, 4).

The recession resulted in membership declines through July 1885, when the Knights had only 551 members in the city. But their membership then skyrocketed, primarily as a result of the success of a Knights-led strike against Jay Gould's western Union Pacific and Wabash railroads. By July 1886, the Knights had eighty-eight local assemblies, a membership of 14,000, and published a weekly paper called the Chicago *Knights of Labor*; they had 25,000 members by the end of the year (Bogart and Thompson 1920, 457).

By the mid 1880s, the Trades and Labor Assembly had admitted Knights assemblies into membership and was cooperating with them to promote moderate labor legislation as the answer to the plight of the working class. One hundred trade union and Knights delegates from around the state responded to the assembly's call to found the Illinois State Federation of Labor. This March 1884 convention was held in Chicago. Chicago delegates were distributed as follows: five each for Cigarmakers Union no. 14, Chicago Typographical Union no. 16, stonecutters, bricklayers and stonemasons, and seamen; four for both painters and coopers; three for carpenters and joiners; and two each for shoemakers and Scandinavian typographers. The following unions had one delegate: iron molders, journeymen horseshoers, woodworking machine hands, trunk makers, tanners, and curriers (Staley 1930, 21).

The Chicago Trades and Labor Assembly was now led almost exclusively by Anglo-American unionists (Nelson 1986b, 3). The conservative printers and construction tradesmen of the Anglo labor aristocracy wished to keep the convention within strict trade union channels; a *Tribune* reporter stated simply that it was "generally understood that no socialists will be admitted" (February 26, 1884; cited in Staley 1930, 23). The platform passed by the convention was reformist and denied the validity of radical socialist and anarchist principles. It included the following planks:

(1) The total abolition of the contract labor system.
(2) The establishment of boards of arbitration to settle disputes between employers and employees.

(3) The enactment and enforcement of a law making eight hours a day a legal day's work, excepting those engaged in agriculture.

(4) To fix the liability of employers for damages for loss of life or limb to the employee.

(5) The enactment of an efficient apprenticeship law.

(6) The prohibition of the employment of children under fourteen years of age in workshops and factories.

(7) The adoption and enforcement of a compulsory education system.

(8) The more rigid enforcement of the laws relating to the ventilation of mines and the safety of miners, and the enactment of penalties for their violation.

(9) The abolition of the conspiracy or LaSalle Black Law [which had been used to prevent union organizing] and the passage of a statutory enactment declaring illegal all iron clad contracts which deprive the workman of the privilege of membership in any peaceably conducted trade and labor organization.

(10) The relief of tax-payers on mortgaged real estate by giving a proportionate lien against the holders of mortgages for taxes paid.

(11) Weekly payments by all corporations for labor performed the previous week, and the complete abolition of the truck system.

(12) The abolition of land monopoly by non-resident holders.

(13) To make it a criminal offense to gamble in or create corners on the necessaries of life.

(14) The legal right of labor organizations, as such, to hold property and conduct cooperative businesses.

(15) A more complete control of the railroads and waterways of the state as common carriers, in the interests of the people.

(16) The appointment of inspectors of workshops and habitations, of food, drink, drugs, etc. (Staley 1930, 192)

These are significant reforms that would greatly improve the condition of the working class if enacted, but they would not alter the basic outlines of the capitalist economic and political systems. For example, only boards of arbitration are suggested for settling disputes between employers and employees; the wage labor system is accepted as legitimate; unemployment is dealt with by measures that would benefit those already in craft unions (such as abolishing contract convict and child labor and instituting the eight-hour day); land monopolies are to be destroyed only if they are held by nonresidents; and the railways and waterways are to be regulated, not nationalized.

The political lines were clearly drawn between reformist Knights and trade unionists in the Trades and Labor Assembly and anarchists in the Progressive Cigarmakers Union. On May 6, 1884, the Progressives, wishing to have a wider forum for their anarchist philosophy and principles, requested membership in the Trades and Labor Assembly. The secretary of Cigarmakers Union no. 14 stated that they had had the "horrible gall" to do this. He need not have worried about their being admitted to the assembly, however. The Progressives' credentials were referred to the executive committee, which reported that, on a thorough examination, they found the Progressive Union of Cigarmakers antagonistic to the executive board and a political body rather than a union. The committee therefore unanimously rejected the Progressives' request for membership. The delegates of the twenty-three unions in attendance, one of whom was from the rival Cigarmakers Union no. 14, unanimously accepted the report (*Cigar Makers Official Journal* June 1884).

Thereupon, the Progressive Cigarmakers Union issued a call to all unions in the city to secede from the conservative Trades and Labor Assembly in order to form a *Central Labor Union* (CLU) with a "more progressive" policy. Several of the city's German unions responded to this call to accept the principles of the Black International; the metalworkers, carpenters and joiners, cabinetmakers, and butchers all sent delegates to the founding meeting. By late June 1884, the German tanners, German tailors, and the German Typographical Union no. 9 had also joined the CLU.*

The CLU adopted a declaration of principles in October 1884 that was modeled closely on the Pittsburgh Manifesto. It suggested that labor created all wealth, that there could be no harmony between labor and capital, and that strikes as presently conducted were doomed to failure. It urged every worker to reject capitalist political parties and to devote his or her entire energy to labor unions in order to resist ruling-class encroachment upon their liberties.

*This collaboration between trade unions and anarchist cells took place only in Chicago, thus giving the Chicago movement a mass base it did not have anywhere else. In fact, the Chicago anarchist movement anticipated the French, Spanish, and American *syndicalist* union movements at the turn of the century. See Bottomore (1983, 476–77) for a description of these movements.

As the CLU openly took its stand with the Black International and the few remaining members of the Socialist Labor party joined forces with the moderate Trades and Labor Assembly, the conflict between the revolutionaries and the reformers intensified. A number of public debates took place between the Anglo-American former socialists and the German anarchists; Pierce (1957, 3: 267) reports that "clashes between the factions led at times to physical violence."

The Social Revolutionary movement achieved new visibility in late 1884 with the founding of the *Alarm*, a publication that is a good source of material on the anarchists' politics. In the paper, Albert Parsons kept up the attack on the Trades and Labor Assembly for condoning a system of "wage slavery" and "slow starvation." He suggested that the "social war has come, and those who are not with us are against us" (cited in Pierce 1957, 3: 268).

Lucy Parsons, one of the founders of the Working Women's Union in the mid 1870s, was also a crucial figure in the socialist and anarchist movements in the city. In a famous article in the *Alarm* entitled "To Tramps," she discussed the situation of the unemployed who constantly wandered Chicago streets searching for work, food, clothing, and shelter. She condemned the Relief and Aid Society for its failure to prevent the deaths of many in the city by starvation and exposure. The previous winter had resulted in the suicide by drowning of many who had chosen to die quickly rather than by slow starvation. Lucy Parsons told the tramp contemplating suicide to learn how to make bombs in order to take a few rich people with him. The essay ended with the admonition to "Learn the Use of Explosives!" (Ashbaugh 1976, 55).

Other authors also wrote of the beneficial effects of dynamite bombs: "What is Dynamite? It is the latest discovery of science by which power is placed in the hands of the weak and defenseless to protect them against the domination of others. One pound of DYNAMITE is better than a bushel of BALLOTS!" (Pierce 1957, 3: 268). Specific directions for manufacturing and setting bombs, as well as recommendations concerning assassination and street fighting, also were published in the pages of the *Alarm*; this caused it to live up to its name among many in the English-speaking population who could now read about the violent pronouncements of the revolutionaries for the first time in English.

The anarchists' bark was much worse than their bite, however. Although their rhetoric was revolutionary, their actual tactics tended toward the usual rallies and militant speeches. For example, the CLU and the Social Revolutionary movement organized a procession of the unemployed on Thanksgiving Day in 1884. From three to five thousand gathered at the joint office of the *Alarm* and the *Arbeiter Zeitung* and listened to several speeches. They simply marched through the South Side, past the homes of prominent Chicago businessmen, including Pullman, Field, Swift, Armour, and McCormick.

In another demonstration at the dedication of the new Board of Trade building on April 28, 1885, Albert Parsons spoke to a group at Market Square, asking, "How many of you could give twenty dollars for a supper tonight? While those men are enjoying a sumptuous supper, we workingmen are starving" (Adelman 1976, 9). Pointing to the black and red flags, the next speaker said that the red one represented the common blood of humanity, the black one, starvation. It was fitting that black flags were unfurled at the opening of the $2 million Board of Trade building, for that structure symbolized starvation for the masses and privileges for the few. The speeches were cheered (Flinn 1973, 226). Someone then proposed forming a line and marching around the "Board of Thieves" building singing the "Marseillaise," to the accompaniment of a brass band, so that the "eaters of twenty dollar pie" could not fail to hear them (Flinn 1973, 228). Finding their way blocked by the police, the marchers made their way to the office of the *Arbeiter Zeitung*, where Parsons suggested that the next time the police broke up a peaceful meeting, the marchers should defend themselves with dynamite (Ashbaugh 1976, 59).

The CLU and the Social Revolutionaries continued their demonstrations in the summer and autumn of 1885. On the Sunday preceding Labor Day, a grand march was organized to offset the parade of the Trades and Labor Assembly planned for the next day. One of the CLU leaders stated: "There is going to be a parade tomorrow. Those fellows [in the Trades and Labor Assembly] want to reconcile labor and capital. They want to reconcile you to your starvation and your shanties" (Flinn 1973, 250).

How strong were the Social Revolutionaries and the Central Labor Union, and who were their supporters? These are not easy questions to answer; there are no surviving documents, certainly no membership rolls of the CLU or the Social Revolutionary clubs. This may have resulted from the atmosphere of political repression, which forced these groups to carry on their activities in secret.

But it is clear that the revolutionary politics of the Central Labor Union did not confine the organization to political marginality. In late 1884, there were six groups of the Black International in the city. By mid 1885, there were seventeen with a total membership of around one thousand. The membership was over two thousand a year later (Commons et al. 1918, 2: 390; David 1958, 110).

Movement strength cannot be measured by Social Revolutionary club membership alone. By the end of 1885, the Central Labor Union, which endorsed the anarchist Pittsburgh Manifesto, was approximately equal in strength to the Trades and Labor Assembly; the CLU consisted of thirteen unions; the Trades and Labor Assembly had nineteen (Commons et al. 1918, 2: 387). By the spring of 1886, with recruiting boosted by the continuing recession, the CLU represented twelve thousand city workers, more than the Trades and Labor Assembly, and had twenty-two unions in its ranks (Ashbaugh 1976, 56; Pierce 1957, 3: 267).

Despite its rapid growth, the anarchist movement never managed to inspire the city's Anglo-American workers. Parsons organized a Social Revolutionary "American Group" in November 1883 with only five members. Even though the membership of that group increased to forty-five by October 1884 and ninety by April 1885, it remained the only native-born club; it is doubtful whether the native born ever constituted more than one-tenth of the anarchist strength in Chicago during this entire period.

In contrast, Germans gave the anarchist movement strong support, as indicated by the circulation figures of the Social Revolutionary newspapers. The English-language *Alarm* had a circulation of three thousand a week at its height; but the German-language *Arbeiter Zeitung* published between five and six thousand copies a *day* between 1883 and 1886, and its Sunday edition, *Die Fackel*, published between nine and twelve thousand. The *Vorbote*, another German weekly, had a circulation of between seven and eight thousand in the mid 1880s (Commons et al. 1918, 2: 390).

The anarchist movement derived its real strength from the close association of the Social Revolutionaries with the city's German and Bohemian trade unions. In April 1886, the Central Labor Union included the eleven largest unions in the city representing the following trades: German printers, fringe and tassel workers, fresco painters, cabinetmakers, bakers, Bohemian lumber shovers, laborers, hod carriers, brewers and maltsters, coopers, brick makers, both Bohemian and German carpenters, wagon workers, harness makers, butchers, metalworkers, and the union that had started it all, the Progressive Cigarmakers (Commons et al. 1918, 2: 391).

The Eight-Hour Movement

All three of the major Chicago labor coalitions—the Central Labor Union, the Trades and Labor Assembly, and the Knights of Labor—soon were able to mobilize a powerful movement around one of the most important labor demands of the nineteenth century: the eight-hour day. Demands for shorter hours were heard in the United States as early as 1825, when the issue was the ten-hour day. The movement alternated between periods of great strength and weakness in the decades that followed. In Chicago, there was agitation for the eight-hour day in both the sixties and the seventies; the early trades assembly successfully lobbied for a state law mandating the eight-hour day that was never enforced, and the eight-hour demand was heard frequently during the July 1877 strikes.

The Trades Council of 1879 demanded the reduction of working hours from ten to eight, holding a three-day demonstration with Ira Steward, the most prominent eight-hour theorist, as a speaker. The workers founded a short-lived Eight Hour League in 1879, and the furniture workers national union made it a key demand; forty-nine furniture factories in the city instituted the eight-hour day for a brief period in that year (*Chicago Tribune* July 6, 1879).

Labor had several goals in mind in demanding the eight-hour day; in fact, the idea of shortening the hours of labor eventually became a panacea for all the ills suffered by the working class. Ira Steward suggested that the increased leisure resulting from the shortening of the workday would create a better social order. Workers could not be intelligent citizens unless they had the leisure time to attend night school, to read, to discuss political questions, and to attend political meetings (Cahill 1932, 14). The eight-hour day would also ease the physical and mental strain caused by hard physical labor and by the tedious mechanized production process. Healthy workers would be more productive workers.

The argument for increased leisure time was also supported through reference to suburbanization. Workers needed to participate in the more healthful and more natural suburban family life; the longer journey to work from the suburbs necessitated a shorter workday as well. Steward argued that decreased hours would give the workers the time to observe the life-style of the largely native-born middle class. Their wish for that more affluent way of life would lead to successful demands for higher wages on the part of the working class, which would in turn create buying power that would stimulate the economy.

These arguments appealed to many workers, especially to the Anglo-American labor aristocrats who could realistically aspire to middle-class status. But the broader appeal of the eight-hour movement—to those of all economic statuses within the working class—came from the argument that a reduction in hours would solve the unemployment problem by spreading the available work among a larger number of workers (Cahill 1932, 18).

The precursor of the American Federation of Labor, the Federation of Organized Trades and Labor Unions, took the lead in the eight-hour movement in 1884 when it resolved that "eight hours shall constitute a legal day's labor from and after May 1, 1886." They included no provision for attaining this objective, but they eventually chose the general strike.

Chicago unions began active agitation for the demand on November 11, 1885, when the Bricklayers and Stonemasons Union resolved that they would work only eight hours a day after May 1, 1886 (*Chicago Tribune* November 12, 1885). On November 17, George Schilling of the Trades and Labor Assembly spoke on the issue at a meeting of the Carpenters and Joiners Union, suggesting the need for an organization to agitate for the demand; on Sunday, November 22, a number of trade unionists in the Trades and Labor Assembly heeded the call and organized the *Eight Hour Association.*

The association issued a manifesto calling on all workers to help establish the eight-hour day. The Eight Hour Association did not see shorter hours as a means of restructuring the capitalist system;

they were viewed as a reform that would reduce unemployment and provide workers with more leisure time. The association was initially organized by the native born, as is clear in this statement from the manifesto: "Has machinery in your trade abolished the demand for skilled artisans and craftsmen? Have the native American skilled workers in your trade been supplanted by cheap labor from Europe and Canada? Are wages sufficient for the support of native American families?" (*Chicago Tribune* November 23, 1885, 35).

Because of the power of the issue and the tremendous organizing momentum created by the movement, all the major labor organizations in the city—including the Trades and Labor Assembly, the Knights of Labor, the Central Labor Union, and the Social Revolutionary clubs—were soon involved in agitating for the eight-hour day (David 1958, 182). But the issues that had split the labor movement did not disappear under the impact of this movement, and factionalism between the reformers and revolutionaries continued.

Initially, the anarchists had been skeptical of the movement, feeling that a reduction in hours would not solve the problems of the working class because it would not transform the existing system of wage labor or the oppressive state. As Albert Parsons and August Spies argued in the *Alarm* of November 21, 1885 (cited in Flinn 1973, 260):

The private possession or ownership of the means of production and exchange places the propertyless class in the power and control of the propertied class, since they can refuse bread, or the chance to earn it, to all the wage classes that obey their dictation. Eight hours, or less hours, is, therefore, under existing conditions, *a lost battle*. The private property system employs only to exploit (rob) it, and while the system is in vogue, the victims—those whom it disinherits—have only the choice of submission or starvation.

We do not antagonize the eight hour movement, . . . we simply predict that it is a lost battle, and we prove that even if the eight hour system should be established at this late day, the wage-workers would gain nothing. They would still remain the slaves of their master.

In fact, the Social Revolutionaries never accepted the idea that the eight-hour day could be the answer to all the ills of the working class. But the Chicago revolutionaries could not be content to remain aloof from the most widespread and well-organized worker movement in the city's history. They determined to use it as a tool to agitate for their own more revolutionary beliefs; the organizational tool for such agitation was the Central Labor Union.

While the CLU was attempting to convince Chicago workers of the necessity of social revolution, the Trades and Labor Assembly counseled moderation. The assembly issued a circular to all manufacturing firms and employers in mid January 1886. It suggested that the presence in the city of large numbers of unemployed was a constant source of evil in the community and that Congress had supported the movement by making eight hours a legal day's work for government employees. It stated that the adoption of the eight-hour day would give employment to one-fifth more workers, many of whom had been displaced by machines. The circular ended as follows: "The workingmen of Chicago are ready to make sacrifices in wages in order that more people may find employment and for the general good of the whole community. Surely such a self-sacrificing spirit should meet with a cordial response from the employing class" (*Chicago Tribune* January 19, 1886, 5).

This moderate stand, suggesting that workers would be willing to sacrifice wages in order to gain the eight-hour day, was to become the basis of a political split between the Trades and Labor Assembly's Eight Hour Association and the Central Labor Union. By the movement's peak in April and May 1886, most of the city's German and Bohemian unions were demanding ten hours' pay for eight hours' work; the elite Anglo-American unions were declaring their willingness to settle for a proportionate wage cut along with the reduction in hours.

By March 1886, the eight-hour movement was mobilizing an unprecedented proportion of the Chicago working class for meetings and demonstrations. The Trades and Labor Assembly sponsored a demonstration at a West Side Turner hall. By eight o'clock on March 15, four thousand crowded into a hall meant for two thousand; three thousand more gathered outside, necessitating the erection of several speakers' platforms. The *Tribune* reported the presence of at least twelve hundred from the Bricklayers Union, five hundred from the Shoemakers Union, five hundred from the Cigarmakers no. 14, and three hundred from the boxmakers—all carrying banners and transparencies with moderate reform messages such as "Oppose Child Labor!" "Equality to All!" "Look How You Vote Next Fall!" "Down With Convict Labor!" (*Chicago Tribune* March 16, 1886, 10).

The meeting adopted the following resolutions:

Whereas—The reduction in the hours of daily labor to eight would . . . afford steady employment to all industrious men and women, create steady markets for the manufacturer, the farmer, and the merchant and dissipate the portentious clouds of discontent that too frequently of late obscure the social and political horizon, and

Whereas—While we fully recognize the oft-repeated assertion that under any and all circumstances the wages of labor are likely to fluctuate, we hold as a fact established beyond dispute by history that every step gained by the toiling masses in reducing the hours of labor is never lost but is permanent and enduring be it

Resolved—That we are heartily and determinedly in favor of the eight hour work day from and after May 1, 1886 and now pledge ourselves to use all fair and honorable means to secure its general adoption by every trade and occupation and,

Resolved—That we invite the cooperation of the press and the pulpit and earnestly urge upon all thinking people the necessity of a dispassionate and candid discussion of this momentous question. (*Chicago Tribune* March 16, 1886, 12)

This moderate statement indicates that, despite their presence in the same movement, the political split between the reformers and the revolutionaries remained. The Eight Hour Association wanted moderate reform, not revolution, considering the capitalist system perfectly acceptable. Their position lacks class consciousness, suggesting as it does that all classes have an interest in reducing hours of labor and enlisting the aid of such "working class enemies" as the middle and upper classes, the press, and the pulpit.

The Eight Hour Association held an even larger rally on April 10. More than seven thousand attended, and again thousands more blocked the doors. The meeting was attended by more than a thousand of the Bricklayers and Stonemasons Union, six hundred from the upholsterers, five hundred clothing cutters, and numerous other unions and Knights assembly members. The platform was occupied by over a hundred union, Trades and Labor Assembly, and Knights officers. As Nelson (1986a, 1) reports, 48 percent of those on the platform had Irish surnames, 32 percent had British names, and only 14 percent were immigrants from continental Europe.

Speakers repeated the same moderate themes from the earlier rally, and the assembly got its wish concerning the clergy's support. There were a number of clergy on the platform, and three Protestant ministers spoke to the crowd. All speeches were in English. One minister stressed the importance of temperance and self-improvement:

It's hard to work fourteen hours and then go home and read a book. My heart goes out to you workingmen who love your books and are denied the time to gratify it. But we must get the leisure first. I don't believe in drinking myself, but for all that I don't believe that all of you are teetotallars, nor do I believe that if you had the leisure you would spend your time in the saloon. (*Chicago Tribune* April 11, 1886, 32)

An Irish-born Knights of Labor leader also stressed the temperance theme and reiterated the importance of gaining the support of the clergy and press: "I tell ye fellows what to boycott, whisky! Quit crookin' your elbows and buildin' brick houses for saloonkeepers an' ye'all eat porterhouse steak instead of liver. We don't have to make this fight alone. We've got friends—people, and preachers, and papers" (*Chicago Tribune* April 11, 1886, 32). Both of these statements were greeted with wild cheers, cheers that would not have been forthcoming at a rally of antitemperance German or Bohemian workers.

The Central Labor Union and the Social Revolutionaries did not support the Trades and Labor Assembly effort. They wanted to use the movement as a stepping stone to revolution. They did not accept the reformers' call for a pay reduction and for temperance, and they did not support the attempt to recruit the clergy, the middle and upper classes, and the bourgeois press into the movement. So the CLU held a counterdemonstration on Sunday, April 25, 1886. About five thousand formed a procession six to eight abreast on Randolph Street. Red banners were flying as twenty-five mounted marshalls rode up and down the line giving instructions to the workers; bands played, and thousands watched as the parade marched through the city center to the lakefront.

The *Tribune* reported that *none* of the members of the Trades and Labor Assembly attended this gathering. Nearly all the marchers were German, Bohemian, and Polish; "there was scarcely an American, Irishman, Scandinavian, or Scotchman among them" (*Chicago Tribune* April 26, 1886, 19). The workers carried banners reading "The Brewer Works All Day and Night and Hardly Gets His Rest!" "Our Civilization—The Bully and the Policeman's Club!" "The Fountain of Right is Might!" "Workingmen Arm!" "Right is Might, We're the Strongest!" The sentiments were clearly more militant than those at the Trades and Labor Assembly rally.

Twenty-three unions were represented, showing the great strength of the CLU at this point. The following list indicates the number attending from each union:

Furniture Workers Union (German)	1,200
International Carpenters and Joiners (with Bohemian Turners Band)	1,000
German Bakers Union	900
Bohemian Lumbershovers	800
Brewery Workers	700
Lumberyard Workers no. 1	600
Metalworkers Union (German) (with Lassalle Band)	600
Butchers Union no. 1	300
Hand Labor Union no. 1	300
Cabinetmakers Union	300
Progressive Cigarmakers (German)	200
Bohemian Bakers Union (with the Meinken's Germania Orchestra)	200
Brewers Union no. 1 (with the Cadet Band)	200
Bohemian Workingman's Association	200
Beerkeg Coopers Union	150
Bohemian Carpenters	125
Bohemian Bricklayers	120
Saddlers Union (with the West Chicago Band)	90
Typographical Union no. 9 (German)	60
Carpenters of Cook, Hallock, and Gannon (with Bohemian Pilsen Band)	60
Metal Workers of Pullman no. 1	35

(*Chicago Tribune* April 26, 1886, 18)

The CLU managed to mobilize over eight thousand workers for a march in support of its principles. The dominance of Germans and Bohemians is obvious, with five unions being clearly identifiable as German and seven as Bohemian. The unions not clearly identifiable—the Hand Labor Union, Lumberyard Workers, Cabinetmakers, Metal Workers, Brewery Workers, Beerkeg Coopers, Saddlers, and Butchers—are all known to have had a high proportion of Germans and Bohemians in their trades (Illinois Bureau of Labor Statistics Report, 1884). The strength of anarchism was due largely to the anarchists' ability to mobilize unskilled and skilled workers within the German and Bohemian trade union movement.

The rally itself drew approximately twenty-five thousand Germans, Bohemians, and Poles (Nelson 1986b, 2). The most militant speeches of the day were in German; there had been *no* German speeches at the Trades and Labor Assembly events, clearly indicating the lack of German support for their reformist politics. Speakers at the CLU rally refused to accept the eight-hour day as the only goal of the Chicago labor movement. As August Spies suggested: "If you by your combination tear down the existing state of things, if you have obtained this little bit—the eight hour day—then on, on along the road of victory until the last stone of this bastille of order of the present lies in ruins" (*Chicago Tribune* April 26, 1886, 22). All the speakers argued that the movement had to be continued until the social order was overthrown.

Employers all over the city were becoming concerned. Facing an increasingly powerful and militant labor movement, they began to organize themselves into manufacturers associations. The pattern was for employers to organize and pass a resolution stating that they would lock out their workers if they demanded the more radical CLU-supported demand (the eight-hour day with no change in pay). But many workers defied their employers and refused to withdraw their militant demands; included in this group were the boot and shoemakers, three thousand German and twenty-five hundred Bohemian lumber shovers, the largely German furniture workers, German cigar makers, brick makers, bakers, lathers, and thousands of mainly Irish freight handlers. The result was strikes and/or lockouts in each of these trades.

Some workers, including the largely Irish stockyard workers and the mainly native-born machinists, agreed to accept the eight-hour day at reduced wages, with future wage rates to be negotiated. The unions of boxmakers, clothing cutters, carpenters and joiners, picture frame workers, and patternmakers achieved the eight-hour day with a 20 percent pay reduction. Some workers, including those at the Armour packinghouse (other packinghouse workers remained on strike), some of the brick makers, and the cigar makers, were granted ten hours' pay for eight hours' work. Finally, some workers—most of the clothing workers, many of the iron and steel workers, and the cloak makers—were on piece rates; the eight-hour movement was not seen as applicable to them at all (*Chicago Tribune* April 28–May 3, 1886).

As the movement gained strength, the split between the CLU and the Trades and Labor Assembly intensified. On April 28, George Schilling discussed the eight-hour question at a meeting of stockyard workers that included coopers, butchers, and laborers. On behalf of the Trades Assembly and the Knights of Labor, he advised those present not to press for ten hours' pay and not to strike unless absolutely necessary (*Chicago Tribune* April 29, 1886). The *Arbeiter Zeitung* was not as moderate, advising workers in late April:

In this hour we call upon the workers to arm themselves. We have but one life to lose. Defend it with every means at your disposal. In this connection we should like to caution those workingmen who have armed themselves to hide their arms for the present so that they cannot be stolen from them by a minion of order as has happened repeatedly. (*Chicago Tribune* May 2, 1886, 22)

A few days later one of the members of the Social Revolutionary clubs stated what had become obvious concerning the ethnic political splits that persisted despite the movement's growing power.

The German and Bohemian workers are thoroughly organized and armed and will fight to achieve their end. The brewers, maltsters, butchers, and bakers have already achieved the eight hour day. The employers won't shut down for more than a day or two, they can't risk losing their trade to the eastern cities.

The Knights of Labor are principally American and Irish; they don't train with the Germans and the Bohemians, and we can't get them to do aggressive work in the movement. They hang back and take what they can get, while the Germans and the Bohemians go out and get what they want. (*Chicago Tribune* May 1, 1886, 5)

Both the Trades Assembly and the Central Labor Union held meetings on Sunday, May 2. The assembly's meeting opened with a resolution to form an executive committee of representatives of *all* trades. But this attempt to unify the assembly and the CLU failed.

One speaker suggested that he "hoped the Assembly would not destroy the hope of achieving the eight hour system by joining with anybody for whom the American flag was not good enough" and that the "Trades and Labor Assembly ought to recommend that unions drop their unreasonable demands" (*Chicago Tribune* May 3, 1886, 16). Although most workers were advocating the more radical ten hours' pay demand, another speaker suggested that those advocating no pay reduction were actually against the eight-hour movement and that if the unions had followed the assembly's advice in asking for eight hours' pay for eight hours' work, there would have been no trouble. The movement's ethnic split was becoming more severe and rhetoric more strident as each faction strove to lead the movement down its chosen path.

Through its Eight Hour Association, the assembly distributed this circular:

If ever there was a time in the history of the labor movement when prudence should control your counsels, the present is that time. A false or ill-advised move at this juncture may defeat the very object you have in view. Under these circumstances we deem it our duty to request you to keep this important fact in mind and shape your demands accordingly.

Our advice is that where a disagreement as to terms exists, interview the employer or employers through a committee composed of your most trusted, most discreet and reliable representatives. Base your demands on justice. Present a united front. Determine to secure the adoption of the eight hour system even if concessions to attain it be made. Act like rational men, as law-abiding citizens should.

Discountenance all resort to violence, remembering you cannot afford to offend that public sympathy which is essential to your success. Remember also, if you refuse to act upon these suggestions you will have yourselves to blame if the present golden opportunity passes unimproved. (*Chicago Tribune* May 4, 1886, 28)

The assembly was now advocating polite bargaining with employers to win the eight-hour reform, even if the workers had to give up previously won gains to achieve the reduction in hours.

This was not the position of the Central Labor Union. They also held a meeting on Sunday, May 2, at which a major topic was the ethnic split bedeviling the movement. The German branch of the Carpenters and Joiners Union reported it had attempted to work with its English-speaking counterparts; the attempt had been un-

successful because the English-speaking union had considered the
German demand for ten hours' pay too radical. The German carpenters had decided to work for their own interests as a result. A
similar report was made by the German Typographical Union no.
9, which charged the American Chicago Typographical Union no.
16 with working in the interests of the bosses (*Chicago Tribune*
May 3, 1886). In fact after January 1885, the Chicago Typographical Union no. 16 had refused to honor German union members'
cards, claiming the International no longer recognized the German
union (Chicago Typographical Union no. 16 minutes, January 25,
1885). The CLU decided to appoint a committee to exchange information with the Trades and Labor Assembly but to give up all attempts to work with the assembly politically.

The Central Labor Union then sent a message to the city's workers that had little in common with the Trades and Labor Assembly
circular. The CLU called on all to support the eight-hour movement and suggested that piecework must be instantly abolished because it was "slavish" and "abominable." It went on, "the laboring
class will not be free from misery and want until the right to hold
capital is abolished and society is merged into one class." It ended
by suggesting that ministers and priests uphold the present social
system, so workers ought therefore to keep away from churches
(*Chicago Tribune* May 3, 1886, 17).

Chicago's eight-hour movement was strong despite these political differences. *Bradstreet's* reported that well over sixty thousand
workers in the city were involved, including twenty and a half
thousand clothing workers, seventeen thousand of whom were
women, ten thousand lumber shovers and laborers, ten thousand
metalworkers, seven thousand furniture and upholstery workers,
twenty-five hundred Pullman car workers, six hundred steamfit-
ters, and twelve thousand in miscellaneous trades. From forty to
forty-five thousand had gained some sort of hours reduction by the
end of the first week of May. Chicago was the center of the national
movement, having nearly one-third of all those demanding the
eight-hour day and over one-fifth of all those receiving the reduction in hours (*Bradstreet's* May 15, 1886, 1).

The depth of the movement in the city's working class made it
likely to succeed. The strike was close to a general one among
workers who had not yet achieved eight hours, and less street ac-

tion was necessary than during the 1877 strikes because the well-planned strike included many workers with scarce skills. But an event soon occurred that temporarily stalled the movement for a reduction in hours and destroyed the anarchist movement in the city—the Haymarket affair.

The Haymarket Affair

I shall not review the history of the Haymarket affair in great detail; Henry David (1958) and Paul Avrich (1984) have done that. I shall consider how the incident and the reaction to it illustrate the ethnic split in the Chicago labor movement between moderate Anglo-American and Irish workers and revolutionary Germans and Bohemians.

The trouble started at the McCormick Harvester factory. Because of a dispute over the discharge of union activists, the plant had been shut down in February 1886, and fourteen hundred employees had been locked out (David 1958, 187). McCormick workers called a strike, but the plant reopened in March with hundreds of new workers and Pinkertons to protect them. On May 3, the lumber shovers arranged a meeting near the works to discuss the eight-hour day. As August Spies was winding up a speech on the topic, the bell for the end of the shift rang; workers at the meeting attacked the strikebreakers with sticks and stones and drove them back into the plant (David 1958, 190).

Inspector Bonfield, the most repressive of Chicago's police captains, arrived, and the strikers fled; but they were pursued by the police, who killed one and wounded half a dozen others. Spies witnessed this and, thinking at least six workers had been killed, wrote his famous Revenge Circular, which called on all workers to "destroy the hideous monster that seeks to destroy you" (David 1958, 191–92). Arrangements were made to have a meeting on the evening of May 4 in Haymarket Square to protest police brutality.

When Spies arrived to speak at this meeting, only a few hundred workers were present. The speakers gave relatively moderate speeches; Mayor Harrison actually attended and agreed that no police action was necessary (David 1958, 199–202). As Samuel Fielden was finishing his remarks, he was interrupted by the approach of 175 police. Only two hundred workers remained, the rest having left when a rain cloud approached. Bonfield ordered the meeting to disperse. At that moment, a dynamite bomb exploded near the first rank of the police, killing one instantly and wounding many others. The remaining police began firing indiscriminately, killing four and wounding at least twenty workers and killing and wounding many of their fellow officers (Adelman 1976, 37–38).

Reaction to this incident led to the city's and the nation's first "red scare." The anarchists were charged with a conspiracy to overthrow the entire U.S. political and economic system through the use of dynamite bombs and other violent means. An important component of the reaction was nativism; the city's middle class and the press blamed the foreign born, particularly the Germans, for advocating violent revolution and for lacking an adequate understanding of American economic and political institutions.

The city's press held the anarchists responsible for the incident, even though the culprit who threw the bomb was never identified. The *Inter-Ocean* "reported":

The anarchists of Chicago inaugurated in earnest last night the reign of lawlessness which they have threatened and endeavored to incite for years. They threw a bomb into the midst of a line of 200 police officers, and it exploded with fearful effect, mowing down men like cattle. Almost before the missile of death had exploded the anarchists directed a murderous fire from revolvers upon the police as if their actions were prearranged, and as the latter were hemmed in on every side—ambuscaded— the effect of the fire upon the ranks of the officers was fearful. . . . The collision between the police and the anarchists was brought about by the leaders of the latter, August Spies, Sam Fielden, and A. R. Parsons, endeavoring to incite a large mass-meeting to riot and bloodshed. (Cited in David 1958, 206–7)

There is scarcely one supportable assertion in this paragraph; the other daily papers presented similar stories of the incident. The *Tribune* (May 5, 1886, 1) denounced the anarchists as "vipers," "ungrateful hyenas," and "serpents," and it called the "toleration" they had enjoyed "excessive and ill-considered." It would be necessary to crush both anarchism and communism, or else "the people of Chicago must expect an era of anarchy and the loss of their property, if not their lives."

The nativist component of the political attack was clear in the *Chicago Daily Herald* (May 5, 1886, 1) account, which suggested that the anarchist movement was composed of the "off-scourings of

Europe" and that the philosophy "menaced the very foundations of American society." The middle and upper classes were a sympathetic audience for these "red scare" messages. A temporary madness seemed to engulf them, convincing them the revolution, led by a band of dark, shady, German-speaking foreigners, was at hand (Sennett 1969).

Perhaps more surprising was the reaction of the Anglo-American and Irish workers in the Trades and Labor Assembly and in the Knights of Labor. "Respectable" workers, they felt it necessary to distance themselves from the "evil" represented by anarchism. The Knights were particularly strong in their condemnation of the anarchists even though Albert Parsons had been the first registered Knight in the city. The Chicago *Knights of Labor* (May 8, 1886, 1) printed this disclaimer in capital letters on its front page following Haymarket:

LET IT BE UNDERSTOOD BY THE WORLD THAT THE KNIGHTS OF LABOR HAVE NO AFFILIATION, ASSOCIATION, SYMPATHY OR RESPECT FOR THE BAND OF COWARDLY MURDERERS, CUTTHROATS AND ROBBERS KNOWN AS ANARCHISTS. THEY SNEAK THROUGH THE COUNTRY LIKE MIDNIGHT ASSASSINS STIRRING UP THE PASSIONS OF IGNORANT FOREIGNERS, UNFURLING THE RED FLAG OF ANARCHY AND CAUSING RIOT AND BLOODSHED. PARSONS, SPIES, FIELDEN, MOST AND ALL THEIR FOLLOWERS, SYMPATHIZERS, AIDERS, AND ABETTORS SHOULD BE SUMMARILY DEALT WITH!

The editorial went on to say that these anarchists deserved to be treated as "human monstrosities not entitled to the sympathy or consideration of any person in the world" and that they ought to be "blotted from the surface of the earth." This vendetta continued for years; in October 1886, the Knights condemned the anarchists again; they blamed the anarchist movement for the failure of the eight-hour day as late as 1889 (Chicago *Knights of Labor* January 26, 1889).

The other leaders of the labor reform movement in the city condemned the anarchists nearly as vociferously, despite the lack of concrete evidence against the anarchist leaders. The Chicago Typographical Union no. 16 passed the following series of resolutions after Haymarket, even though one of their former members—Albert Parsons—had been involved in the incident:

Resolved—That Chicago Typographical Union #16 condemns in unmeasured terms the heinous acts of the mob at the hay market [*sic*] May 4.

And we declare the men who have by their uncivilized teachings, caused this red letter day in the history of our city to be the greatest enemy the laboring man has.

Resolved—That Chicago Typographical Union #16 hereby offers a reward of $100 for the apprehension and conviction of the scoundrel who threw the bomb that caused the death and maiming of so many officers of the law.

Resolved—That our delegates to the Trade and Labor Assembly are hereby instructed to present these resolutions to that body and ask its cooperation and endorsement in order that justice may be meted out to those violators of law and civilization. (Chicago Typographical Union no. 16 minutes, May 9, 1886)

The lack of unity in the labor movement made it possible for employers and city government to destroy the eight-hour movement, both its reformist and revolutionary tendencies. Mayor Harrison ordered all gatherings, processions, and workers' meetings broken up. Infantry regiments were put on alert, and citizens' neighborhood patrols were revived. By May 6, the police bragged that they had raided over fifty socialist and anarchist gathering places and apprehended over two hundred suspects. Many prominent anarchists—including Spies, Parsons, Fielden, Michael Schwab, Adolph Fischer, George Engel, Oscar Neebe, and Louis Lingg—were arrested without warrants and held without specific charges. Police officers looking for publicity manufactured a variety of anarchist plots (David 1958, 223–24). All anarchist papers, including the *Alarm* and the *Arbeiter Zeitung*, were shut down; the former did not resume publishing until November 1887.

The nature of the scare meant that socialists, anarchists, strikers, and even conservative reform unionists were condemned; the various political tendencies in the Chicago labor movement were not differentiated. This hurt the eight-hour movement specifically and the labor movement generally. Unions were forced to distance themselves from labor militancy of any kind for years to come. As the Chicago *Knights of Labor* complained:

How often must the workingmen as a class deny their connection or sympathy with anarchy? It does seem as though the press at large has taken upon itself the task of convicting workingmen of socialism, anarchism, communism, and all the other *isms* society is heir to, regardless of the denials or protests, and it is high time that such wholesale misrepresentation ceased. (August 28, 1886; cited in Staley, 1930, 70)

The bomb caused a revulsion of feeling against the eight hour agitators and actually ended the struggle among a great number of trades and occupations. . . . A reign of terror came upon the "agitators." Tommy Morgan and other speakers did not dare to speak or write in the cause of shorter hours, and the movement then subsided. (Chicago *Knights of Labor* January 26, 1889; cited in Staley 1930, 70)

In the short term, the authorities' repressive strategy ended the eight-hour movement in the city. Most trades and unions lost their struggle for the eight-hour day. Employers felt free to rescind gains previously won by workers because there was no possibility of militant strikes in the immediate post-Haymarket period. In fact, labor activists of all stripes now found it impossible even to meet without police interference. At its peak, the movement had achieved some form of hours concession for seventy thousand workers in Chicago; by the end of the year, only ten thousand workers in the *state* were working the eight-hour day (Pierce 1957, 3: 289).

The *Chicago Daily Herald* declared that the bomb ended the eight-hour movement because after that incident the public became concerned with destroying the anarchists and became unconcerned with any question of hours and wages (David 1958, 535). And destroy the anarchist movement they did. The police and the criminal justice system charged a number of anarchists with conspiracy to murder the one policeman who was killed instantly by the bomb. David and Avrich document the many inequities in the trial of the anarchists; for example, the jury selection process was designed to ensure that only those who had already judged the defendants guilty would be chosen (David 1958, 235). The anarchists were essentially tried for their political beliefs; once the criminal justice system accepted that premise, they were doomed. The jury found seven of the defendants guilty (five Germans, one American, and one Englishman) and assigned them the death penalty: August Spies, Michael Schwab, Adolph Fischer, George Engel, Louis Lingg, Albert Parsons, and Samuel Fielden.

Much of Chicago rejoiced at the news of the verdict, and one headline read, "The Scaffold Waits—Seven Dangling Nooses for the Dynamite Fiends!" (David 1958, 319). The *Tribune* reiterated the nativist theme in editorializing:

The bearings of this verdict, however, extend far beyond local limits. It has killed Anarchism in Chicago, and those who sympathize with its horrible doctrines will speedily emigrate from her borders or at least never again make a sign of their sentiments. It goes still further than this. It is a warning to the whole brood of vipers in the Old World—the Communists, the Socialists, the Anarchists, the Nihilists—that they cannot come to this country and abuse its hospitality and its right of free speech without encountering the stern decrees of American law. The verdict of the Chicago jury will, therefore, check the emigration of organized assassins to this country. (Cited in David 1958, 320–21)

Organized labor continued to distance itself from the plight of the anarchists; only the greatly weakened Social Revolutionaries and the Central Labor Union remained consistently on the side of the condemned men. The Knights of Labor resolved the following in October 1886: "Resolved, That while asking for mercy for the condemned men, we are not in sympathy with the acts of the anarchists, nor with any attempts of individuals or associated bodies that teach or practice violent infractions of the law, believing that peaceful methods are the surest and best means to secure necessary reform" (David 1958, 325). Labor moderates did not come to the condemneds' defense until their last appeal had been denied, by which time it was too late. Spies, Fischer, Engel, and Parsons were hanged on November 11, 1887. Lingg had already committed suicide, and Schwab and Fielden's sentences had been commuted to life imprisonment.

The Haymarket Legacy

The Haymarket affair and its aftermath effectively ended the German anarchist movement, and it never reappeared. As the *New Yorker Volks-Zeitung* reported, "the trade union movement, which in Chicago had been stronger than in any other city in the country before Haymarket, was now at a completely low tide. The Central Labor Union had more than 40,000 members in the spring of 1886. Now a mere 5,000 are left on paper, and of these, not even 1,000 will show up at demonstrations" (cited in Keil 1986, 23). Even the *Alarm*, when it was finally published again on November 5, 1887, felt compelled to give up its advocacy of the use of force in the fight to emancipate the working class. Other radical organizations faced similar problems. The German American Turner Association complained of a "moral state of siege dating from the lamentable events in Chicago. Since that time anything smacking of dissatisfaction with the public order has been banned; anyone who dares express his sympathies for the masses and their struggle for salvation is declared a revolutionary and anarchist worthy of the gallows" (cited in Keil 1986, 23).

Employers now had a free hand in crushing militant strikes; they received even greater support from the passage of various repressive labor acts, including the Merritt Conspiracy Bill, which made it a crime to conspire to perform an act of force or violence dangerous to human life, person, or property. Even a speech or written article could make one liable under the act. The Coles Anti-Boycott Law affixed penalties of $2,000 and/or two years imprisonment for anyone conspiring with another to institute a boycott (Pierce 1957, 3: 289–90).

Haymarket and its aftermath simply ruled out the more militant socialist and anarchist choices within the labor movement; the movement's reformers now defined the only major tendency. They were active on both the economic and political fronts. Politically, the Trades and Labor Assembly founded the United Labor Party in August 1886. It was a coalition of various factions, including the remnants of the Greenback movement of the late 1870s. The party polled twenty-five thousand votes in the fall 1886 elections, electing one state senator, seven members of the house, and five judges. The party lobbied successfully for reformist legislation, including an anti–convict labor law, a law against the use of private detectives to put down labor disturbances, a law to prevent discharge for engaging in union activities, and an anti–sweatshop labor act; but there were few enforcement provisions.

On the economic front, there were now no competitors for the reform unionists. The Central Labor Union had been destroyed, and the Knights of Labor in Chicago were soon dead as well. The Knights' intensive organizing in 1886 had in fact been very haphazard; they had simply induced many existing unions to affiliate with them. In 1887, skilled unions, seeing the Knights assemblies as competition, demanded that all workers affiliated with the Knights also affiliate with the skilled trade unions in the city or face exclusion from the craft. Most Chicago craftsmen obeyed the order by withdrawing from the Knights altogether, which destroyed the mixed assemblies because the unskilled were unable to support them using their own resources. By the end of 1887, District 24 had only thirty-five hundred members, and only five hundred by 1889. The Trades and Labor Assembly expelled all Knights assemblies from the coalition in 1888 (Bogart and Thompson 1920, 467–73).

This left the labor movement in the control of the Trades and Labor Assembly unions. By 1890, sixty-five thousand Chicago workers belonged to these unions (Pierce 1957, 3: 297), which were now affiliated with the American Federation of Labor. The printers had provided the model for relationships with one's employers. In February 1885, as part of a strike settlement, the union ratified the first contract in the city between a union and an employer when it received a closed shop in return for a guarantee that the union would not engage in any sort of strike, boycott, or other job action against the *Telegram* (Chicago Typographical Union no. 16 minutes, February 8, 1885). In early 1887, the Chicago Typographical Union became the first in the city to engage in collective bargaining with an organization of employers, the Chicago Daily Newspaper Association. The price scale agreed to was to remain in effect for five years, subject to change at the end of each year. All other disputes between the parties would be submitted to arbitration if they could not be resolved by committee; strikes and boycotts were ruled out as a means of resolving disputes.

Similar trade agreements were soon worked out in the building trades and among mill workers, marine trades, machinists, woodworking, and garment workers. The agreements gave workers greater employment security and wage increases; employers received the assurance that production would not be interrupted by strikes or business hurt by boycotts. These conditions came at the cost of accepting the basic outlines of the capitalist economic system and all the problems that system would create for workers.

Conclusions

Clearly, Chicago did not have a unified labor movement in the 1870s and 1880s. There were at least three distinct tendencies. One was a *reform union* path that accepted the basic outlines of the economic and political systems. Reformers were conciliatory in their relations with their employers and worked for minor adjustments in the system through legislation and elections. Reform unionists aimed at higher wages, shorter hours, and a variety of changes that would make capitalism more tolerable to workers. The tendency can be traced through the skilled craft unions and mutual benefit societies of the printers, machinists, and construction trades unions and through several trades coalitions, including the General Trades Assembly in the 1860s and the Council of Trades and Labor Unions and the Trades and Labor Assembly of the 1870s and 1880s.

This reformist model of economic action and political organizing was weaker in periods of economic distress, such as the 1873–1879 depression, when many craft unions were destroyed. But the Lassallean tendency, *strongest* during the depression, had much in common with the reform union tendency. It proposed cooperation as a means of making the workingman competitive with capitalists already dominating the marketplace, and it encouraged workers to use their votes within the existing governmental framework to elect those sympathetic to working-class interests.

The constituency of the reform union tendency was primarily skilled Anglo-American workers in the aristocratic trade unions. The tendency was led by the printers of Chicago Typographical Union no. 16 in the General Trades Assembly of the 1860s and the Council of Trades and Labor Unions and the Trades and Labor Assembly of the 1870s and 1880s.

German skilled workers did participate at times in these trades coalitions, and some Germans cooperated with the Anglo-American workers for a while in the 1870s by defining moderate Lassallean politics. But they soon rejected moderate labor reform and defined a *revolutionary union* tendency. They questioned the basic laws of industrial capitalism in the city and argued that fundamental structural changes were necessary to make the system more just and equitable. The revolutionaries were class conscious, believing they should strive to emancipate the entire working class; they did not believe that they ought to work for benefits within each trade, as the reformers did. Although the revolutionaries acknowledged the possibility of using peaceful means to gain benefits for the working class, they moved increasingly toward the position that a violent revolution would be necessary to achieve the total emancipation of workers.

This tendency can be traced from the cells of the Marxist International of the early 1870s, through the more militant German wing of the Socialist Labor party, the Lehr und Wehr Verein and other armed resistance groups, and finally the anarchist Social Revolutionary clubs and the Central Labor Union. These groups used mass marches, militant strikes, armed resistance militia, and finally proposed the use of dynamite bombs in defense of working-class interests.

A third tendency, mobilized mainly by the unskilled, can also be defined: the *mass strike*. The unskilled were largely unable to participate in organized labor politics because craft union membership was usually the basis for such politics. The absence of an economic organizational base led the less skilled to resort to noninstitutional means of influence: crowds to intimidate strikebreakers, massive protest rallies by the unemployed to demand public jobs, and the general strike enforced by roving committees in working-class industrial districts.

Anglo-American workers rarely participated in these mass strikes. For example, the July 1877 strike was largely begun by Irish-born railroad workers and then dramatically escalated by other foreign-born workers, including Irish, Bohemian, Polish, and German outdoor laborers in Chicago lumberyards, coal yards, brickyards, and packinghouses. The native-born railroad workers, especially the engineers and conductors, as well as all the city's Anglo-American skilled unions remained aloof, ignoring the strike or arguing against it. Those few skilled unions that did discuss the eight-hour day and higher wages near the end of the strike were German.

One explanation of the mobilization pattern in the Chicago labor movement is that the labor aristocrats in the strongest, highest paid, longest lasting unions were the constituency for the reform tendency; that low-status skilled workers suffering skill degradation, low wages, and high unemployment used their weak unions to mobilize a revolutionary response to industrialization; that the unskilled, without strong unions, participated in mass strikes for higher wages.

But it is not possible to account for the mobilization pattern through an examination of workers' economic position alone. *Workers in the same trades, at the same skill levels, facing the same eco-*

nomic conditions for the same reasons chose different political paths based on their ethnic origins. The Bohemians and Irish were mostly unskilled. Both engaged often in militant strikes, which were the only possible means of improving the economic position of largely unorganized, unskilled laborers in the city. When they did finally enter organized politics through the creation of unions of unskilled Bohemians and the mobilization of many unskilled Irish in the Knights of Labor, the two groups chose very different political paths. The Irish were reformers, and many of the Bohemians were militant revolutionaries.

Similar political differences arose among Chicago's skilled workers. The split in the cigar makers union between German and Anglo-American workers is a good example. A group of workers in the same trade facing similar working conditions, the same vulnerability to mechanization and sweatshop cigar manufacturing, and similar economic status were unable to join in a common political cause. There was a significant tendency for skilled workers to join either the reformist or the revolutionary tendency based on their ethnicity, with the Anglo-Americans in the reformist faction and the Germans in the revolutionary group. In the 1880s, the German printers, carpenters and joiners, cigar makers, bricklayers and stonemasons, coopers, and painters were all active in the Central Labor Union; the Anglo-Americans in those trades were in the reformist Trades and Labor Assembly.

The rest of the evidence tells the same story. The militant 1873 unemployed marches were led by the International, an organization without an Anglo-American section but with three German, one French, one Scandinavian, and one Polish section. The split between the Marxists and Lassalleans in the 1870s was based partly on ethnicity; the Marxist tendency was overwhelmingly German. Later in the 1870s, the militant strikes by coal heavers, lumber shovers, and brickyard workers led to the development of the mass strike model used in 1877. The most active workers in those strikes were foreign born, especially Irish, German, and Bohemian. In the late 1870s, when the Socialist Labor party militantly called for the nationalization of much of U.S. industry, it was largely German. Most SLP electoral support came from heavily German and Bohemian sections of the city.

The anarchist tendency was the most revolutionary of the period, arguing for the total destruction of the capitalist system, the abolition of class rule, the replacement of the economic system by a system of autonomous producer groups, and the elimination of the state. The strength of the Chicago anarchist movement by the mid 1880s was due to the use of strong German and Bohemian community and trade union networks to mobilize the movement.

The ethnic fragmentation in the Chicago labor movement was also obvious during the eight-hour movement, when a split developed between the largely Anglo-American and Irish workers in the Trades and Labor Assembly and the Knights of Labor and the Germans and Bohemians in the Central Labor Union and the Social Revolutionary clubs. The Anglo and Irish reformers wished to gain the eight-hour day as a reform to decrease unemployment and increase leisure time; they were willing to accept pay reductions if necessary to gain their goal. The Germans and Bohemians wished to use the eight-hour agitation to promote total revolution and stuck to the more militant demand of no pay cuts. Both tendencies were strong, mobilizing thousands for marches in support of their demands. The factionalism was resolved only by the use of repressive force against the anarchist movement. Significantly, the repression was accepted, even applauded, by the Anglo-American and Irish reformers. Eliminating the anarchists from the labor scene strengthened reform unionism, which has dominated labor politics from 1886 to the present day.

Chapters 1 and 2 have analyzed the mobilization pattern in the Chicago labor movement during industrialization. The crucial importance of ethnicity in the mobilization of that movement has been documented, but the reasons for the role of ethnic origins have yet to be identified. What about ethnicity made it a factor in determining whether a worker remained inactive or joined revolutionary or reformist movements? The list of possibilities is nearly endless. Was it the economic, cultural, or political background in the country of origin that determined the immigrant's political choice in the Chicago movement? Did those from skilled trade backgrounds tend to become revolutionaries, and those of peasant origins become reformers? Were Germans revolutionaries because they had been socialists and anarchists in Germany?

Was the immigrant's situation in Chicago the key factor? Did ethnic background determine economic position in the Chicago labor market? Perhaps a cultural division of labor was created so that ethnic origin determined economic situation, which in turn determined political choice. Perhaps the reformism of the Anglo-American workers can be explained by their position in the labor aristocracy. Or were noneconomic factors, such as the impact of nativism and the exclusion of ethnic groups from influence in the Chicago polity, also important? Perhaps cultural and language differences simply made it impossible for workers from various ethnic groups to communicate adequately. Employers' divide and conquer strategies might have effectively prevented working-class solidarity. What was the role of ethnic residential segregation in determining political choice in the movement? The next few chapters determine some reasons for the importance of ethnicity as a decisive factor in political mobilization in the labor movement by analyzing the specific political choices of Anglo-American, Irish, and German workers.

Chapter Three

Anglo-American Labor Reform
in Chicago

When they were active in the labor movement, the native-born and non-Irish immigrants from the British Isles were usually reformers. These workers founded and led many of the early craft unions, which often tried to establish good relations with their employers in the economic sphere and proposed legislative reform and attempted to elect sympathetic candidates to office in the political realm. But few Anglo-American workers supported actions to overturn the existing economic and political institutions; unlike the predominantly German socialists and anarchists, they accepted capitalism and representative democracy as institutions that served the interests of the working class.

It is important not to oversimplify the complex politics of the Anglo-American workers. Some labor reformers were attracted to somewhat more radical schemes, such as producer cooperatives, or flirted with socialism during the 1870s depression. Others supported various panaceas to solve the problems experienced by workers in the industrial revolution, such as Greenbackism and the eight-hour day. A small number, Albert Parsons among them, joined the socialist and anarchist movements.

But these were exceptions. Those who became revolutionaries—for example, both the native-born Albert Parsons and the English-born anarchist Samuel Fielden—had early experiences that radicalized them. Parsons had been active in the abolitionist movement and was married to a black woman, Lucy Parsons, who was one of

86

the most important revolutionaries of the period (Ashbaugh 1976); these experiences made it less likely that he would follow the reformist path of his fellow printers. And Fielden had been a child laborer in a British cotton mill for thirteen years beginning at age eight and had been influenced by the abolitionist movement as well (Roediger and Rosemont 1986, 57).

Anglo-American workers with unexceptional lives accepted the system as given. A variety of factors—including the impact of British immigrants, the high *average* economic status of the group, their acceptance of ideologies that legitimated the system, residential dispersion, and their ability to gain some political influence in the Chicago polity—convinced the overwhelming majority of Anglo-Americans that reform would be enough.

British Immigration to the City

The non-Irish immigration from Great Britain has a special importance in Chicago history because most of the native born in the city had migrated from eastern states and had British ancestors. Unlike many subsequent immigrant groups, the original English U.S. settlers did not have to adjust to a foreign identity; rather, they came as colonizers who hoped to reproduce most aspects of English society and culture in their new home (Steinberg 1981, 7). According to the best available estimate, 61 percent of the white population of the United States in 1790 were of English descent, and another 17 percent were Scotch or Irish (Steinberg 1981, 7). Ninety-nine percent of the colonists were Protestant.

There was a variety of reasons why those from England, Scotland, and Wales decided to try their luck in the United States. Underpopulation was an important problem in the early days of the colonies; many of the early immigrants were indentured servants, paupers, vagrants, and convicts who had been recruited by emigration agents to fill unskilled jobs in this country (Steinberg 1981, 10–11). Other immigrants came in search of political and religious freedom. Most of the early settlers were from the middle part of the English class structure. The lower classes (the rural poor) could not afford to emigrate, and the upper classes (the royal aristocracy) had no motivation to do so.

This petite bourgeoisie of small farmers and small businessmen brought with them a classical liberal ideology; the more entrenched feudal beliefs, which might have encouraged viewing society in class terms, were more likely to be held by the aristocrats and serfs who had been left behind in England. Middle-class ideology rejected theories of society that emphasized the importance of class conflict and celebrated the growth of laissez-faire capitalism and a system of political democracy in which each small landowner or businessman had an equal say in the governmental process (Garner 1977, 30–33). Puritanism, with its suggestion that those who work hard will get ahead and be among those chosen by God for salvation, also found a comfortable home in this environment (Laurie 1979). These middle-class ideas had a profound impact on the Anglo-American working class.

Large numbers from the top of the British working class—skilled craftsmen—also emigrated to the United States. In fact, U.S. industrialization could not have proceeded without the British worker; there simply were not enough native-born workers with the appropriate skills. As Erickson suggests, "nearly every new industry begun in America before 1840 was fertilized with British skills." The British skilled worker was used to "nurse a new industry into life, to oversee or superintend a new factory or mill, to operate or service complicated machinery, or to add a new process or a finer make of goods to an existing industry" (Erickson 1957, 4).

No expense was spared to import skilled craftsmen from England and Scotland. Transportation expenses were guaranteed. Lucrative three- to five-year contracts were drawn up, guaranteeing the artisan high levels of pay regardless of the success of the venture or trade conditions prevalent at the time. Many others were induced to come to the United States with extravagant profit-sharing bonuses (Erickson 1957, 5).

Partly because of the power their scarce skills bestowed on them, the English craftsmen soon came to be regarded as the "prima donnas" of the labor force; they often refused to instruct native apprentices, objected to having other workers working near them, or quit to found their own businesses. Employers were even forced to bargain with the trade unions in England over wages and working conditions.

By the mid nineteenth century, British workers were being pushed as well as pulled to the United States. Problems at home included crop failures, overpopulation due to declining death and high birth rates, and most important, the impact of industrialization on British and Scottish craftsmen (Johnson 1966, 54). The spinning jenny, water frame, mule, and power loom revolutionized the work of both the hand spinner and the hand weaver in the textile trades. The introduction of steam power moved most production into industrial cities and out of villages. Unemployment was soon as high as 50 percent for weavers and nearly as high for other village craftsmen (Johnson 1966, 54).

Approximately thirty thousand Englishmen and Scotchmen came to the United States from 1853 to 1860, over forty-four thousand from 1861 to 1870, sixty-four thousand from 1871 to 1880, and nearly one hundred ten thousand from 1881 to 1890 (Johnson 1966, 347). Many wound up in Chicago. Non-Irish immigrants from the British Isles made up as much as 8.3 percent of the Chicago population in 1850, then declined to 5.7 percent in 1860, 5 percent in 1870, and 3.6 percent in 1880 and 1890 (Beijbom 1971, 114). Data on the class and skill backgrounds of migrants are unavailable for the nineteenth century; statistics for the first decade of the twentieth century indicate that over 38 percent of British migrants were professional and skilled workers, the highest percentage skilled of any immigrant group (U.S. Senate 1911, 4: 28).

The many British craftsmen who immigrated to the United States and to Chicago brought their strong trade union traditions. The nature of that tradition is the subject of a stimulating debate among English social historians (Anderson 1980; Calhoun 1982; Foster 1974; Thompson 1963). The weight of evidence, according to both non-Marxists such as Calhoun (1982) and Marxists such as Anderson (1980), suggests that early radical resistance to British industrialization was based on a strong reaction by the trades to the undermining of their economic and social status. But these revolutionary sentiments were transformed by mid century into Chartist reformism. Such moderate politics were based on the political leadership of a segment of the British working class, the labor aristocracy, which had been able to gain a privileged economic and social position through strong union control of certain crafts.

Engels had recognized this phenomenon and commented on it as early as 1852 in a letter to Marx. As he suggested in his preface to the *Condition of the Working Class in England:*

The engineers, the carpenters and joiners, the bricklayers are each of them a power, to the extent that . . . they can even successfully resist the introduction of machinery. That their condition has remarkably improved since 1848 there can be no doubt, and the best proof of this is in the fact that for more than fifteen years not only have their employers been with them, but they with their employers, upon exceedingly good terms. They form an aristocracy among the working class; they have succeeded in enforcing for themselves a relatively comfortable position, and they accept it as final. (Engels 1958, 368)

Lenin later echoed this sentiment: "The English proletariat is becoming more and more bourgeois, so that this most bourgeois of all nations is apparently aiming ultimately at the possession of a bourgeois aristocracy and a bourgeois proletariat as well as a bourgeoisie" (Lenin 1966, 252).

Perhaps alone among the working classes in the industrializing nations, the British labor aristocracy had moved into a stage of accommodation to capitalism at the time of the industrialization of Chicago. Musson (1976) points out that labor aristocratic unions developed early in English history in the iron, engineering, and cotton industries among the millwrights, steam engine makers, textile machine makers, iron founders, boilermakers, and cotton spinners. The main concerns of these unions were wages, hours, apprenticeship regulations, and working conditions in their particular trades. Collective action across trade lines occurred only when support was needed for strikes, not out of class consciousness.

This British model of labor economic and political action was familiar to many of the skilled workers who immigrated to Chicago, and it was implemented in the city's printing, machine, and construction trades. The British Amalgamated Society of Engineers had a union with ninety-seven members in Chicago by 1866; the Amalgamated Society of Carpenters had three hundred members in the city by 1870 (Schneirov 1984, 37). These and other Chicago unions instituted another characteristically British innovation: benefit systems. These systems explicitly favored self-interest over class consciousness as a means of promoting active union membership and participation. The *Workingman's Advocate* commented as follows regarding this *new model unionism:* "Perhaps the strongest reason why such a feature [benefit systems] has proven successful is that self-interest controls, to a great extent, all human action; and when the benevolent is combined with the protective, as in this instance, selfishness, if no more honorable instinct, prompts active and continued membership" (July 4, 1868, cited in Schneirov 1984, 38). The great impact of new model unionism is indicated by the fact that a variety of unions, including the iron molders, sailors, shoemakers, bricklayers, tailors, printers, stonecutters, painters, and ship carpenters, implemented benevolent features between 1869 and 1872 (Schneirov 1984, 39).

Ethnic Segmentation in the Chicago Labor Market

New model unionism was effective in elevating the economic status of a certain portion of the Chicago working class. But because of its stress on self-interest and trade interests, the use of the model inevitably created severe economic disparities within the working class as a whole. Craft unionism, as practiced by the British- and native-born elite, excluded from their trades everyone except close male friends and relatives. Their control of many of the elite craft unions—as in printing, the machine trades, and construction—meant that Anglo-American workers, both British and native born, were on the average more privileged than other European immigrants.

Table 9, which shows the occupational structure of each of the major ethnic groups in the city for 1870, 1880, and 1890, illustrates that the most privileged group by far was the native born of native-born parents. Next in status come the British immigrants, then the Germans, the Scandinavians, and finally the Irish. The native born manage to place an extraordinarily high percentage in the middle and upper classes, about 45 percent for the three census years, compared to approximately 30 percent for the city as a whole. The British do less well in this regard; they are close to the city averages in the upper and middle classes, placing from one-quarter to one-third in that category.

Another measure of status is the capacity to avoid the city's worst unskilled jobs; again the native- and British-born groups do very well in this respect. Both have about one-quarter in the category in 1870 and about one-fifth in 1880 and 1890, compared to around one-third for the city as a whole. The British, although not able to enter the middle and upper classes in large numbers, partially

TABLE 9. *Chicago's Occupational Structure by Nativity,*
1870, 1880, 1890
(in percentages)

Class	United States	British	German	Scandi-navian	Irish	Other	Total
1870							
Upper middle and upper	22.2	9.9	10.2	4.2	5.6	8.9	12.7
Lower middle	25.3	14.9	13.0	5.5	10.2	18.5	16.5
Labor aris-tocracy	15.1	31.9	18.2	30.5	13.8	15.1	18.3
Low-status skilled	13.7	18.1	26.2	21.6	12.2	24.6	17.9
Un-skilled	23.7	25.2	32.4	38.2	58.2	33.0	34.5
Total	100.0	100.0	100.0	100.0	100.0	100.1	99.9
N	32,831	10,061	22,772	6,610	20,258	5,193	97,725
1880							
Upper middle and upper	16.0	11.6	10.8	4.2	7.4	9.9	12.2
Lower middle	25.0	17.2	13.0	5.8	10.0	13.1	17.7
Labor aris-tocracy	18.5	31.0	15.4	24.1	14.1	12.4	18.3
Low-status skilled	20.4	20.6	31.3	33.6	15.5	33.8	24.0
Un-skilled	20.0	19.4	29.5	32.3	53.0	30.7	27.8
Total	99.9	99.8	100.0	100.0	100.0	99.9	100.0
N	72,171	14,041	36,160	11,545	21,219	11,362	166,498

TABLE 9, *continued*

Class	U.S., native parents	U.S., foreign parents	Total United States	British	German	Scandinavian	Irish	Other	Total
1890									
Upper middle and upper	19.9	10.0	14.3	11.4	10.9	4.9	6.3	11.9	11.5
Lower middle	35.3	26.5	30.4	22.4	11.7	8.1	13.8	7.7	20.1
Labor aristocracy	18.5	20.1	19.4	27.6	21.2	26.8	12.4	14.4	20.0
Low-status skilled	9.6	19.4	15.1	19.2	23.7	22.9	11.6	30.3	19.1
Unskilled	16.7	24.0	20.8	19.4	32.4	37.3	56.0	35.8	29.3
Total	100.0	100.0	100.0	100.0	99.9	100.0	100.1	100.1	100.0
N	74,767	95,658	170,425	31,709	74,649	40,463	36,169	39,654	393,069

Source. 1870 Census of Population, Table 32, p. 782; 1880 Census of Population, Table 35, p. 566; 1890 Census of Population, Table 118, p. 650.

compensate for this failure by having a high proportion in the labor aristocracy (around one-third) compared to the city average (one-fifth).

The elite position within the working class enjoyed by the native born and British is shown by the extent to which they dominated the labor aristocratic trades in the city. They were 73 percent of the printers, 69 percent of the railroad workers, 60 percent of the machinists, and 63 percent of employees of manufacturing establishments; but they represented only 26 percent of laborers. Railroad industry data also indicates that the native born and British were a low proportion of the low-status railroad laborers and freight handlers and a high proportion of the elite trades—engineers and conductors (Illinois Bureau of Labor Statistics Report 1884).

The result of this pattern of occupational representation was that Anglo-Americans—native born and non-Irish immigrants from the British Isles—dominate the occupational categories in the upper reaches of the class structure. The native born alone account for over half of the upper-middle and upper classes in all three census years and from one-half to two-thirds of the lower-middle class. If British immigrants are included as part of this English-speaking, largely Protestant elite, the percentages balloon to around two-thirds of the middle and upper classes. Within the working class, this elite ethnic group was also well represented within the labor aristocracy; over half were native born or British, and well over half of the two lower-working-class groups are from non-Anglo ethnic groups.

Anglo-American workers were also more widely dispersed throughout the occupational structure; other ethnic groups tended to be confined to a small number of low-status job categories. The truth of this proposition can be shown through the use of a statistic that measures the degree to which each ethnic group was evenly distributed throughout the occupational structure. Using such a dispersion measure on the detailed occupational categories of the 1880 Census reveals that the native born were most evenly distributed with a low score of .33, Germans have a score of .53, Scandinavians have a score of .70, and the Irish have a score of .95.* The high scores of the Irish and Scandinavians reflect the fact that the Irish and Swedes in the city were generally of peasant background; former peasants were heavily concentrated in undifferentiated unskilled categories in the census (such as "laborer").

The Anglo-American worker was in a privileged economic position throughout the period when compared to first-generation immigrants. But what about the second generation? Unfortunately, the 1870 and 1880 Censuses have no breakdowns for the first and

---

*This measure is defined as follows:

$$X_1 = 10 \left[\sum_i^{66} \left(\frac{N_{ij}}{N_j} - \frac{1}{k} \right)^2 \right]$$

where N_{ij} is the number of individuals in ethnic group j employed in occupation i; N_j is the number of individuals in ethnic group j; and k is the number of occupational categories, in this case, the sixty-six nonagricultural occupations listed in the 1880 Census.

second generations. However, the 1890 Census did report on occupation for the native born of native-born parents, and the comparison with second-generation immigrants is most instructive. The native born of native-born parents are the elite of the Chicago class structure, placing a remarkable 55 percent of their number in the middle and upper classes and having only 17 percent in the unskilled working class. Those of foreign-born parents do much less well, placing 36 percent in the middle and upper classes and having one-fifth of their number in the unskilled category.

Richard Sennett's analysis of a middle-class community on Chicago's West Side reinforces this conclusion. Using city directories to trace the occupational status of fathers and sons in Union Park, Sennett concludes: "The situation of the sons of the foreign-born was . . . clear-cut. Starting from a base similar to that of the children from native families, they had a steadily worsening position in their occupational profiles, relative to sons of native-born fathers" (Sennett 1974, 228).

Thus, there was an *ethnically segmented labor market* in Chicago in this period; ethnic origin was highly correlated with position in the labor market. The average differences in occupational status were reflected in income levels that varied according to ethnic group. Figures for overall earnings have been obtained from the 1884 Bureau of Labor Statistics (BLS) report. Unfortunately, this report, based on voluntary submissions, heavily overrepresents the skilled categories within the working class. The BLS report indicates that the Chicago working class was 47 percent labor aristocrat, 31 percent low-status skilled, and 22 percent unskilled. The 1880 Census, a much less biased source because it used census takers and not voluntary returns, indicates that the working class was probably closer to 26 percent labor aristocrat, 34 percent low-status skilled, and 40 percent unskilled. Thus, the BLS report overestimates the average income of any ethnic group with a large proportion in unskilled laborer positions.

To correct for this problem, earnings means were weighted using the more accurate 1880 Census proportion for each ethnic group within each working-class sector. This procedure results in British-born workers having the highest earnings, at $598 a year, followed by the native born, with $549, Scandinavians with $517, Germans with $476, and Irish with $447. The unweighted Bohemian figure is $436. Although there is little census data on Bohemians, manuscript census analysis and BLS returns indicate that their occupational statuses and earnings were similar to those of the Irish (Schneirov 1975).

The fact that the British worker seems more privileged than the native-born worker should not come as a surprise. The BLS report included only data on the working class, within which the British had the highest proportion in the labor aristocracy of any ethnic group (44 percent in 1880 compared to 31 percent for the native born and 26 percent for the city as a whole). But outside the working class, the British were much less able to penetrate the middle and upper classes than were the native born. In other words, the ability of the native born to reach the middle and upper classes is not reflected in these income figures. If average earnings across all classes could be computed, the native born would probably have a higher average income than any group because of their high proportion in the top classes in the city.

The average of over $400 for the Irish and Bohemians conceals the fact that many unskilled laborers made much less than this, probably around $350 to $400 per year. For 1882, unskilled laborers in the city made an average of $386 per year, and railroad laborers made $367. Less than half of what many of the elite working-class trades made, this was generally not enough to support one's family (Illinois Bureau of Labor Statistics Report 1882).

There are at least two possible explanations for these ethnically based earnings differences. Hechter's (1975, 1978) cultural division of labor thesis would predict that they were due to these ethnic groups' having different occupational distributions and thus different earnings. Ethnic competition theory (Olzak and Nagel 1986) would propose that they were due to wage discrimination based on ethnicity, that certain ethnic groups made less than others when they worked in the same jobs in the same trades.

Table 10 reports on earnings by head of household for each ethnic group in the city for 1884, controlling for working-class sector. These figures should be interpreted with caution because the numbers involved are small. The most dramatic fact is the high earnings for all the ethnic groups in the labor aristocrat category, yearly earnings often $200 to $300 higher than those in the unskilled and low-status skilled jobs. The key to earning power was the ability to

TABLE 10. *Earnings of Head of Household by Ethnic Group and Working-Class Sector, 1884*
(in dollars)

Ethnic Origin	Earnings	N
Labor Aristocrat		
Native born	673.81	52
British	783.00	16
German	710.88	17
Scandinavian	719.33	9
Irish	741.33	36
Bohemian	637.50	2
Other	704.00	1
Total	712.72	133
Low-Status Skilled		
Native born	545.04	29
British	486.25	4
German	478.03	31
Scandinavian	416.00	6
Irish	468.67	9
Bohemian	402.86	7
Other	450.00	1
Total	489.13	87
Unskilled		
Native born	438.08	12
British	420.00	1
German	351.92	13
Scandinavian	471.57	7
Irish	362.33	18
Bohemian	380.00	3
Other	260.63	8
Total	375.81	62

Source. 1884 Bureau of Labor Statistics Report.

enter an elite trade rather than ethnic group per se. In other words, occupational distribution, not wage discrimination, explains the earnings differences between various ethnic groups.

There was no strict ethnic caste system in Chicago in this period; position in the class system or even within the working class was not strictly determined by ethnic group. But certain groups, especially the Anglo-American workers, were more likely to succeed in the Chicago labor market. This was primarily because they could enter and succeed in the higher status crafts, not because of wage discrimination within occupational categories.

One explanation for the reformist politics of the Anglo-American workers would then be that they simply understood that the system was working in their interests. Why should they challenge an economic system that was meeting their needs? The difficulty with this argument is that the economic situation of Anglo-American workers was much more varied than their almost invariably reformist politics.

In other words, such a proposition fails to account for the reformist politics of lower status skilled and unskilled Anglo-American workers. Why would native-born cigar makers support reform politics despite the fact that the business cycle and mechanization would soon destroy their union, indeed would soon destroy the trade itself? The answer is that the politics of native-born cigar makers were influenced by a variety of noneconomic factors, including residential patterning, cultural and ideological beliefs, and Anglo-American workers' ability to influence the political system.

Residential Dispersion of the Anglo-American Workers

Residential patterning is crucial to understanding political mobilization because community-based social networks were often used in the mobilization process. The Chicago labor movement certainly did not confine itself to workplace networks in its political organizing efforts. Community-based networks were especially important in the more militant movements; both the 1877 general strike and the 1880s anarchist movement were mobilized in foreign-born residence areas. The pattern of residential concentration or dispersion varied significantly by ethnic group. The more dispersed groups, such as the Anglo-Americans, tended to accept more moderate politics; the groups concentrated in more ethnically homogeneous neighborhoods were more likely to espouse revolutionary politics.

The process of ethnic residential settlement is illustrated in Maps 1, 2, and 3, which show the settlement pattern for selected ethnic groups for 1860, 1870, and 1900.* The maps do not indicate population densities; no neighborhood was ethnically homogeneous. Rather, the noted areas were neighborhoods or communities with distinctive ethnic institutions: stores, clubs, bars and saloons, social organizations, and so on. White areas represent the primary settlements of the native born.

The 1860 map indicates clearly the propensity of the native born to settle near the city's center along the lake and on the West Side; this was to be a pattern throughout nineteenth-century Chicago history, as succeeding maps indicate. These two areas contained the city's most desirable housing, which the native and British born were able to obtain because of their higher average economic status. Apartment buildings were constructed near the central business district (CBD) as early as 1868. These "family hotels" or "French flats," as they were called at the time, allowed the worker to "keep up appearances" by avoiding living in a small, low-status cottage (Pierce 1957, 3: 57–58). Living in or near the CBD also meant proximity to many of the city's higher status jobs, which the Anglo-American workers could reasonably expect to acquire.

As Sennett has suggested, the alternative, living in the river wards, was not desirable for other reasons:

Most large cities are located on or near rivers; in the case of Chicago, the Chicago River's two branches converge at what was then the center of town. In the nineteenth century, the river was used as an open sewage and refuse canal; that meant it smelled. To someone with a sensitive nose and ample means, it was an obvious move to get as far away from the river as possible, on open high land like that of the West Side. (Sennett 1974, 12–13)

Another reason Anglo-American workers did not want to live in the river wards was that they did not want to be near the rapidly

---

*These maps are from the Chicago Department of Development and Planning publication *Historic City* and are based on census data, parish and congregation records, and general histories of Chicago.

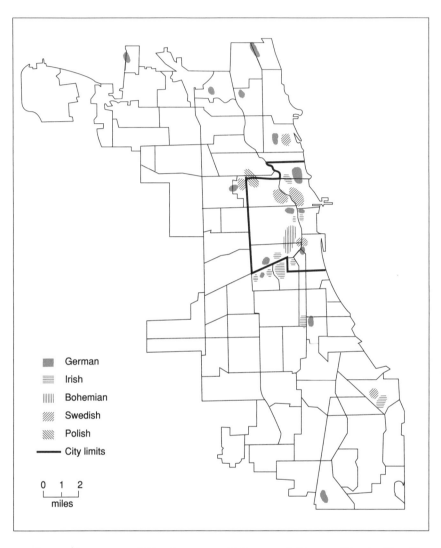

German
Irish
Bohemian
Swedish
Polish
City limits

0 1 2
miles

Source. Department of Development and Planning of Chicago, *Historic City: The Settlement of Chicago* (Chicago: Department of Development and Planning of Chicago, 1976), p. 15.

Map 1. Chicago ethnic community settlement pattern, 1860.

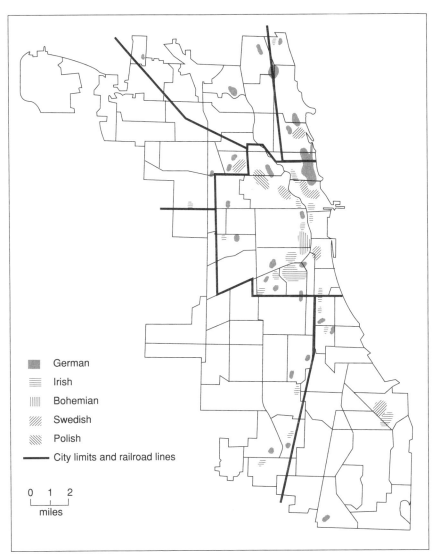

German

Irish

Bohemian

Swedish

Polish

City limits and railroad lines

0 1 2
miles

Source. Department of Development and Planning of Chicago, *Historic City: The Settlement of Chicago* (Chicago: Department of Development and Planning of Chicago, 1976), p. 39.
Map 2. Chicago ethnic community settlement pattern, 1870.

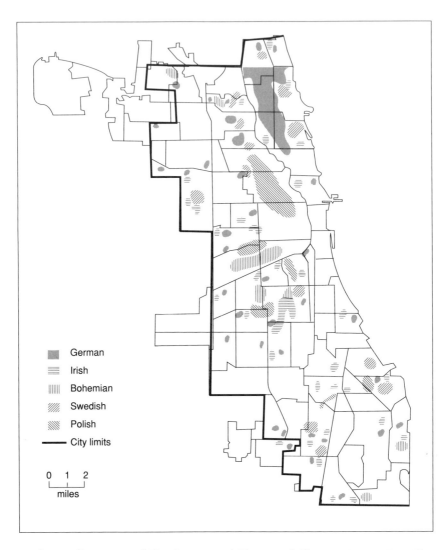

German

Irish

Bohemian

Swedish

Polish

City limits

0 1 2
miles

Source. Department of Development and Planning of Chicago, *Historic City: The Settlement of Chicago* (Chicago: Department of Development and Planning of Chicago, 1976), p. 61.

Map 3. Chicago ethnic community settlement pattern, 1900.

growing residential areas of newly arrived immigrants; such non-Anglo, Catholic immigrants were considered bad neighbors because they were viewed as dirty, uncouth, uneducated, immoral, and generally un-American.

As in the occupational sphere, the native born had more residential choices than the foreign born. Some lived in the CBD, but the native and British born were more likely to be able to afford the more expensive, spacious, newer housing in the city's outer wards. Many Anglo-American families chose the West Side because it offered good transportation to CBD jobs (Hoyt 1933, 91); a number of them, for example, acquired neat, single-family homes in the West Side community of Union Park (Sennett 1974).

An index of residential segregation using the 1884 Chicago School Census documents the greater residential concentration of the city's Irish and German residents. The index varies from 0 to 1, with ethnic groups that are more concentrated in fewer wards having a higher index than those more dispersed in a higher number of wards.* The results are .41 for the Germans, .48 for the Irish, but only .28 for the native born.

Katznelson (1981) has argued that the separation of work and home, which occurs with residential dispersion, has a moderating impact on the worker's politics. He argues that militant movements are nearly always based simultaneously in both workplaces and communities.

Another reason this residential pattern may have contributed to the moderation of Anglo politics is that it meant that Anglo-American workers lived in class-heterogeneous neighborhoods. Living in the peripheral, more prestigious communities meant that Anglo workers were more likely to interact with and identify with middle-class residents. They were more likely to accept moderate, reformist, middle-class ideas about the system than were foreign-born workers, who lived in exclusively working-class residence areas.

*This measure is defined as follows:

$$X_1 = 10 \left[\sum_{i}^{18} \left(\frac{N_{ij}}{N_j} - \frac{1}{k} \right)^2 \right]$$

where N_{ij} is the number of individuals in ethnic group j residing in ward i; N_j is the number of individuals in ethnic group j; and k is the number of residential areas, in this case, the eighteen wards in the 1884 Chicago School Census.

Cultural Factors

Certainly, the institutionalization of new model unionism, ethnic segmentation in the labor market, and residential dispersion all played roles in Anglo-American workers' acceptance of reform politics. But there were other reasons as well. Anglo-American workers, even when they faced nearly insurmountable economic problems, generally accepted a *hegemonic ideology* (Gramsci 1971). This ideology suggested that those in low-status jobs making little money were undisciplined, lazy, stupid, or drank too much beer or whisky; it blamed economic problems faced by the largely Protestant Anglo-American worker on competition from the Catholic foreign-born peasantry. It suggested that radical ideas were un-American, that they were espoused by crazy foreigners who had no understanding of American institutions.

Many Anglo-American workers accepted a cohesive ideology that convinced them to accept the system as given; it included a strong work ethic, nativism, temperance, and a virulent antiradicalism. Each part of this ideology will be reviewed in turn, beginning with the work ethic, but the individual components were not really separable in practice.

One good way of studying this hegemonic ideology is to examine the beliefs of the city's native-born printers in the Chicago Typographical Union no. 16. The printers were the leaders in the reform union tendency; their beliefs about the source of such economic problems as unemployment or low wages, as well as their proposals about how to solve those problems, were important because these printers held dominant positions in the various labor assemblies formed throughout the period. Many of them expressed their thoughts on these questions in the *Inland Printer,* which the union endorsed in 1884 (Chicago Typographical Union no. 16 minutes May 25, 1884), and they received dozens of letters supporting its opinions from printers in the city. The first issue suggested it was "by and for printers in the Midwest." The statements in the journal are the best source of evidence on the beliefs of the English-speaking printers in Chicago.

The printers in the Chicago Typographical Union no. 16 generally aspired to higher economic status; many hoped someday to own an office of their own and believed it was a real possibility. One means to such status was to work hard.

Look around the office where you are working. You will see a fellow who, whenever there is any fun going on is in for having a time of it for a day or two. If there is any extra work or unpleasant task to do, he is ready to swear that as there is no pay in it he is not the fellow for it. . . . His luck will be just to occupy the same position if not a poorer one, as long as he lives. If you want to have good luck, make it yourself. (*Inland Printer* February 1884, 11)

More than hard work is needed to lead one down the road to success; one must also be educated.

The printer must read up on his trade in order to be proficient. Who would employ a physician or a lawyer who did not keep up in his respective profession? The condition in the craft in a degree accounts for the low wages paid, and one of the first steps toward advancement is to increase our knowledge. More reading will produce better workmanship, and better workmanship will bring better wages. (*Inland Printer* March 1884, 8)

[A printer ought to] possess such a general knowledge of scientific subjects to make him a worthy member of the cultured classes, and bring him closer to the mental level of the individuals which are accustomed to come and go in any of the large printing establishments. (*Inland Printer* September 1885, 538)

Printers did aspire to become members of the "cultured classes," and they had many of the same social attitudes as those of Puritan middle-class background or orientation. They believed that self-improvement through hard work and education could lead to upward mobility.

The day has passed when the members of the craft can safely be sneered at on account of the place they occupy, either in society or the vast machinery of the business world. Whatever of odium may have been attached to the men composing it . . . has been effectively silenced in these later years. Now printing can boldly throw down the glove and challenge comparison with any and every trade or profession for sobriety, respectability, the calling to high places of trust and honor, as it has ever been able to do for education, intelligence, genius and the rare dowry of brains. (*Inland Printer* July 1886, 607)

The printers' beliefs and striving for status made sense; they were perhaps the most powerful and privileged trade in the city. But their influence went beyond their trade; because of their powerful union and their positions of influence in the various trades assemblies, they convinced many in the lower status trades to accept the idea that education and hard work would lead to upward mobility.

The Anglo-American cigar makers, for example, rejected the revolutionary politics of the Progressive Cigarmakers Union in favor of an analysis of their condition emphasizing that mobility based on individual effort was possible. "What position are we, the cigarmakers, to hold in society? Are we to receive an equivalent for our labor, sufficient to maintain us in comparative independence and respectability to procure the means with which to educate our children and qualify them for playing their part in the world's dream?" (*Cigar Makers Official Journal* January 1882, 31).

The cigar makers asserted that the purpose of their union was

to rescue our trade from the condition into which it has fallen, and raise ourselves to that condition in society to which we as mechanics are justly entitled . . . to place ourselves on a foundation sufficiently strong to se-cure us from further encroachments, and to elevate the moral, social and intellectual condition of every cigarmaker in the country. (*Cigar Makers Official Journal* January 1882, 31)

Such hope for bettering their economic condition through improv-ing the morals and education of every cigar maker was unrealistic; structural factors—technological advances and tenement house cigar manufacturing—would soon destroy the jobs of even the most moral, best educated, and hardest working cigar makers.

Employers made the same argument concerning hard work and education; it was obviously to their benefit to convince their work-ers to work hard and accept the notion that failure in the labor mar-ket was due to employees' individual deficiencies rather than em-ployer decisions or problems within the capitalist system as a whole. Some of the most effective employer attempts to disseminate these hegemonic ideas were made by powerful railroad companies to the overwhelmingly Anglo-American engineers and conductors.

Railroad management tried to convince all their workers that the road to success lay in working hard for the day when the worker would be promoted to a higher place in the company. Firemen were told they would someday become engineers; brakemen were told they had only to wait for the time when they would be conduc-tors; engineers and conductors were counseled that they had a good chance to become top managers. The management-oriented

Railway Age (August 21, 1885, 533) made this argument: "When vacancies occur, promotions will be made from the most competent and deserving men of our own line. Remember there is always room at the top, and the officers who have obtained the highest rank in the service are those who have worked their way up from the lowest round of the ladder." The journal argued that hard work was the means to such mobility: "The young man who enters the railway service determined to make it the business of his life, who in twisting a brake or throwing coal into the fire bay, studies to do it in the best possible way and who shows himself interested in whatever work is given him and competent to do it will sooner or later find his full reward" (*Railway Age* May 15, 1884, 308).

Railway Age even published a biographical dictionary of railroad officials to provide examples of what hard work could do for these "poor boys." These biographies did indeed show that many of the top railroad officials had worked for a time at lower levels of the companies. The fact that there were far fewer jobs at the top than at the bottom, thus restricting the chances for advancement, was not emphasized, however. In 1880, the Illinois Central, for example, had 1 division superintendent, 1 assistant division superintendent, and 4 train masters in their Chicago division, which included 55 conductors, 100 brakemen, 60 baggagemen, 80 switchmen, and 172 laborers (Illinois Bureau of Labor Statistics Report 1880, 216–17). Few of the unskilled and semiskilled would be able to move up, but the workers could be convinced to work hard and not complain about working conditions if they thought they had a chance for individual upward mobility.

Education was viewed as a way of getting ahead, but an effort to get educated substituted individual for collective economic or political action. *Railway Age* was explicit about the fact that education would exert a conservatising influence on the railroad worker:

Nothing is more certain than that the sole influence powerful enough to prevent the gradual separation of the people of this country into classes—with a vast, dull-eyed hopeless multitude of toiling serfs at the bottom—is education. . . . The man who has received the full benefit of these institutions has no need to loudly assert that he "is as good as any capitalist," for everybody knows that he is and he never imagines that anyone will doubt it. To such men capital will concede their rights as a matter of course.

The communistic movement will end when the educating influences here succeed in enlightening the vast multitudes. (*Railway Age* June 25, 1885, 402–3)

The work ethic and the supposed leveling influence of education were important components of an ideology that convinced workers they had a real chance to make it through their own efforts. But another important piece of the hegemonic ideology of the period was *nativism*, defined by John Higham (1977, 4) as "intense opposition to an internal minority on the ground of its foreign (i.e., 'unAmerican') connections." At various times in Chicago history, nativism was linked to anti-Catholicism, antiradicalism, and the temperance movement. Immigrants became scapegoats and were held responsible for all the ills society faced: depressions, revolutionary movements, unemployment among the native born, drunkenness, political corruption, gambling, prostitution, and poverty.

Nativist attitudes had various institutional expressions. The anti-immigrant "Know-Nothing" parties, such as the American party, often competed for political office in early Chicago history. The Anglo-American working and middle classes created the nativist American Protestant Association. The upper class founded the United Order of Deputies, which viewed the foreign born as "uncivilized heathen from pre-industrial lands" (Schneirov 1984, 276). The Protestant City Missionary Society placed a full-time missionary in the Southwest Side Pilsen community in order to convert Bohemian freethinkers (atheists) to Christianity; the Catholic church viewed its priests in the Irish stockyards district in a similar way (Schneirov 1984, 276). Even trade unions, such as the carpenters, viewed their organizers as missionaries (Schneirov 1984, 277).

Immigrants were thought to be immoral; that was considered the real reason for their problems and those they supposedly caused the Anglo-American workers. Anglo-American labor reformers viewed their movement as a means of uplifting the mass of lazy, impulsive, poor, immoral immigrants. Eight Hour Association leaders in the mid 1880s successfully appealed directly to Protestant religious leaders to support their movement for hours reduction, which they suggested would also result in the "moral reform" of the immigrant (Schneirov 1984, 439).

America, the *Native Citizen*, and the *British American* were nativist newspapers that argued against Catholic customs and lifestyles and for immigration restrictions (Funchion 1976, 21).

These organizations and papers successfully convinced many Anglo-American workers that the economic and social problems they faced stemmed from Catholic immigration; as a result, the new industrial capitalist system itself was not blamed for those problems. The nativist, antiradical sentiment of the Chicago English-language press is clear in this statement in the *Chicago Daily Herald* about Italians, Russians, and Poles: "This country extends a cordial welcome to honest, industrious, and intelligent people from all parts of the world (China excepted), but it cannot afford to become a land of refuge for criminals, paupers, and barbarians, whose highest ambition is to overthrow law and authority of every kind" (Feldstein and Costello 1974, 171).

The Anglo-American workers expressed much hostility toward their foreign-born brothers and sisters, some of it because of the economic competition the latter represented. The printer A. C. Cameron's attack on the foreign born when the Trades and Labor Assembly rejected Central Labor Union affiliation is a good example of nativism within the city's labor movement:

I am one of those who do not think it a crime to be an American, or worse than murder to speak the English language. I am opposed to any movement toward joining with those that carry the red flag of Socialism of Europe to the democratic republicanism of America. The Trades Assembly will be certainly smirched if it takes on such a responsibility. (*Chicago Tribune* May 3, 1886, 16)

Nativism was also tied to opposition to the more militant ideas and tactics within the labor movement, thus effectively reducing the likelihood of native-born acceptance of revolutionary ideas. The close ties between nativist and antiradical sentiments are shown in the following quotes from the *Chicago Times* and the *Chicago Tribune*:

To put into practice the criminal doctrine of the "red flag" by Germans, Czechs, Poles, or any stranger to our shores is offensive foreignism. (*Chicago Times*, quoted in Illinois *Staats Zeitung* May 25, 1887, 3)

The way to prevent the spread of communism here is to close our seaports against the further ingress of European vagabondage. Perhaps we might enact laws whereby no one should be permitted to emigrate here who could not show sufficient credentials as to his not having been either a thief, a pauper, or a vagabond in the country from which he comes. Had there been some such law in force, eleven-twelfths of those communistic gentlemen in our city would never have reached our shores. (*Chicago Times* February 19, 1874, 44)

The *Chicago Tribune* suggested the following about a speech made by the socialist candidate for mayor, Ernst Schmidt, in 1879:

It was an appeal to them to encourage a feeling of enmity to the law and government of this country. . . . This speech would have been an impudent, insolent, disgraceful harangue delivered by anybody, but delivered by a man of alien birth of alien principles, to an alien audience, in a foreign tongue, was doubly infamous and scandalous and can find no sympathy from the great mass of Germans. . . . Schmidt will soon discover how universal is the American abhorrence of socialism and of the blatant ignorance on which it is founded. (*Chicago Tribune* June 25, 1879, 25)

Many problems, including the poverty of the foreign born, were blamed on immigrants' propensity to drink beer and whisky. In the seventies and eighties, the largely Anglo-American, upper-class Protestant Citizens Association, the Union League Club, the Women's Christian Temperance Union, and the Citizens League for the Prevention of Sale of Liquor to Minors lobbied for temperance legislation, for the passage of Sunday closing laws, and even for Prohibition. The Anglo-American printers clearly accepted the idea that drinking was one of the reasons for the low economic position of many of those in the city's working class. "Absolute sobriety is a prime essential to success, and a drunken printer is a foul disgrace to the art and all the high and honored names it has canonized" (*Inland Printer* July 1886, 609).

Temperance also had a tremendous impact on the railroad trade. By the seventies, alcohol was banned even off the job for most railroad employees (Lightner 1977, 161). The Anglo-American elite brotherhoods accepted the temperance argument; both the Order of Railway Conductors and the Brotherhood of Locomotive Engineers made drinking a sufficient cause for dismissal from their organizations. Those dismissed for drinking were blacklisted by both the employers and the unions (*Railway Age* October 10, 1884, 668).

The temperance ideology, like the work ethic, was used to good advantage by powerful railroad employers, who argued that their interest in it was solely because of the danger that drunken railroad employees might cause accidents. But the fact that they often required *total* abstinence indicates they may have had other motives;

enforcing this requirement for one's workers had the effect of barring workers from pubs and saloons, where much union organizing and working-class political activity took place.

Acceptance of this hegemonic ideology—the work ethic, nativism, temperance fanaticism, and antiradicalism—was promoted directly by employers under the cover of their supposed concern about their employees' "morals." Perhaps the most interesting attempt along these lines was railroad managements' creation of railroad Young Men's Christian Associations (YMCAs). By the late seventies and early eighties, railroad companies were contributing heavily to and serving on the boards of the YMCAs, which established centers that lured railroaders by the promise of clean beds, hot baths, and comfortable reading rooms. There the men were forced to listen to "edifying lectures, Bible study groups, and hymn feasts to nourish the spirit" (Lightner 1977, 275). The Illinois Central Railroad donated $600 to the Cairo Illinois Y in 1882 in order to "accomplish some good in that ungodly place" (Lightner 1977, 276). Managers could rest assured that few unions would be organized in such settings; and it is unlikely that Lassalle, Marx, or Bakunin were featured in the reading room.

The railroad managers did not do this solely to make their men more religious. They increased the influence of morally "correct" self-improvement associations among the railroaders in order to prevent the rise of more economically oriented, class-conscious trade unions.

The company which can afford to see that their engines are carefully supplied with coal and oil and kept in their best repair can equally well afford to take pains that their men shall have needed rest and a chance to get proper food at reasonable rates and the advantages afforded by a Christian Association. I rejoice that no guild of railroad men is likely to sink to the level of mere trades unions, the sole object of which is to affect the prices of labor. (*Railway Age* June 15, 1882, 331)

Managers understood the economic value of successful attempts to control the morals of their workers.

All railroad officials will bear cheerful testimony to the value of the work of the railroad Young Men's Christian Associations. From a strictly utilitarian point of view, the work pays. . . . A temperate man is better than one who is godless. One of the best engineers I ever knew, a man who could be relied upon for any emergency, whose engine never was in trouble and who was always ready to obey orders and perform whatever duty was there expected of him, never got on his engine without a testament in his pocket and is now filling a pulpit most acceptably in a Christian church in this state. Such men make good men from a purely business standpoint, and every agency that tends to the development of such men is of value and deserves the hearty support of the railroads. (*Railway Age* March 19, 1885, 185)

Undoubtedly, "emergencies" were considered to include running trains during the course of strikes by other railroaders.

The railroad managers supported forty-six Railway Ys by 1882, donating $50,000 annually to maintain them (*Railway Age* July 13, 1882, 387). The Chicago branches of the Ys were extremely active; in 1883, they reported over eighty-five thousand visits to their facilities, many of which included attendance at meetings, education classes, Bible classes, gospel meetings, lectures, and so on. During the same year, over a thousand books were withdrawn from their libraries, over a hundred thousand papers, tracts, and pamphlets were distributed, and over twenty-seven hundred visits were made to railroaders at workplaces and homes by YMCA staff members (*Railway Age* January 24, 1884, 61).

Certainly, the Ys had a significant impact on the lives of Chicago's railroad workers; many must have spent much of their leisure time in these institutions. Similarly, requiring the use of company hotels, company stores, and company restaurants was also economically profitable for the companies because it both generated revenue directly and limited railroaders' ability to find a time and place to organize against the companies.

The great resources at the railroads' disposal allowed them to experiment in efforts to control the patterns of association of their men, their drinking, the ideas workers had concerning their work, their chances for upward mobility, their attitudes toward foreign workers and toward their superiors, and their religious beliefs. These efforts successfully promoted individualism, a work ethic, a lack of class consciousness, and nativism in the railroad workers.

The acceptance of a cohesive, multifaceted, hegemonic ideology by a large portion of the Anglo-American working class was based on the ability of employers and aristocratic trade union leaders in the Trades and Labor Assembly to convince workers that the system worked for those who worked hard, got educated, stayed sober, and were God fearing and that those who did not make it were mainly lazy, uneducated, drunken, Catholic peasants. Foreigners who suggested otherwise were labeled irrational radicals with little understanding of the fine American institutions that provided such tremendous economic opportunities.

Political Access for the Anglo-American Worker

Unlike many of the foreign-born workers, especially the Germans, there was little in the relationship of the Anglo-American workers to the Chicago political system to make them conclude they should become revolutionaries and overthrow the state. Anglo-American votes usually counted, and police repression was visited mainly on those of non-Anglo background; this convinced Anglo-American workers to lobby for the passage of legislation favorable to the working class or, failing that, to try to elect sympathetic candidates to office.

Organized labor's first political successes came as early as 1866, when the ward-based eight-hour leagues associated with the Trades Assembly elected aldermen who supported the eight-hour de-mand in five out of sixteen wards. The city council passed an eight-hour law that same year, and with the support of the governor and attorney general, the state passed it in 1867 (Schneirov 1984, 20–21). Despite strikes designed to gain compliance, the laws were not enforced. But the Anglo-Americans felt encouraged by the fact that they had elected aldermen who passed legislation shortening the workday.

By the 1880s, Anglo-American reformers had developed what Schneirov (1984) calls "political collective bargaining," the public sphere counterpart of their cozy relationship with employers in the private sector. The idea was to use the large numbers of working-class voters as leverage in bargaining with party bosses for the en-actment of moderate labor legislation and other benefits.

Many Anglo-American workers rejected the militant proposals of German socialists and anarchists but accepted a close relation-ship with the Democratic party and with Mayor Carter Harrison, who had defeated both the employer-supported Republican and German working-class-supported SLP candidates in 1879. In the fall elections of that year, the Trades and Labor Council and the Greenback party endorsed Harrison, thus contributing to the defeat of socialist Ernst Schmidt. Harrison remained in office until 1887, supported by many middle-class as well as Anglo-American and Irish working-class voters.

Anglo-American workers supported Harrison because he was willing to back moderate reform proposals and because he was willing to appoint them to patronage jobs. Soon after his election, Harrison appointed six Greenbackers and eight-hour advocates in the Trades and Labor Assembly to city jobs; and he appointed many more labor reform leaders to jobs as factory and health inspectors later in the 1880s (Schneirov 1984, 350).

These labor leaders viewed their positions as good platforms from which to pursue reform; they were, however, denounced for a "sordid betrayal of class ideals" by the remains of the Socialist Labor party (Schneirov 1984, 124). Relations between the German socialists and the Anglo-American Democrats on the city council were not improved when the predominantly German socialists were denied the privilege of appointing election judges. Knowing that this meant they would be unable to prevent election fraud against their party, the socialists walked out.

Working-class political strength, especially in the Anglo-American and Irish communities, meant a decline in the political power of the city's upper-class employers. The employer-dominated Citizens Association and various political reform clubs lamented the rise of "political corruption," which came with the rise of *machine politics;* but what upset them most was their inability to get the city administration to take their side in labor disputes. In 1885, the Citizens Association noted that police could not be used to suppress "rioters" (*sic*) because they were also voters (Schneirov 1984, 373). There was some truth to their charge; the Trades and Labor Assembly often successfully lobbied city hall to support their strikes. For example, in 1882, Harrison refused to send police to support a streetcar company during a strike by largely Anglo-American conductors and drivers; in 1884, largely Irish police refused to intervene in a strike by Irish iron molders (Schneirov 1984, 373–74).

The fact of political access for the Anglo-American working class had political consequences; it created and sustained support for moderate labor reform. As the next chapter illustrates, the city's

Irish workers enjoyed even greater levels of political influence and, not coincidentally, also supported reform labor politics.

Conclusions

One explanation for the reformist politics of many Anglo-American workers would be that it was in their interest to accept the system because it gave them economic advantages. This group's overall position was excellent; many of their number were in the middle and upper classes, and the economic prospects of Anglo-American children were the best of any group in the city. Even those confined to working-class positions were often in the labor aristocracy because Anglo-Americans dominated exclusionary new model unions in the Chicago labor market.

It is not too surprising that Anglo-American labor aristocrats were conservative in their dealings with both their employers and the political system; that they emphasized upward mobility for themselves, their families, and their trade and rejected class-conscious alternatives; and that they aspired to middle-class status and respectability. Their vulnerability to middle-class Protestant ideals and arguments may have been reinforced by residential patterning in the city because aristocrats were likely to live in dispersed, predominantly Protestant, middle-class communities. Here they were far from their workplaces and far from the possibility of social interaction with their foreign-born co-workers, interaction that might have strengthened class identification.

But this argument cannot be used to explain why lower status Anglo-American workers accepted reform politics because such workers' economic prospects were often bleak. The explanation of their acceptance of reform politics lies in their belief in a hegemonic ideology that was borrowed from the middle class and articulated by labor aristocrats in the various trades assemblies. This ideology blamed individuals for their low economic position; the poor were assumed to be immoral, to lack a strong work ethic, to have failed to educate themselves, or to be drunks, atheists, or Catholics. Broad religious differences were also a crucial basis for political divisions between reformist Protestant Anglo-Americans in the Trades and Labor Assembly and freethinking Germans and Bohemians in the revolutionary Central Labor Union.

The ethnic political fragmentation was also reinforced by nativism, which suggested that the economic problems facing American workers were due to competition from the foreign born rather than basic defects in the capitalist system of production. Nativism was reinforced by ethnically based labor market segmentation and residential segregation, as well as by language differences, which made it unlikely that most Anglo-American workers would interact extensively or meaningfully with non-Anglo workers.

Thus, Anglo-Americans generally accepted a conservative collective bargaining approach in both the economic and political spheres, and they tended to reject class-conscious, revolutionary German trade unionism, socialism, and anarchism. Even though it was not working for them, low-status Anglo-American workers saw no reason to reject an economic system that was working for their *reference group*—Anglo-American members of the labor aristocracy and the middle class. Their reformist tendencies were reinforced by a positive political experience, especially in the 1880s—the election of a sympathetic mayor, the appointment of labor reformers to patronage jobs, and mayoral and police support for some of their strikes.

Most Irish workers also rejected revolutionary politics. But an argument that the Irish did this because the economic system worked for them is even harder to sustain than in the Anglo-American case. The Irish as a group had the lowest economic status of any ethnic group in the city. The Irish did not accept Puritan-oriented, middle-class ideologies; they were in fact one of the groups against which nativist, temperance, and anti-Catholic attacks were directed. What then explains the reform politics of the Irish workers in Chicago?

Chapter Four

Irish Labor Reform

The pattern of Irish participation in the labor movement was in some ways like that of Anglo-American workers. Both groups tended to reject revolutionary politics in favor of labor reform. Irish workers often became politically active through Knights of Labor assemblies, which demanded better wages, shorter hours, better working conditions, and union recognition, not the restructuring of the economic and political systems. In the 1880s, nearly all Irish activists supported the reformist, Anglo-American–led Trades and Labor Assembly rather than the revolutionary Central Labor Union. In fact, it was the Chicago Knights of Labor, with its largely Irish leadership, that condemned the anarchists most vociferously after the Haymarket affair.

Most of those in both the Anglo-American and the Irish working class rejected anarchism. But in other ways, the Chicago Irish movement participation pattern differed from that of the Anglo-Americans, most importantly in that the Irish were less active in the more organized political activities of the skilled workers. In the 1870s, there was little Irish participation in the Marxist International, the Workingmen's Party of Illinois, and the Socialist Labor party. At the height of Irish participation, the SLP was only 10 percent Irish; there were only eleven Irish Labor Guards in the workers defense clubs, compared to three hundred Germans and two hundred Bohemians.

This lack of Irish participation in organized labor politics is not too surprising given the fact that the Irish were overwhelmingly unskilled; because they were so easily replaced, they found it difficult or impossible to organize unions, and unions were often the organizational basis of participation in labor politics. Only a few unions (the seamen, iron molders, packinghouse workers, freight handlers, and horseshoers) had large numbers of Irish members, and most Irish-dominated unions that were formed were short-lived.

Because they lacked the scarce skills that would have enabled them to use craft unions to gain economic and political power, the Irish developed an alternative, the *mass strike model*. As described previously, this tactic involved forming crowds to roam among workplaces to convince workers to join the strike, convince employers to shut down their operations, and physically intimidate scabs (Schneirov 1984, 148). Many of the less skilled workers who used this model in the 1870s and 1880s were Irish, including the railroad switchmen and freight handlers, packinghouse employees, iron and steel workers, coal heavers, and brickyard laborers.

The mass strike depended on community support as well as support from Irish workers. Irish community–based guerilla warfare was used against the police in the 1877 mass strike; more than a third of those arrested during that strike were Irish. As Schneirov (1984, 165) reports, during the Halsted Street conflicts, the police were forced to order every window on the street closed because they received so many missiles and pistol shots from the houses in the Irish community there.

So the Irish used militant tactics, but only to improve their lot under the existing system, not to replace that system with another. One possible explanation for Irish workers' reformism is that unskilled workers are unable to develop coherent revolutionary politics. This is an inadequate hypothesis because the few Irish who were skilled workers, such as the iron molders, were also overwhelmingly reformers. Yet the largely unskilled Bohemians, whose average economic status was similar to that of the Irish, were active participants in the highly organized, revolutionary socialist and anarchist movements in the city. A full explanation of the Irish participation pattern in labor politics is possible only by analyzing both Irish immigrants' backgrounds and the economic, social, and political bases of labor politics in the Chicago Irish community.

Irish Immigration to Chicago

The set of events that brought thousands of Irish immigrants to Chicago differed from the circumstances that led to British immigration. The most relevant factor was English colonization, which resulted in the economic underdevelopment of Ireland. Beginning in the 1500s, the effect of English policies in Ireland was to reduce a majority of Irish Catholics to a progressively more economically deprived state. Plantations were granted to English Protestants in Ireland as early as 1541. In the 1600s, Scottish Presbyterian settlers were sent to colonize Northern Ireland; they confiscated so much land that by mid century only 14 percent of all land in Ireland was still Catholic owned (See 1979, 137–42).

In the eighteenth century, worry over Irish economic competition and the possibility of Catholic succession to the English throne led to the passage of the Penal Laws and the use of an English puppet government to rule Ireland. Catholics were denied the right to vote, hold office, teach, trade, enter the professions, or bear arms. The Catholic clergy and all Catholic schools were outlawed, leaving most Catholics uneducated. The few Catholic estates that remained were broken up through restrictions on inheritance and ownership; Catholics were even barred from owning a horse worth over £5 (Fallows 1979, 13; See 1979, 144). By the time of repeal of these laws in the late eighteenth century, many Irish Catholics worked very small plots of land and were poor and illiterate.

Other measures, including embargoes on dairy products, woolens, meat, butter, cheese, and a heavy tariff on linen, created additional economic problems for Ireland. The British stifled industrial growth to prevent competition between British and Irish manufactured products. The result was that the working class developed much more slowly in Ireland than in England and the rest of Europe. Many, though not all, Irish Catholics were forced to accept lives as poor peasants and were prevented from entering the skilled trades or even semiskilled factory labor. Unlike Britain and Germany, which saw the growth of large industrial working classes in this period, Ireland actually witnessed a decline in industrial workers from 1.7 million in 1821 to 1.6 million in 1841. Agricultural workers increased in number from 2.8 million to 3.5 million (See 1979, 212).

Colonialism created a near-caste society in Ireland, with absentee English landlords at the top, Scottish Protestant traders, small craftsmen, and small business owners in the middle, and Irish Catholic tenant farmers and agricultural laborers at the bottom. The destitution of much of the Irish Catholic peasantry was exacerbated by a tremendous population surplus. In the century before the Great Famine of 1845, Ireland's population increased from 2.5 million to over 8 million (Clark and Donnelly 1983, 26). In an economy stunted by colonial exploitation, there were too few jobs for the growing number of workers (Funchion 1976, 6). The Catholic peasants were forced to subdivide their already meager holdings still further; by 1841, only 6 percent of all tenant farms were over thirty acres, and 30 percent included only one acre (See 1979, 216–17). Laborers and farmers holding twenty acres of land or less constituted 75 percent of all adult males in the agricultural sector of the economy (Clark and Donnelly 1983, 27).

Under these oppressive conditions, the peasantry barely subsisted. Few ate bread, meat, or salt; many of their huts on the small plots had no windows and often no chimney; disease was common; illiteracy was high. Lack of capital, backward farming methods, and the fact that improvements benefited only the owner meant that farms were not improved. Many Irish Catholic peasants migrated seasonally to England to work in the fields or as laborers on the railroads and canals; others resorted to begging (Wittke 1956, 5). Even the Protestant attorney general wrote the English king that the Irish were "in a state of oppression, abject poverty, sloth, dirt and misery not to be equalled in any part of the world" (See 1979, 147).

The Irish fought against these conditions; in fact, the record of collective action by Irish Catholic peasants in the late eighteenth and early nineteenth centuries was unequaled in Europe (Clark and Donnelly 1983, 26). There were uprisings against the English crown and the Scottish settlers in Ulster as early as 1590 and 1641 (See 1979, 138–41). The Irish peasantry created secret societies in order to take revenge for high rents and engaged in violence called "Whiteboyism" to prevent evictions by landlords trying to consolidate their holdings. Irish peasants ostracized tenants who collaborated with such landlords; the model of economic action later known as the *boycott* was built on these practices. The British were able to crush the open rebellions but unable to suppress the secret gangs, which had broad support throughout the countryside. By the end of the eighteenth century, battles between these covert Catholic defense associations and the Protestant Orange Order were common.

In the 1790s, the United Irishmen movement, inspired by the French Revolution, attempted to establish a popular republic in Ireland. In response, the British proposed the unification of the British and Irish legislatures, convincing the Irish that their interests would be respected in the new united parliament. When that respect failed to materialize, the Irish patriot Daniel O'Connell created the Catholic Association, which mobilized the peasantry and the small Catholic middle class in a fight for political emancipation (Funchion 1976, 23; O'Ferrall 1985). The key factor in O'Connell's success was the Irish peasantry's strong ties to the Catholic church (Clark and Donnelly 1983, 15). Those ties had been reinforced by centuries of religious oppression; Irish priests often said mass in the fields and were forced to depend on their neighbors for economic support during this time.

O'Connell won a series of elections using his grass roots organizing approach, and he mobilized tens of thousands for political rallies (O'Ferrall 1985, 132–33). But he soon was forced to accept a bill that granted the vote to "ten pound and over" freeholders, thus disenfranchising the peasantry (See 1979, 229). Later, using the same organizing techniques, O'Connell founded the National Repeal Association in order to dissolve the British-Irish parliamentary union. By 1843, the movement was the most significant yet seen in Ireland, drawing hundreds of thousands to its rallies. But the organization came to an end when the British banned its meetings.

Thus, most Irish peasants did not know a trade, but many had extensive political organizing experience; the political skills they developed in Ireland would later be of use in establishing the political machine in Chicago. These political skills did not help stave off disaster for the Irish Catholic peasantry in the mid 1840s, however. Many Irish peasants had been forced to depend on the only crop, the potato, which could be grown productively on their small, rocky plots. When the potato famine hit in 1845, it nearly wiped out the Irish Catholic population. Nearly one million Irish died, and another million quickly emigrated to avoid starvation (Funchion 1976, 7). From 1841 to 1880, an incredible four million Irish, the overwhelming majority unskilled, emigrated to the United States.

Many could not afford the $12 to $15 passage fee, but their way was paid by landlords and public officials anxious to get as many as possible off the relief rolls (Schaaf 1977, 188).

Thus, while across the English Channel the English and German working classes were trying to define a political response to industrialization, Irish peasants were struggling to find enough to eat. When they got to the United States, skilled workers from England and Germany expected to become well-paid artisans, but poor Irish peasants simply wished to survive. In fact, one of the main U.S. attractions for the Irish was the abundance of food. Letters from previous emigrants expressed sentiments like the following: "If a man likes work, he need not want for victuals." "There are a great many ill conveniences, here, but not empty bellies." One popular emigrant song included these lines, "They say there's bread for all, and the sun always shines there" (Wittke 1956, 11).

The *American Daily Advertiser* listed cheap land, high wages, and freedom from military service, as well as plenty of food, as the most important reasons for immigration to the United States. A pamphlet entitled "Hints to Irishmen who Intend With Their Families to Make a Permanent Residence in America" was published in Ireland as early as 1816. It stressed the need for farmers and artisans and the good treatment accorded foreigners. Labor recruiters advertised for workers at what were considered high rates of pay, leading many Irish to see the United States as the promised land (Wittke 1956, 112).

Political rights and freedom from oppressive British rule were seen as positive benefits as well; there was a great deal of positive feeling for the United States because of its ability to throw off the yoke of British rule a century before, something the Irish people had not been able to do (Fallows 1979, 25). In the 1860s, there were reports that the U.S. government was sending recruiters to Irish towns to sign up soldiers for the Union cause. Supposedly, these enlistments were encouraged by recruiters' promises that the U.S. government would aid in freeing Ireland from British rule once the southern rebellion was put down (Piper 1936, 4). Many of the emigrants may have come to the United States expecting to return as liberators of Ireland.

Chicago was a natural destination for the Irish. Canal and railroad construction provided thousands of job opportunities for the unskilled and quickly established the Irish as a large proportion of the railroad industry labor force. Some of the Irish were recruited from eastern cities where they had been working; others were recruited by Chicago employment agents as they stepped off the boat in New York (Funchion 1976, 10). There were 6,098 Irish in the city by 1850, 19,889 by 1860, and 39,998 in 1870. By then, most of the Irish who were to immigrate to Chicago had already done so; there were only an additional 5,000 by 1880 (Piper 1936, 2).

The Economic Position of the Irish

Once in Chicago, most Irish were unable to enter middle- and high-status working-class jobs because of their lack of skills and nativist discriminatory practices. Apprenticeships with the skilled craft unions were monopolized by Anglo-American workers. Discrimination was often blatant; most job advertisements in nineteenth-century Chicago papers ended with the phrase "No Irish Need Apply." The result was that, despite their early arrival in the city, the Irish had the lowest average occupational status of any major ethnic group in the Chicago labor market as late as 1890.

The Irish had much lower economic status than the native born, as is indicated in Table 9. They were overwhelmingly (over 80 percent) working class in all three census years. In a period when the native born had approximately one-fifth to one-fourth of their number in the low-skill, lowest wage jobs, the Irish had over half; those Irish who managed to escape unskilled work generally moved only as high as the skilled working class. The average Irish worker was also in a much lower position than the average German; Germans had a higher proportion of their number in the higher working-class categories because most of them were from skilled trade backgrounds.

The low occupational status of the Irish was reflected in their disproportionate representation in the lowest status trades. The Irish were about 13 percent of the Chicago population but were 28 percent of all laborers in the city. The Irish were overrepresented in other unskilled trades such as servants (19 percent), teamsters (23 percent), freight handlers (65 percent), hod carriers (29 percent), and lumber vessel unloaders (28 percent) (Illinois Bureau of Labor Statistics 1886; U.S. Census of Population 1880). They were also overrepresented in some of the lower status skilled trades such as blacksmiths (19 percent), coopers (17 percent), and iron and steel workers (19 percent). They were able to break into only one labor aristocrat trade; 20 percent of the bricklayers and stone-masons in the city were Irish (U.S. Census of Population 1880).

The Irish were almost totally unable to enter middle- and upper-class jobs in Chicago. A survey of the ethnic origins of Chicago physicians in the late nineteenth century showed that only 5 out of 161 were Irish Catholics. Only 30 of 494 of the city's leading lawyers, 6 of 222 members of the Chicago Board of Trade, 2 of 42 bankers, and 4 of 44 building contractors were of Irish Catholic origin (Funchion 1976, 14). The lack of choices for Irish workers was reflected in their high score of .95 on the occupational dispersion measure; they were overwhelmingly confined to a few low-status, unskilled jobs.

Low occupational status translated into very low average annual income for Irish families. Irish working-class (weighted) average annual earnings were $447, compared to $598 for the British born and $549 for the native born. Average incomes conceal the fact that many unskilled Irish laborers made around $350 a year, assuming they could find any work at all (Illinois Bureau of Labor Statistics 1882). The Relief and Aid Society said that the Irish were always at the top of the list of those requiring assistance, and the *Chicago Tribune* (February 14, 1875; cited in Schneirov 1984, 160) reported, "there is probably as much real poverty in Bridgeport as anywhere in the town."

If lack of economic success in the labor market determined propensity to accept revolutionary politics, one would expect the Irish to be the most revolutionary group in the city. But they were not. Specific features of their social, cultural, and political life prevented the Irish from supporting a movement to overthrow the Chicago and U.S. economic and political systems.

The Social and Cultural Bases of
Irish Labor Reform

In this period, German socialists and anarchists proposed class-based, radical solutions to the plight of Chicago workers. The city's Irish workers did not support such revolutionary solutions, in part because they utilized ethnic, community-based, not class-based resources to better themselves. Their identification with the Irish community was stronger than their identification with the city's working class.

Ethnic identification among the Irish was high in part because they, like other Chicago ethnic groups, were forced to defend themselves against aggressive nativist attacks. Nativist groups such as the American party (the Know-Nothings) seized upon the strong Irish commitment to Catholicism to explain such social problems as drunkenness, political corruption, gambling, prostitution, and crime. Irish poverty led to their being stereotyped as lazy, dirty, drunken, brawling criminals with no respect for common decency. Chicagoans declared that Great Britain was exporting Irish paupers and criminals in order to get rid of them; there were even calls for the Irish to be sent to Canada (Fallows 1979, 25). More concretely, the Irish were denied jobs, equal access to social positions and clubs, and the opportunity to enjoy Irish cultural pursuits; unsuccessful attempts were also made to limit Irish influence in politics.

The Irish fought against these attacks just as they had in Ireland; but in Chicago, they were able to utilize high-density urban residential communities as an effective organizing base. Because of their low incomes and consequent inability to afford commuting costs and high rents, the Irish were forced to live near the river and walk to their jobs in the packinghouses, stockyards, docks, coal-yards, brickyards, and lumberyards. As mentioned previously, the Irish had a higher score (.48) than the native born (.28) on the residential dispersion measure, indicating a greater concentration of Irish residents in fewer wards.

The Irish had established a residential community near their river workplaces as early as 1842; in that year, work on the Illinois and Michigan Canal had to be suspended due to economic difficulties (Funchion 1976). This led to an Irish squatters' settlement near Chicago in an area called Kilgubbin just southwest of the city. Most residents built small frame huts, and here these "shanty Irish" endured the worst living conditions in the city. By the 1870s, this community was known as Bridgeport (see Map 2).

The establishment of Bridgeport led to the reinforcement of exclusive Irish social networks; this social isolation made a distinctive Irish labor politics more likely because it limited the interaction of Irish and non-Irish workers. No community area within Chicago was ethnically homogeneous; by the 1860s, some skilled German butchers had moved into Bridgeport in order to find work in the nearby packinghouses. Eastern Europeans, especially Poles and Lithuanians, arrived in the 1880s and 1890s (Holt and Pacyga 1979, 114). But many crucial community institutions in Bridgeport, including the political machine, the saloon, and the Catholic church, were controlled by the Irish; and other important Bridgeport organizations addressed narrowly Irish concerns. Thus, Irish self-help organizations such as the United Sons of Erin Benevolent Society and the Hibernian Benevolent Emigrant Society tried to help the Irish poor; Irish nationalist organizations like the Fenians, Clan na Gael, and Irish National Land League attempted to liberate Ireland's Catholic population; the St. Patrick's Society planned the annual St. Patrick's Day celebration; and the Montgomery Guards, the Emmet Guards, and the Shields Guard conducted Irish military exercises (Funchion 1976, 17; Piper 1936, 10, 17).

Despite the lack of perfect ethnic homogeneity in the neighborhood, these various organizations combined to create a cohesive Irish social and political life well into the twentieth century. As Holt and Pacyga (1979, 116) suggest:

Emphasis on communalism was a strong characteristic of Bridgeport history during the latter part of the nineteenth century and has continued to be so ever since. The geographic neighborhood . . . has continually faced problems which have had to be dealt with by groups rather than individuals. Inadequate housing, poverty, and labor problems have led Bridgeport residents to seek remedies through the communal network of the local Democratic machine on the one hand and through offices of organized labor on the other. In Bridgeport, as in other working-class neighborhoods, these institutions reinforced each other precisely because they were based in the community and in familial relationships.

Such extended and overlapping relationships were particularly apparent in the Hamburg section of Bridgeport. This area . . . continues to be predominantly Irish. . . . So strong were the social and spatial associations in enclaves like Hamburg that they resembled small self-contained villages located in the midst of a large city. . . . The strength of such affiliative structures cannot be overestimated. This set of linkages continues to provide the basis for neighborhood organizations, labor unions, and political parties.

Perhaps the most important Irish social organization was the Catholic church.

The Catholic Church

As in Ireland, the Irish response to anti-Catholic sentiment and politics was fierce loyalty to the Catholic church and its associated organizations. The Chicago Catholic church was controlled by the Irish in this period; the first parish in Bridgeport was founded by the Irish in 1846, and St. Patrick's Church was built in that same year (Funchion 1976, 16; Holt and Pacyga 1979, 114). The bishop for the Chicago area was Irish from 1854 through the end of the century, as was the first archbishop, who served from 1880 to 1902 (Funchion 1976, 17).

The church served more than a religious function; it was also central to Irish community life. It established orphanages, temperance societies, and schools; sponsored lectures; founded libraries and reading rooms; and published three Catholic papers (Piper 1936, 59–60).

Commitment to the church increased the social and cultural isolation of the Irish from non-Catholic ethnic groups in the city, isolation that was already high due to the polarized conflicts that had resulted from nativist attacks. Catholic priests reinforced such isolationism, suggesting that there was much in American life that could contaminate Irish faith. They banned certain books and plays and strongly and successfully encouraged Irish youth to attend Catholic parochial schools and school events (Funchion 1976, 17).

The impact of nativism, residential isolation, membership in ethnically homogeneous social organizations, and commitment to their church may be parts of an explanation for why Irish workers mobilized a distinctive tendency in the labor movement. All these factors contributed to reinforcing exclusively Irish social ties and to weakening ties to non-Irish workers and their political movements.

But these factors do not explain why the distinctively Irish labor politics that was created was reformist. The reasons for Irish reformism have to do with the nature of such Irish community organizations as the Catholic church, the Knights of Labor, the Irish nationalist groups, and the political machine, as well as the relationships between these groups.

For example, the Knights of Labor were often forced in a more conservative direction because they hoped to recruit Irish Catholic members. Terence Powderly and other Knights leaders responded to church pressure by keeping the Knights from espousing radical or socialistic beliefs (Browne 1949; Grob 1976). In April 1883, the treasurer of the Chicago Knights wrote to Powderly:

> For some time past I have received private reports from reliable sources that the clergy of the Catholic Church have been and are now tampering with quite a number of members of our Order, and so much so, that a very large proportion of our assemblies have become decimated in numbers, and it is strongly hinted that in a short time a manifesto will be issued against the Order in this diocese. (Browne 1949, 85)

Showing that he understood the crucial role played by the Irish Catholic in the Knights, the treasurer went on to suggest that such a manifesto would be a "death blow to the Order, not only in Chicago, but in the States at large." In its second issue, the *Chicago Knights of Labor* expressed similar worries:

> Archbishop Kendrick of this Catholic diocese, which is very large, in reply to questions today asking his opinion of the Knights of Labor, was very emphatic in his denunciation of the order as regards its relations to the Catholic Church, and while not speaking officially stated very positively that he was opposed to any member of his diocese becoming a member of the Knights of Labor under any circumstance. He added that he considered the Knights of Labor a most dangerous organization. (Chicago *Knights of Labor* March 1886, 20)

In fact, the church rarely distinguished between the more radical and more moderate labor organizations, often lumping freethinking (atheist) socialists and anarchists with the moderate Knights (Browne 1949, 89). The Catholic church naturally was worried about the atheistic nature of the revolutionary labor movement and was also suspicious of any social or political movement that was not tied closely to its own network of loyal Catholic social organizations.

The necessity of appeasing the Catholic church led the Knights to abandon their secret oath-bound features in the early 1880s; it also caused them to avoid being perceived as too radical. The virulence of the attacks on the anarchists by the Knights after Haymarket clearly illustrated the Knights' defensive struggle to differentiate themselves from revolutionary socialism and anarchism in the city. Failure to do so would have meant the wholesale defection of one of their most important constituencies: the Irish Catholic working class.

Irish Nationalism

Next to the Catholic church, the most important Irish social organizations were the Irish nationalist groups. Like the church, they influenced the Irish working class to choose reformist politics in Chicago. Revolutionary class consciousness involves understanding that one's economic plight is shared by all members of a class, that a class enemy is responsible for that plight, and that only revolutionary political action can remedy the situation. The Irish nationalist organizations provided all these things. But there was one catch: That enemy was not in Chicago or even in the United States. The Irish nationalist groups identified the British social system, not American society, as the source of Irish oppression.

The Irish accepted the Puritan argument that they would make it economically in the Chicago labor market when they acquired the appropriate skills. They blamed English colonialism for their lack of skills, believing that Ireland's economic development had been arrested because of English exploitation of the Irish economy. They also made invidious comparisons between the democratic polity in the United States and British totalitarianism. Reinforcing this choice of the British as the culprits was the Catholic church leadership, which for years had strongly supported the liberation of Catholics in Ireland but gave less support to efforts to liberate workers in America.

The nationalist organizations made it unlikely that the Irish would accept the plausible explanation that their economic problems were the result of anti–Irish Catholic prejudice or the failure of the capitalist system in Chicago. The strength of the nationalist groups made it nearly impossible for Chicago's German socialists and anarchists to recruit Irish workers into their revolutionary movements; the Irish were too busy trying to overthrow the economic and political systems that were oppressing their relatives and friends in Ireland.

The U.S. Irish nationalist movement benefited from strong Irish ethnic identification in this country (Funchion 1976). Anti-Irish prejudice and the mixing of Irish from all parts of Ireland led to a U.S. nationalist movement that was less affected by the parochial conflicts dividing the movement in Ireland. Also, the Irish revolutionary in the United States was able to formulate ideas and engage in political action against the British with little fear of interference or repression from the British government. That made the Irish nationalists more radical in both tactics and ideology than their counterparts in Ireland, who were forced to compromise with powerful Protestant settlers and the British government.

For example, when O'Connell's repeal campaign failed in 1843, the Chicago Irish quickly expressed their support for the revolutionary Young Ireland campaign, although that movement had little support in Ireland (Funchion 1976, 28). In the 1850s and 1860s, the Irish in Chicago had a strong branch of the Fenians, another revolutionary group that had far greater strength in the United States than in Ireland. The Fenians, dedicated to the sole purpose of achieving Irish independence, had three hundred members in Chicago by 1863 (Piper 1936, 18). They held meetings twice a week, held the national Fenian convention in Chicago in 1863, and managed to raise $54,000 for the cause of Irish independence during a two-week period in March and April 1864 (Piper 1936, 20). The group conducted military drills and purchased arms and munitions in preparation for a strike against England.

But the somewhat farfetched idea of a military strike against England soon resulted in factionalism in the Chicago order. Some favored an attack on England itself; others believed an invasion of the English colony of Canada was more feasible. Incredibly, the latter strategy was finally adopted, and a navy was formed in Chicago to "sweep the lakes of British commerce" (Piper 1936, 23). Chicago Fenians furnished three regiments of infantry, two batteries of artillery, and a naval brigade—a total of a thousand men and $600—to the 1866 attack on Canada (Piper 1936, 23). The invasion was a dismal failure; a U.S. circuit court subsequently declared that the invasion had violated the Neutrality Act, and President Andrew Johnson issued a proclamation forbidding American citizens from taking part in such activities (Piper 1936, 25). Despite the order, there was an abortive second invasion attempt in 1870, to which the Chicago nationalists again contributed troops (Funchion 1976, 25).

The Fenian movement was in decline by the late sixties, in part because of the weakness of the movement in Ireland itself. When the Fenians dissolved, another revolutionary organization sprang up to take its place: the Clan na Gael. Because it was believed that publicity had hurt the Fenians, the Clan, founded in New York in 1867, was organized as a secret society. Both it and the early Knights of Labor had secret rituals (initiation ceremonies, handshakes, ciphers, and other masonic rites) that made them popular among former Irish peasants who had organized against landlords in clandestine rural societies in Ireland.

The Clan met with opposition in many U.S. Catholic dioceses because of the pagan overtones of some of its rituals; some Catholic leaders viewed it as a religious competitor to the church. But no such opposition occurred in Chicago, where Archbishop Feehan became a vehement defender of Irish nationalism (Funchion 1976, 40). The strength of church support for nationalism is shown by the fact that the editors of the *Western Catholic*, the major Irish Catholic paper in the city, suggested at one point that dynamite should not be used in the Irish struggle against England; rather, London should be set ablaze because that would result in somewhat less loss of life (Funchion 1976, 40). Church support made the Chicago nationalist movement particularly strong and particularly radical.

By 1881, Chicago was the undisputed center of Irish revolutionary nationalism in the country (Funchion 1976, 29). For every nationalist organization in Ireland, there was a Chicago counterpart, and the groups were generally stronger in the latter location. Boycotts of stores selling British-made goods were organized (Schneirov 1984, 221). The Irish National Land League, a group working for Irish Catholic peasant control of Irish land, held meetings like this one in the early 1880s:

A very large and highly enthusiastic meeting of Irish American citizens under the auspices of the Dillon Branch of the Irish National Land League was held in the hall of Father Cartan's Church of the Nativity on 37th St. last Monday evening. Father Cartan was called to the chair and delivered a logical and eloquent opening address in which he said that the time had come for earnest action on the part of every man with Irish blood in his veins.

There was no use in meeting and dispersing again without result. They must organize and organize powerfully in order to counteract the coercive policy of the English government in Ireland. He hoped that no man within hearing of his voice would leave the building without enrolling his name as a member of the Dillon branch of the Irish National Land League. (Great cheering) (*Citizen* [Chicago] January 14, 1882, 16)

On this one occasion, two hundred and fifty new members were enrolled in the organization, making a total membership of four hundred in this one club. Full church participation was crucial in such successful mobilizing efforts in the Irish nationalist movement. Three other clubs met this same week, with similar successful recruiting results (*Citizen* [Chicago] January 14, 1882).

These nationalist organizations engaged in militant activity in support of the Irish cause. The goal was to humiliate England in every way possible, through terrorism if necessary. Traditional parliamentary solutions had been rejected because of the defeat of the Irish legislators at the hands of the English and because of the suspension of Irish civil liberties following the murder of several British officials. So the Clan sent many of its members abroad on bombing missions, successfully dynamiting Britain's Local Government Board, the offices of the *London Times*, Victoria Station, Scotland Yard, London Bridge, Parliament, and the Tower of London (Fanning 1978, 145).

Many of the bombers were from the Chicago Clan na Gael. Sounding almost eerily like the German anarchist papers, the *Arbeiter Zeitung* or the *Alarm*, the major Irish nationalist paper in the city, the *Citizen*, defended the bombings, saying, "deeds, not words should be weighed. . . . It is only dynamite or some other blessed agency created by God, utilized by science, and wielded with heroic purpose that makes them thump their craws and talk about measures of redress" (June 7, 1884; cited in Fanning 1978, 146). To the Irish Catholic parliamentarians who condemned the bombing campaign, the editors of the *Citizen* replied that the American Irish did not have to follow blindly the directions of their cousins at home, for they had their own score to settle with England. Settle it they would, they asserted, with or without the approval of their fellow Irish across the sea (Funchion 1976, 33). The *London Times* clearly understood the revolutionary nature of the U.S. Irish movement, saying in 1885 that "the Irish question is mainly an Irish-American question" (Brown 1976b, 327).

The bombings were finally called off because of the possibility of the success of an Irish Home Rule Bill slated to be introduced in May 1886, but the U.S. Irish nationalist movement remained revolutionary. The nationalists continued to believe that dynamiting symbols of English nationalism was justified, but dynamiting (largely Irish) policemen in Chicago was totally unjustified. As the editor of the *Citizen* argued with regard to the Haymarket affair:

Chicago during the current week has been a theater of great sensations. The moral conflict between capital and labor has been taken advantage of by a few hare-brained extremists to precipitate a physical conflict between the forces of anarchy and those of law and public security. To strike for shorter hours and for higher wages is not looked upon by the general public with disfavor, but to attack manufacturing establishments with the object of destroying them, and to throw dynamite bombshells into the ranks of the protectors of the city's peace, with inevitably murderous effect, meets with the unstinted condemnation of all good citizens whether they be merchants, manufacturers, professional men or members of labor organizations who have in view not anarchy but national reform. Indeed we are sure that no class of men will more heartily condemn the violent proceedings of the extremists on Monday afternoon and Tuesday evening than the chiefs of the Knights of Labor. It is horrible to have it recorded of Chicago that such acts could be committed almost with impunity within her limits and it appears most extraordinary that any man pretending to the slightest modicum of reason should prefer the bludgeon and the mob to the convention and the ballot in this free and enlightened country. How much better and stronger it would be to take the advice of Henry George and carry the labor grievances into politics! To that no citizen can make consistent objection. The ballot must decide the struggle one way or the other in the end. Anarchy can never do it. (*Citizen* [Chicago] May 8, 1886, 4)

The editor felt that the political system could be successfully influenced by any and all of Chicago's citizens; comparisons between the political situations of workers in Chicago and the native Irish in the British Isles were viewed as ludicrous. The editor ends the editorial by congratulating the Irish citizens of Chicago for their failure to support anarchism and by referring explicitly to the heroic role of Irish policemen during the Haymarket incident:

The *Citizen* cannot close this editorial without congratulating the Irish-American element of this city on the splendid bearing throughout the deplorable history of the week. In no case has an Irish name appeared in

connection with the disturbances that have again advertised this city far
and wide. No men in America as we have often declared are more loyal to
American law and government than the Irish. In the ranks of the police,
the long list of the fatally injured or seriously wounded shows a majority of
Irish names and two of them at least . . . were members of the MacManus
Fenian Guards twenty years ago in this city. (*Citizen* [Chicago] May 8,
1886, 4)

As I shall illustrate, one reason for Irish support of the American
and Chicago political systems was their ability to garner jobs on the
public payroll, including positions on the city's police force.

Relationships Between Irish Organizations

The three key social institutions in the Irish community—the
church, nationalist organizations, and the Knights of Labor—co-
existed peacefully in Chicago. It was easy for those who belonged
to all of these groups to feel that they were following a consistent
set of social and political norms and values; Catholic faith, labor reform, and anti-English sentiment fit into one coherent worldview.

The church supported nationalist activity, providing both space
for meetings and priests as speakers. The church allowed the Irish
to join the Knights once that organization was no longer a secret,
oath-bound society and was willing to espouse moderate labor politics. Irish nationalists in editorials in the *Citizen* supported the
Knights' approach to labor reform by condemning those capitalists
who overworked or underpaid their employees (Funchion 1976,
37). The Knights and the Clan had similar positions on the revolutionary labor movement in Chicago, and both strongly condemned
the anarchist movement in the immediate post-Haymarket period.

Nationalists supported the church by railing against freethinking
anarchists. The editor of the *Citizen* argued just after the Haymarket incident that the Irish would never support a German anarchist movement in which atheism played an important part:

We are, as a race, free from atheism and anarchy. We do not always live
up to the high standard of Catholic excellence, and we are often impatient
and unjust in political partisanship, but we have never advocated either
individually or collectively, the destruction of all government and the
blasphemous dethronement of the most high God. (*Citizen* [Chicago]
May 15, 1886, 29)

Leadership circulated freely between nationalist and Knights' organizations. During the early months of 1886, several Clansmen were prominent speakers at Knights and Trades and Labor Assembly rallies. On the national level, the leader of the Knights, Terence Powderly, was a senior guardian of his local Clan na Gael camp. In Chicago, Richard Powers, president of the Seamen's Union and an active member of the Trades and Labor Assembly, was a member of the Clan as well as the Irish National Land League. Elizabeth Rodgers helped organize the original Working Women's Union during the 1870s and in 1886 was the master workman (*sic*) of the Knights' Chicago district 24 as well as the president of the 8th Ward Irish National Land League (Funchion 1976, 38).

In combination, the Irish dedication to Irish nationalism and Catholicism made it unlikely that the Irish would ever support a revolutionary movement in Chicago. Much discontent regarding their poor economic position in the city was defused by means of a radical nationalist movement; nearly all Irish revolutionaries in the city were fighting for the emancipation of Ireland from England, not for the emancipation of the Irish working class in Chicago. Also, the Catholic hierarchy demanded political moderation in the city (if not in the more remote Ireland and Britain) and barred Irish Catholics from participating in an atheistic socialist and anarchist movement. These organizations successfully promoted Irish labor reform, but one more crucial determinant of Irish labor reform politics must be discussed: the Irish role in city politics.

The Irish Role in Local Politics

Although the Catholic church may have provided spiritual sustenance and the nationalist organizations some measure of revenge against the British, neither could provide a general solution to Irish poverty. The economic self-help associations such as the benevolent societies did not have enough resources to make a difference; unskilled unions were ephemeral and rarely able to use their mass strikes to gain more than a few cents a day raise. The Knights were a hopeful experiment because they used the resources of the skilled to support economic action of the unskilled; but the skilled inevitably defected to their exclusive craft unions.

Given the absence of purely economic solutions to their plight, the Irish were forced to innovate in order to achieve some measure of upward economic and social mobility. Because advancement in the private sector was so difficult, they looked to the largely unexplored territory of the public sector to move up; they perfected the *political machine*.

The key to the power of the machine was its use of a variety of incentives to convince voters to vote for its candidates. At the bottom of the machine hierarchy were the precinct captains and workers, whose role was to round up voters to vote the Democratic ticket on election day. Inducements were offered during the year to ensure voter loyalty (the traditional ham and turkey on Easter and Christmas and help with burials, christenings, weddings, getting the street fixed, or getting the garbage collected in front of one's house). The machine was not beyond using more direct material incentives, including $.50 or $1, a glass of beer or a shot of whisky, or lodging for a few days before the election. But voters did not necessarily view it as simple economic exchange, favors for votes; rather, they considered the machine operative a friend and voted Democratic to help him (Rakove 1975).

Above the precinct captain were the ward committeemen and the aldermen, who controlled the major source of voting discipline: the *patronage job*. Chicago, of course, had many public sector jobs, from police and fire department positions to the sewer and water department, the parks department, the court system, and the administrative apparatus of the Democratic party itself. Voting practices were controlled by distributing jobs to those willing to vote for and, more important, work to ensure that others voted for, the machine ticket. Because the more jobs distributed, the more votes controlled, the most powerful in machine politics were those who controlled the largest number of patronage jobs.

The unskilled (and so most of the city's Irish residents) needed patronage jobs more than the skilled. City jobs provided exactly what private sector unskilled jobs did not: good pay and working conditions. Because basic city services had to be performed even during depressions, they were also secure from the threat of unemployment. The patronage job became the road out of poverty for many of the city's unskilled Irish residents; it was well worth giving up one's vote and working for the machine candidates on election day to get such a meal ticket.

The machine was very successful at electing its candidates to office, rolling up its greatest vote margins in the poor, foreign-born, river wards where voters were most apt to take advantage of economic inducements to vote the machine slate. There were further economic inducements beyond wages and salaries for those largely Irish officials who managed to attain high positions in the machine. One of the most profitable endeavors was the "boodle." The aldermen received kickbacks for approving franchises for a variety of private operators to provide such profit-making city services as gas, electricity, water, railroad lines, streetcar lines, and telegraph service. As Stead (1964, 176–77) describes the process:

The method of boodling as prevailing in the City Council of Chicago for many years is very simple. Some man or some corporation wants something from the city. It may be some right of way or it may be a franchise for tearing up the streets in order to lay gas pipes, or it may be an ordinance sanctioning the laying of a railroad down a street or to make a grade crossing across one of innumerable thoroughfares of the city. He can only obtain permission by obtaining it from the City Council. Now the majority of the City Council consider that they are not in the Council "for their health." As each of them went into it "for the sake of the stuff" and for whatever there was "in it" for themselves, they think these favors should not be granted without the receipt of a corresponding *quid pro quo*. Hence it is necessary, if you wish to get anything through the council, to "square" with the Aldermen. The "squaring" is done discreetly and with due regard to the fundamental principle which sums up the whole law of the boodler, namely: thou shalt not be found out.

In rapidly growing Chicago, the opportunities for such boodles were great; city council members, who included some non-Irish, were known as the "grey wolves" for their practice of illegally selling such franchises (Fanning 1978, 108). There were other opportunities for payoffs as well, such as granting "licenses" for the illegal operation of gambling and prostitution halls.

The Irish quickly came to dominate the political machine in Chicago, and they managed to exclude other ethnic groups from infringing on their power for generations to come. There were various reasons they were able to accomplish this. For one thing, they had greater motivation to gain control of more secure, tax-revenue-supported public jobs because they seemed to have no other road to economic security. Even the relatively unskilled jobs on the public payroll (such as police and fire department jobs) accorded the worker more status and more security than the best job the typical Irish worker could obtain in the private labor market.

Another factor explaining Irish dominance of the machine was their political experience in mid nineteenth-century Ireland. O'Connell had used a similar model of grass roots organizing in building his Catholic Association, and the Irish had long been used to having their landlords tell them how to vote in any given election (Funchion 1976, 42). Survival during the famine years had also dictated the development of a spirit of reciprocity, of "I'll scratch your back if you'll scratch mine"—the same attitude necessary for the successful operation of the political machine.

Also, unlike most other immigrants, the Irish spoke English and were used to the English system of law and justice (Rakove 1975, 32). They were adept at finding ways around a political-legal system in order to maximize private gain for themselves and their countrymen. Unlike the more idealistic Germans, they had no illusions about the objective fairness of such a system, and they were willing to use any and all means to manipulate it to their own advantage, just as they had done in Ireland.

The Irish were also able to use their Catholicism to their great advantage. They had faced Protestant anti-Catholicism in Ireland and were not surprised when the Know-Nothings and other nativist groups used anti-Catholic strategies in politics. They combated such attacks by using the natural identification of southern European Catholics with others of their religious persuasion to gain valuable votes for Irish Catholic candidates; the Irish were outside the usual ethnic antipathies that affected those central and southern European groups. As one Irish machine operative put it: "A Lithuanian won't vote for a Pole, and a Pole won't vote for a Lithuanian. A German won't vote for either of them—but all three will vote for a 'turkey,' an Irishman" (Rakove 1975, 33).

Another important Irish political tool was the bar or saloon. The political value of the saloon derived from its role as the crucial public meeting place in the Irish community. Bars served this function for early labor unions, especially the ephemeral unions of the poor, less skilled workers who could not afford to build their own meeting halls. They were often used as strike headquarters (Duis

1975, 642) and as labor exchanges, where the out of work could find jobs. In 1889, 44 percent of the city's employment agencies shared a building with a saloon, and another 22 percent were within two doors of one (Duis 1975, 644). Workers cashed their checks at the corner saloon, and the saloon often served as a relief agency, supplying lunches to the hungry for free or for the price of a nickel beer.

The saloonkeeper was in a position to provide favors to those who were out of work, hungry, or cold or who needed a loan, bail money, or a paycheck cashed. The saloonkeeper often became a politician or a friend of politicians because of his important economic and social functions and his place at the center of Irish social networks in the city. He was the center of verbal communication, and face-to-face interaction was what got out the vote in a multi-language city where many did not speak or read English.

In fact, Chicago politicians often talked of the difference between the *river wards* (poor areas of the city that always voted Democratic) and *newspaper wards* (where readers made candidate newspaper endorsements important to the election results). In the river wards, precinct captains went door to door to get out the vote while the office seeker generally went from bar to bar, often buying votes with a beer or whisky. Saloons also lodged casual laborers and drifters for days before the election in order to ensure an impressive vote total for the Democratic candidate (Duis 1975, 761).

Machine bosses who wished to ensure the election results made sure that polling places were either in or near the saloon. Duis (1975) estimates that half the city's polling places were located in bars in the eighties. Even the Anglo-American reformers understood the importance of this for the Irish machine; they tried to increase license fees for saloons and also made the removal of polling places from bars part of their political reform package in the mid eighties.

The Chicago machine of the seventies and eighties was far less centralized than it became in later years. There were many political "bosses," not just one; bosses were individuals who controlled a large number of patronage jobs and thus more voters. Many of these politicians were saloonkeepers, such as the most powerful boss of the time, Mike McDonald. Other influential Irish politicians, including Bathhouse John Coughlin, Michael "Hinky Dink" Kenna, Barney Grogan, and P. J. Cullerton, were also associated with the saloon business.

The decentralized nature of the machine made it possible for other Irish social organizations to become minimachines, supporting small political cliques in return for a greater share of the patronage pie (Funchion 1976, 44). As Funchion points out, almost every prominent member of the Clan in the eighties, and undoubtedly the Fenians before them, was deeply involved in machine politics.

The leader of the Clan in Chicago, Alexander Sullivan, was appointed clerk of the board of public works in 1873, reflecting his work in the effort of the People's party to defeat the temperance-oriented Law and Order party. Sullivan made deals with various politicians, promising them Clan support in return for patronage; and the patronage at his disposal then increased his popularity among the Irish. In the early 1880s, he backed Mayor Harrison and was rewarded by being permitted to appoint several of his friends to the police department. He secured countless positions for Clansmen in several other city and county departments, including the board of election commissioners and the superior court (Funchion 1976, 45).

Other Clan members also had large numbers of patronage jobs at their disposal, including jobs in the county commissioner's office, Cook County Hospital, the city treasurer's office, and the sheriff's office. Some were elected to aldermanic positions; others were on the Cook County Central Committee of the Democratic party. In fact, Funchion (1976, 46) argues that many members of the Clan joined for the sole purpose of getting a job. The Clan thus helped defuse Irish labor radicalism in two ways. It provided an outlet for Irish militancy, encouraging many Irish to blame their Chicago problems on the English. It provided public sector jobs to the unemployed.

For all these reasons, the Irish dominated city politics. By 1885, fourteen of the eighteen members of the Democratic Central Committee were Irish; this allowed control of who was elected to the city council and other key city and county posts. By the 1890s, twenty-four of the twenty-eight individuals in sole control of the city's wards were Irish (Funchion 1976, 42).

Other Chicago ethnic groups, especially the largely Anglo-American reformers, fought unsuccessfully against Irish control of the political machine. The prominent role of the Irish in city politics was resented as early as 1838 (Funchion 1976, 18). In 1840, the Chicago *American*, a nativist publication, suggested that the Irish had too important a role in the outcome of elections. It charged that many Irish were exercising their right to vote before they could do so legally. Successful prosecutions of several Irish machine politicians for vote fraud reinforced the idea that the Irish were dominating the machine through illegal means (Levine 1966, 145).

One Democratic mayoral candidate suggested as early as 1846 that foreigners should have to live in the United States for twenty-one years before becoming voting citizens (Funchion 1976, 18). The Know-Nothings attempted to counter the Irish Catholic influence in politics by passing laws requiring that applicants for municipal jobs be born in this country.

A variety of Anglo-American political reform and temperance groups (the Citizens Association, the Commercial Club, the Republican Union League Club, the Democratic Iroquois Club, the Women's Christian Temperance Union, and the Citizens Law and Order League) carried the fight against the machine into the 1880s. In 1885, the Irish machine suffered a temporary setback when many of the political reformers' proposals, including election reform, unbiased election judges, smaller precincts, and the creation of an election board, were passed at the state level (Schneirov 1984, 370). Despite occasional challenges to their dominance, however, the Irish continued to control Chicago politics well into the twentieth century.

Conclusions

Characterizing Irish labor politics as "militant reform" is not as contradictory as it sounds. The Irish were militant in their tactics, but reformist in their goals. They were the leaders of the mass strikes of this period; the lack of separation of workplace and community among the unskilled Irish facilitated the use of community-based kinship, neighboring, and social organizational networks in these strikes. They demanded not the transformation of the economic and political systems, but union recognition, higher wages, shorter hours, and better working conditions. Without scarce skills, achieving even these moderate goals was difficult for the Irish. Despite their aggressive tactics, they remained at the bottom of the city's occupational and income structure.

Their search for a solution to their problems forced the Irish to draw on other resources in their community. An effective response was facilitated by the fact that the Irish had faced an aggressive nativist attack by Anglo-American Protestants. The defensive response to that attack fostered an increasing level of Irish ethnic identification and a greater sense of social solidarity and common fate within their community. The Irish pulled together, believing that their future was tied to the success of their ethnic group and not necessarily to their class or trade.

The resources used in this community-based response included social and political institutions such as the Catholic church, the Irish nationalist organizations, the Knights of Labor, the saloon, and the political machine. These distinctively Irish institutions became *havens* within which a unique response to the plight of the Chicago Irish was mobilized. They contained the cohesive social networks needed to communicate with potential recruits when political action was necessary. The solidarity among those in these organizations made their recruitment to such action likely when they were contacted.

Irish solidarity facilitated political mobilization within the Irish community. But the cultural and political characteristics of these institutional havens resulted in a reformist rather than a revolutionary response to Irish problems. The Catholic church had for centuries been the social organizational basis of the Irish defense against the economic, political, and cultural imperialism of Protestant Scottish settlers and the British government. Labor politics mobilized through church social networks had to be conscious of the church's antipathy toward any political movement with atheistic or pagan tendencies (such as the anarchist movement and oath-bound secret societies such as the early Knights of Labor). The church provided space for meetings and social networks for recruitment to labor politics, but it also used its influence to make Irish labor politics more conservative, to limit its aims.

The Irish nationalist organizations fostered reformism in the city by promoting revolution against Britain. They convinced the Chicago Irish that they ought to blame their lack of skills and their poverty on British and Scottish Protestants. The relative invulnerability of the Chicago Irish to British repression and British arguments concerning the Irish meant that the Chicago nationalist movement was more radical in ideology and tactics than the native Irish movement. Radicalism was displaced; English and not Chicago political and economic institutions were blamed for the plight of the Chicago Irish. Irish dynamiters attacked London Bridge rather than the Chicago police in Haymarket Square.

The Irish working class was reformist only because its members viewed political institutions in Great Britain, the United States, and Chicago very differently; denial of Irish political access in the British Isles was contrasted to the Irish ability to ascend to positions of political leadership in Chicago. The Chicago political system did not provide only political influence for the Irish; it also provided upward economic mobility. The key to the strength of the Chicago political machine was the fact that it provided long-term, stable, well-paid employment to unskilled Irish peasants who had never before had job security.

Many of those jobs were in the Chicago Police Department. It would have been absurd to question—as the anarchists did—the very political system that had provided the Irish with their first real chance for economic success. It made more sense to form a coalition with more moderate labor reformers in the Trades and Labor Assembly who did not call for the overthrow of the state, as the Knights of Labor did during the early 1880s eight-hour movement. As suggested by the insightful fictional Irish bartender of the period, Mr. Dooley:

I see by this pa-per," said Mr. Dooley, "that anarchy's torch do be uplifted an' what th' 'ell it means, I dinnaw. But this here I knaw, Jawn, that all arnychists is inimies iv governmint an' all iv thim ought to be hung up be th' nick. What are they anny how but furiners an' what r-right have they to be holdin' tor-rch-light procissions in this land iv th' free an' home iv th' brave? Did ye iver seen an American or an Irishman an arnychist? Naw, an' ye niver will. Whin an Irishman thinks th' way iv thim la'ads he goes on th' polis force an' draws his eighty three-thirty three f'r throwin' lodgin' house bums into th' pathrol wagon. An' there ye a'are. (Schaaf 1977, 109)

Chapter Five

The Roots of
Revolutionary German
Labor Politics

Throughout the entire period of industrialization, German workers provided both leadership and rank-and-file participants for the most class-conscious, revolutionary labor politics in Chicago. But they never managed to convince most of the non-German members of the working class to join in their effort. Despite their class-conscious rhetoric, both the revolutionary socialist and anarchist movements recruited mainly German members using social networks within the German community and drawing extensively on German cultural traditions.

Chapters 1 and 2 have provided extensive evidence that Chicago's revolutionary labor movement was primarily German. A German political club founded in 1857, the Social Democratic Turnverein, was the first in the city to espouse Marxist principles. The German carpenters and Social Political Workingman's Union formed sections of the Marxist International in the early 1870s; in 1873, three of the six sections of the International were German.

In the mid 1870s, fifteen of twenty-two sections of the Workingman's Party of the United States were German; the party's radical German-language paper, the *Vorbote*, had thirty-six hundred subscribers by 1876. Over 40 percent of those arrested during the 1877 strikes had German or Bohemian last names. The German cabinetmakers, cigar makers, stonecutters, and coopers exhibited a degree of class solidarity with the less skilled by expressing support for that strike. All candidates actually elected by and a high proportion of the voters for the Socialist Labor party were Germans.

In the 1880s, the great majority of anarchists in the city were German. German-language anarchist papers had a circulation of over twenty thousand in the mid 1880s; twelve of the thirteen anarchist clubs and six of the eight Haymarket martyrs were German. The first union to express anarchist views, the Progressive Cigarmakers Union, was German. The anarchist Central Labor Union was made up primarily of German unions. Most socialist and anarchist meetings actually took place in communities with a high proportion of German residents; hundreds of such meetings were announced in the German-language press and attended by German workers throughout this period (*Arbeiter Zeitung* [Chicago] for this period). In one month (April 1884), there were seventeen meetings of anarchist groups held in German and Bohemian Turner halls.

Throughout the period, German revolutionaries were in direct conflict with Anglo-American reformers on both ideological and tactical questions. Most Germans did not believe that labor reform measures (such as child labor restrictions, stricter enforcement of apprenticeship rules, prohibition of convict labor, and factory inspection) could solve the problems of the city's working class. Germans also were more likely to reject the exclusive craft union organizing model in favor of organizing the unskilled; the Progressive Cigarmakers advocated organizing sweatshop cigar workers, for example. They did not believe that currency reform would help workers much, and they supported the more radical demand of ten hours' pay for eight hours' work during the eight-hour movement in the mid 1880s. Tactically, they denied the efficacy of lobbying legislators, eventually deciding that the electoral system was not an effective arena for working-class political action and supporting the use of armed workers defense associations. The split between the Anglo-Americans and the Germans was finally resolved only because brutal repression effectively crushed the anarchist tendency following the Haymarket bombing.

However, I am not suggesting that most Chicago Germans were revolutionaries. No revolutionary movement, even dramatically successful ones, ever recruits the majority of its potential constituency. The Chicago movement was no exception; many in the city's German working class did not support the socialist and anarchist tendencies even when those movements were at their height. Certainly, few middle-class Germans supported revolutionary politics. Most probably agreed with the sentiments of one of the most powerful German-Americans in the Midwest, Hermann Raster, editor of the moderate *Illinois Staats-Zeitung*, who condemned the socialists and anarchists as follows:

> With their insolent and insane demands, they jeopardize this country's economy and every honorable person's property. Unfortunately it is from the German Reich that these bloody scoundrels, these socialists, communists, and anarchists have come. The Germans in the United States were powerful, esteemed and influential, and although not loved, they were respected. After the founding of Bismarck's Reich . . . , however, their repute has steadily declined, because of the repulsive, offensive, hideous character of newly arriving German emigrants. (Cited in Keil 1986, 18)

Raster also wrote a letter to the governor of Illinois calling for the execution of the Haymarket martyrs and later called for immigration restrictions to keep German immigrant radicals out of the country (Keil 1986, 18–19).

However, although most of the city's Germans were not revolutionaries, most of its many revolutionaries were German. And these revolutionaries were able to mobilize a strong movement that attracted tens of thousands for marches and rallies and that recruited two dozen of the city's largest unions. Obviously, there were factors that made Chicago's German-born workers more likely to accept revolutionary ideologies and tactics within the labor movement. As for the analyses of the labor politics of the city's Anglo-American and Irish workers, an effective explanation for German workers' political choices must consider the background of German working-class immigrants as well as the nature of German economic, community, and political life in Chicago.

The Working Class in Germany

Many workers faced economic hardships in mid nineteenth-century Germany. Unlike Great Britain in this period, Germany was still primarily agricultural, its economy based on the peasant and the farm, the artisan and the craft shop. Most skilled workers belonged to *guilds*, precursors of craft unions that were local monopolies of craftsmen such as butchers, bakers, tailors, shoemakers, and cigar makers. Those who were not members of the guild were banned from working in the trade; and guild masters, the owners of craft shops, were banned from trespassing on other masters' economic territory.

The system was built on *social honor*, the expectation that even low-status individuals were born into social groups that performed important functions for society. Each worker had pride in fulfilling his or her specific role in society; strong sanctions ensured that the individual did not perform functions inappropriate to his or her social rank. Some mobility within the system was expected. In particular, artisans expected that diligent work would result in smooth upward mobility from apprentice to journeyman to master. There were obvious negative economic consequences for the individual craftsman if such mobility was not forthcoming, but it was considered a violation of social honor as well (Moore 1978, 129–30).

By the 1840s, there were trends leading to the dissolution of the German guilds. Improvements in transportation technology and the lifting of various economic restrictions resulted in the expansion of markets to national, even international scope, thus undermining the local monopolies that were the foundation of the guilds. Master craftsmen began to see their businesses fail, journeymen were unable to advance to master status, and apprentices could not find work as journeymen. Many workers were forced to become casual laborers.

Rapid population growth, a trend that affected all of Europe, exacerbated the situation. The German population increased from twenty-three to thirty-five million between 1800 and 1850 (Noyes 1966, 16). Industrialization and urbanization had not progressed far enough to provide jobs for so many new workers. Seventy percent of the German population still lived in the country or in villages smaller than one thousand in 1850 (Noyes 1966, 17). Even the most industrially developed section of Germany—Prussia—had a working class that was less than one-fifth factory workers in 1846 (Noyes 1966, 21).

The result was lower wages, increasing unemployment, and increasing poverty for the craftsmen. The initial penetration of market capitalism into the rural areas of Germany displaced peasants as well; sharecropping and seasonal day labor became increasingly common. These problems were followed by a potato famine, grain failures, and a financial panic between 1845 and 1848, worsening an already bad situation.

Workers viewed these trends as significant threats to their economic and social positions; morally indignant guild members responded by organizing clubs and associations. In fact, organizing various kinds of workers' associations quickly became the panacea for all the ills afflicting the German working class, especially once the German government made all such group associations legal (Noyes 1966). Even singing societies and the patriotic German gymnastic associations called *Turner societies* were politicized.

Both masters and journeymen organized, but the former excluded all journeymen from their groups, tried to force a return to old guild restrictions, and generally promoted policies that would preserve their positions at the expense of the journeymen. The journeymen realized that a return to the old system would not solve their problems; they saw that the penetration of the capitalist market into local monopolies and the severe labor surplus would prevent them from ever becoming masters in Germany.

When it became clear that the guilds would not represent their interests effectively, journeymen began to consider revolution. Few journeymen became revolutionary socialists, but many did feel that basic changes in economic institutions would be necessary to solve their problems. They wanted an end to special concessions and privileges, a system in which every member of society was assured a job at the appropriate social level. Many journeymen tried to organize along with unskilled workers, who were a majority of the German working class, in order to create a new society, a course of action the master craftsmen never considered (Moore 1978, 149; Noyes 1966, 196).

The result of this organizing effort was a series of working-class political actions in 1848 and 1849, following on the heels of the French worker revolts. In fact, this "revolution" never involved a large proportion of the German working class; barricades were erected in only two cities. But the combination of economic deprivation and political repression of the scattered uprisings led to increased political consciousness and intensified organizing efforts among German workers (Noyes 1966, 307).

These efforts culminated in such organizations as Karl Marx's

Revolutionary Communist League, which espoused strong trade union organizing and strikes to fight for a new society and enjoyed much support in the fifties. By the sixties, Lassallean ideas and politics also became popular in the German working class. But all the workers' political organizations were soon repressed or forced underground by the government.

The combination of economic deprivation and political repression did not lead all German workers to revolution in Germany; many decided instead to emigrate to the United States. Emigration from Germany was around twenty thousand per year from the thirties to the mid forties. It increased to nearly one hundred thousand per year in 1847 in response to the previously described conditions. Reasons given for emigration were both political and economic; emigrants mentioned overpopulation, the potato famine, fragmentation of land holdings, decline of the crafts, unemployment of rural farmers, bureaucracy, police repression, taxes, and obligatory military service as reasons for their decision to leave Germany (Walker 1964, 145).

Of course, immigration had its pull side as well. Most immigrants decided on the United States as their destination because they expected this country to offer greater economic opportunites and political freedom. Chicago was a natural destination for the German immigrant. Skilled craftsmen believed that job opportunities in the city and surrounding area would be more numerous than in their native country. Farmers and rural laborers believed it possible to own a farm in the growing west, which was expected to offer freedom for those of various religious and political persuasions, as well as low taxes, cheap land, and the opportunity to achieve a comfortable existence in a short time for oneself and one's children (Hofmeister 1976, 19). Gottfried Duden's *Report on a Trip to the Western States of North America* appeared in Germany in 1829; the book's "streets paved with gold" emphasis apparently led many to make the long journey to Chicago once they reached the United States (Hofmeister 1976, 20).

As pointed out with regard to Irish immigrants, many jobs were created through the building of the Illinois and Michigan Canal and the railroads around mid century. The rebuilding of the city following the fire in the 1870s also meant jobs for construction workers of all skill levels. Enthusiastic letters to relatives back in

Germany convinced many potential migrants to come to Chicago; and agents for the railroad, construction, and other industries were hired to keep the stream of immigrants flowing. As the German community in Chicago grew, the city developed a more complete set of German institutions and support networks, which made it even more attractive to the immigrant craftsmen. Many Germans who had planned to own a farm in the rural west wound up as un- skilled workers in Chicago when their meager funds ran out or when they realized how lonely the existence of a German im- migrant farmer could be. Chicago offered nearness to German friends, relatives, and institutions; the wilderness did not.

In terms of numbers and cultural and political impact, Germans were the most important immigrant group to settle in Chicago in its early history. There were only 5,094 Germans in Chicago in 1850; but their numbers increased to 22,227 in 1860, 53,022 in 1870, 76,661 in 1880, and 168,082 in 1890. By 1890, there were over 320,000 first- and second-generation Germans in the city, rep- resenting one-third of Chicago's total population. Many of these immigrants were undoubtedly skilled craftsmen because 74 per- cent of them were from Prussia, the most industrialized part of Germany (Townsend 1927, 16).

The German Worker's Economic Position
in Chicago

Nearly all the German immigrants to Chicago found themselves in the city's working class (see Table 9). Over three-quarters of the German-born population was working class in all three census years; less than one-quarter was in the middle and upper classes. But unlike the Irish, German workers brought skills with them and were often able to avoid the city's worst unskilled positions. As re- ported previously, this was reflected in an occupational dispersion measure that is somewhat higher at .53 than the native-born figure of .33 but much lower than the Irish figure of .95.

Working-class Germans did have trouble breaking into the Anglo- American-dominated labor aristocracy; from one-quarter to one- third of all German residents were in the unskilled and low-status skilled sectors, and less than one-fifth were in the labor aristocracy. Germans had greater numbers in the low-status skilled category than any other ethnic group. They dominated such skilled trades as cigar making, baking, brewing, cabinetmaking, and harness, saddle, and trunk making—the trades most vulnerable to skill degradation and having lower wages and less employment security than the construction, printing, and machine trades.

Thus, Germans had fewer of their number in the highest status trades and the middle and upper classes than the British- and native-born craftsmen, but fewer in unskilled laboring jobs than the Irish. The average German worker earned $476 a year, which compares unfavorably with the $598 of the British born and the $549 of the native born, but is higher than the $350–$400 earned by the typical unskilled worker.

Despite the rhetoric of the "American dream," the German immigrant's children did not enjoy economic statuses significantly better than their parents. Keil and Jentz have considered intergenerational mobility in 2,222 German households from the 1880 Census manuscripts. Table 11, drawn from their analysis, unfortunately does not differentiate between the low-status skilled and labor aristocrat categories. Still, the table shows that although the second generation had a greater ability to find skilled as opposed to unskilled work, its members were only 3.3 percent more likely to enter the middle and upper classes than were their parents.

TABLE 11.   *Class of First- and Second-Generation German Heads of Households, 1880*

Class	First Generation	Second Generation
Upper middle	1.9	2.8
Lower middle	18.0	20.4
Skilled working	36.5	50.7
Unskilled working	35.7	21.9
Not specified	7.9	4.2
Total	100.0	100.0
N	1,888	142

Source. Hartmut Keil and John B. Jentz, eds., *German Workers in Industrial Chicago* (DeKalb: Northern Illinois University Press, 1983), p. 23.

As in the case of the Anglo-American and Irish workers, individual German workers' economic positions did not predict political choice. It was not surprising, given their economic position, to find that Anglo-American printers supported the continuation of the existing economic and political systems. But it was interesting to find much less well off native-born cigar makers supporting the same reformist politics. Likewise, it is not shocking to find that the low-status skilled German Progressive Cigarmakers led the revolutionary anarchist secession; cigar makers were vulnerable to the negative impact of mechanization and the business cycle. But it is surprising to find that labor aristocrats like the German printers in the Chicago Typographical Union no. 9 also joined the anarchist Central Labor Union. In fact, German workers of all skill levels supported revolutionary politics. There was a distinctively German revolutionary labor politics in Chicago in this period, and it mobilized Germans from the top to the bottom of the working class. The explanation for revolutionary German politics must consider social, cultural, and political factors, and not just economic position.

The Cultural and Social Organizational Basis of the Revolutionary German Labor Movement

Based in German community networks rather than only at workplaces, the revolutionary labor movement was able to capitalize on strong ethnic identification. Just as for the Irish, the strength of such ethnic identification was increased by the need for Germans to respond to nativist attacks, which were mounted primarily by Anglo-Americans who wished to protect their own privileged economic position. But the Irish also waged a successful war to remain the only real power behind Chicago's political machine. Nativism and its associated economic and political discrimination created common German economic, cultural, and political problems and motivated distinctively German solutions.

Nativist Attacks on Germans

Economic problems were created by the policy of excluding Germans from the elite Anglo-American unions. Such discrimination was one reason for the existence of separate unions for each ethnic group in the city and for German–Anglo-American factionalism within the labor movement. The practice may have maintained Anglo-American wages at high levels, but *collectively*, it limited working-class power and increased employer strength. The *Arbeiter Zeitung* commented as follows regarding the propensity of the native-born craft unions to exclude the foreign born from their ranks:

In most factories the laborers are under the supervision of foremen who come from the same country as the laborers and who regulate the shops according to their own ideas and in addition receive a commission from the owners. This procedure will last as long as foreign labor is kept out of the labor organizations or is treated with hostility.

American labor should try to elevate foreign labor to its own standard instead of fighting and suppressing it. (*Arbeiter Zeitung* [Chicago] August 7, 1888, 32)

Germans faced attacks on their culture, especially their practice of Sunday drinking at picnics and in beer gardens. In discussing the enforcement of the Sunday blue laws in the early seventies, one alderman suggested, "The Germans here must submit themselves. It is really impudent considering that they came here poor and in order to make money and that afterwards they always want to be considered Germans only" (*Staats Zeitung* [Illinois] April 17, 1871, 48). A few months later, this same alderman stated, "The Puritans founded the Republic, established freedom, and received the Germans with open arms. The Germans should therefore refrain from wanting to introduce European mores [into the United States and Chicago]" (*Staats Zeitung* [Illinois] June 13, 1871, 39). He went on to say that observation of the Sabbath had made the United States great and that the consequences of its nonobservance could be seen in the sorry state of the European nations.

Nativist sentiments were expressed by the upper classes as well as by the middle and working classes, as pointed out by a German paper in its report on an attempt to oust German and Irish police commissioners from office in Chicago.

If the *Tribune* does not believe that the nativist hatred of foreigners has anything to do with the revolt against the Police Commissioners, let it send its reporters to the gambling hell called the Board of Trade and let them hear how the respectable citizens there use the words "d. . .d

Dutch" [*sic*] or "d. . .d Irish" when they speak of Police Commissioners. (*Staats Zeitung* [Illinois] January 3, 1873, 21)

Attacks on German culture became part of a general attack on German working-class politics. Germans were accused of being radicals who knew little of American institutions and wanted to destroy all of value that Americans had built up. These attacks became especially frequent after the Haymarket affair, as the *Staats Zeitung* suggested in the late 1880s:

> For several years a tendency to hate foreigners has been noticeable in the United States. The fanatical clergy of the majority of American sects—in particular the Methodists, Congregationalists, Presbyterians, and Baptists, have taken advantage of these conditions not only to enforce the blue laws, but also to make them more severe.
>
> This anti-foreign sentiment has been strong enough to influence many Americans who otherwise might have been liberal and progressive. The enforcement of Sunday laws is first of all an attack against the German element because of the custom of going out on Sundays with families to enjoy the out-doors, to listen to good music while drinking beer in a beer garden.
>
> Another cause of the anti-foreign tendency is to be found in the activity of the recently immigrated anarchists and socialists. The American considers the red flag, the banner of anarchists as well as the socialists, and sees a continuous threat against his institutions. (*Staats Zeitung* [Illinois] May 11, 1888, 28)

Just as for the Irish, nativist attacks resulted in a defensive withdrawal into German cultural traditions, community-based social networks, and ultimately a distinctive labor politics.

The German Residence Community

Germans responded to the attack on their culture, their way of life, and their politics by settling in nearly homogeneous neighborhoods where they socialized with fellow countrymen and women, married other German community residents, spoke their own language, and discussed problems unique to themselves. Within this German *ethnic enclave*—segregated by language, cultural differences, and social networks—ethnic identification was strong, perhaps stronger than in Germany itself, which had only recently experienced national unification.

The German residence community founded in the mid nineteenth century lasted well into the twentieth century. The initial German settlement was, like Irish Bridgeport, founded near the Chicago River (see Map 1). But the German community did not remain narrowly confined to the river wards; by 1870 (Map 2), it had expanded significantly to the north. Unlike many of the native-born and British workers, the average German was not able to afford a large single-family home on the West Side or an apartment near the central business district. Many lived in frame housing, in "humble wooden cottages," or in newly built three- to four-story row housing on the city's North Side (Pierce 1957, 3: 52).

As Map 2 also shows, the city's Germans had established another residential outpost on the Northwest Side in the 1860s. Unlike the North Side settlement, which included a large number of skilled craftsmen as residents, the Northwest Side community was settled by mostly unskilled workers. Through the use of manuscript census schedules, Keil and Jentz (1981) found that the unskilled in the Northwest Side settlement segregated themselves by ethnicity, and even by province, regardless of their occupation; by contrast, the somewhat more ethnically diverse North Side settlement had skilled workers of various ethnic origins living on the same blocks, segregated more by trade than by ethnicity.

There was a fully developed set of German community institutions in both the North and Northwest Side residence areas, including German-language schools, churches, meeting places, businesses, and workplaces. Germans were able to live their everyday lives without leaving the German community; many both worked and shopped in their own neighborhood (Harzig 1983, 138). Some worked in the lumberyards, furniture-making plants, iron mills, foundries, brickyards, and breweries that were located near the community's western boundary. Many others established bakeries, saloons, cigar-making, wagon- and carriage-making, tailor, shoe-making, printing, and woodworking shops within the German enclave. The German owners of these small businesses generally employed other Germans, often apprenticing their sons to the trade (Harzig 1983, 135). Young women often worked in the neighborhood-based clothing industry as tailoresses, dressmakers, or machine operators (Harzig 1983, 135). Of 38 bakers and 158 saloon keepers in the German neighborhood in 1880, more than four-fifths were of German descent; and all these German neighborhood bakers and saloon keepers preferred German employees (Harzig 1983, 139).

The German propensity to settle in predominantly German communities in Chicago is shown by their residential dispersion score of .41, which is higher than the native-born score of .28. Some neighborhoods within these two residential areas showed very high levels of ethnic homogeneity. In one eight-block area in the Northwest Side community studied by Harzig (1983, 131), nearly 80 percent of the heads of household were of German origin in both 1880 and 1900. This compares to 26 percent German for the city as a whole. As she puts it, "The comparatively few non-German residents were evenly distributed throughout the area and did not interfere with its German character" (Harzig 1983, 132). The residential stability of the area was high. These residents were not newcomers; in 1880, the head of household had come to the United States an average of nine to thirteen years earlier.

Propensity to marry within one's ethnic group is a good measure of in-group identification and social isolation; in the same neighborhood, 87 percent of all married couples had a first- or second-generation German partner in 1880; 83 percent had such a partner as late as 1900 (Harzig 1983, 132). These German enclaves continued to be the residence area for many first- and second-generation immigrants, at least until the 1920s, in part because of continued German immigration to the city (Keil and Jentz 1981, 15).

Thus, many German residents lived, worked, played, found friends, and organized to try to solve their economic and political problems in their neighborhood. Like the Irish, the Germans founded a variety of ethnic social organizations to deal with their unique difficulties. A German Benevolent Society was established as early as 1847 and a reading club by the next year. Odd Fellows lodges were founded beginning in 1849 and a Masonic Lodge in 1855. In the 1850s, singing clubs, Hermann's Sons Clubs, a tailors club, a cabinetmakers club, the German Society, the Wheelwrights Club, a young men's club, various fraternal societies, an arts and sciences association, and the German Aid Society were all established (Hofmeister 1976, 113–16).

In these organizations, only the German language was spoken, and the tendency toward preserving German cultural and social networks was reinforced by the fact that the majority of German parents sent their children to German denominational schools throughout this period (*Arbeiter Zeitung* [Chicago] May 12, 1883).

Chicago's revolutionary movement was largely German in part because it was mobilized within this socially isolated, culturally cohesive community. The community, with stable German institutions and little separation of workplaces and community life, provided the cultural, social, and political basis for a distinctively German revolutionary movement. Certain social organizations—especially the free thought societies, Turner associations, and antitemperance groups—were particularly important in creating and preserving a tradition of German working-class radicalism in Chicago.

Free Thought Societies

A freethinking society was established in Chicago in the mid 1850s, although no details are known about it (Wittke 1952, 129). Atheism and free thought stimulated radicalism in other areas of life, and, unlike many Irish Catholics and Protestant Anglo-Americans, German freethinkers were insulated from the conservative influences of the church. Free thought and the conservative influence of the Protestant and Catholic churches were common topics of discussion in both socialist and anarchist political clubs throughout the seventies and eighties (*Arbeiter Zeitung* [Chicago] for the period).

Just like their Irish counterparts, Chicago's German Catholic leadership was concerned about the influence of free thought among its flock; the Catholic church in fact viewed all labor movement militants as heathen because of the importance of atheism among the revolutionaries of the city. Their paranoia about the free thought movement, along with their natural political conservatism, caused church leaders to join capitalist employers in condemning all forms of labor agitation. Some of these sentiments are clear in this statement by a speaker at German Catholic Day in 1887:

We have to block the activities of the now-existing labor societies in which the followers of Marx and other Jewish defenders of social economy are the leaders. These labor societies are working toward a revival of slavery, trying to dictate to their bosses. They are bound to revive the Roman and Grecian barbarism through their insistence upon eradicating the religion to which we owe our civilization. The working men have to be won back to the church; peace of mind of which they were robbed by the socialistic agitators can be theirs once again if they attend church instead of attending public meetings on Sunday. But they need the leadership of their employers. (*Staats Zeitung* [Illinois] September 7, 1887, 5)

The competition between the church and the revolutionaries for the allegiance of the city's working class was intensified by the fact that many socialist and anarchist meetings took place on Sunday, the only day off for many workers. Thus, workers had the choice of attending church services or a political meeting. At one point in the movement, German activists actually organized a march for the eight-hour day on Easter Sunday (Nelson 1986b). There may well have been a split between German Catholics and German freethinkers in the Chicago labor movement, with the latter espousing revolutionary politics and the former, reform unionism.

This proposition about the importance of the atheist movement for the mobilization of German anarchists is supported by the fact that other ethnic groups with tendencies to join socialist and anarchist movements also had thriving, ethnically based free thought societies. The Bohemians, who had a particular hatred of the Catholic church because Catholicism had been imposed on them by German invaders, founded the city's most vital free thought movement, and there were also many free thought advocates among socialist Norwegians. However, such advocacy of atheism made the Protestant Anglo-Americans in the Trades and Labor Assembly and Catholic Irish in the Knights of Labor much less likely to join the anarchists (Nelson 1986b, 11).

Turner Societies

Another crucial group of German social organizations supporting the German working-class movement were the Turner gymnastic societies. In Germany, the first Turner societies were founded in the early part of the nineteenth century to facilitate German nationalism and unification. Friedrich Jahn was convinced that there could be no rebirth or reunification of Germany unless its people became patriotic, healthy, and strong through a carefully planned regimen of physical and mental training (Wittke 1952, 147–50). Turner members were active in the revolution of 1848, many fighting on the Dresden and Frankfurt barricades; and these forty-eighters, as they were called, were responsible for founding many Turner societies in Chicago.

The Chicago Turnvereine became centers for German participation in the abolitionist movement in the 1850s; that movement and the participation of Turner members in the Civil War were often recalled in revolutionary speeches of the 1870s and 1880s. So many in the Turner movement died fighting for the Union Army during the Civil War that it took some time to revive the societies in the immediate postwar period. When they finally were revived, the German Turners in the city were more revolutionary than their German counterparts, just as the Irish nationalist organizations were more militant in Chicago than in Ireland.

The Turnvereine were in fact absolutely crucial in mobilizing the socialist and anarchist movements because their members tended toward leftist politics; many forty-eighters used the Turners as a means of advancing their social and political views in the United States. A less obvious but no less important reason for their centrality in revolutionary movements was the fact that the Turner societies were forced to build large halls for their gymnastic exercises and exhibitions, especially in Chicago, where a harsh climate made outdoor exercising impossible for much of the year. These halls quickly became the most important meeting places of the Chicago labor movement, as documented in Chapters 1 and 2.

Turner halls became *havens* where the Chicago working class, especially Germans and Bohemians, could develop their politics in relative isolation from the intrusions of the city's political and business elite. The authorities understood the importance of such meetings; during crisis periods, such as 1877 and the immediate post-Haymarket period, police were often sent into Turner halls to break up peaceful meetings. Even Anglo-American unionists understood the importance of the Turner halls to the German workers:

Our German citizens are the owners of five or six magnificent halls in the city. . . . These buildings have been erected mainly though the energy of the workingmen of one nationality; yet to the eternal disgrace of our

American, Irish, English, and Scotch mechanics, all of them combined are unable to point to a single structure which stands as a monument to *their* independence which they can claim as their *own* property—or which they can use as a resort, without the payment of rent to any landlord. On the contrary, the Germans have their lyceums, their reading rooms, their lecture and music halls, their gymnasiums, where they can meet in social concourse, discuss the political situation, enjoy an intellectual treat and improve their physical conditions without money and without price—because the revenue received from rent more than covers all necessary expenses. (*Workingman's Advocate* [Chicago] January 8, 1876, 12)

A radical emphasis within the Turner movement in the city is obvious as early as 1857, when the Social Democratic Turnvereine was organized in the Northwest Side German residence area. This was the first working-class association to introduce Marxist ideas to German workers in Chicago. The Turners worked for political reform as well as economic emancipation; in the fifties, the American Turners suggested that they would strive for the ideal republic that had been denied them in Germany and use the Constitution and the Declaration of Independence as tools in that struggle (Wittke 1952, 151). Turners also helped political refugees from Europe and fought for women's rights, labor reform, the eight-hour day, factory and child labor laws, progressive political parties, fair income and inheritance taxes, direct election of the president and senators, and public ownership of public utilities. The Aurora Turner hall initiated a collection on behalf of the anarchist defendants and families after the Haymarket arrests. The Turners were indeed havens for progressive politics in this period.

The various social organizations in the German community did not work in isolation. There were connections between the free thought, Turner, and socialist movements, as was made clear at an 1882 meeting celebrating the fifteenth anniversary of the Vorwaerts Turner Society. The first speaker, a *Freethinker* editor, said, "Although we are living under a republican form of government (a government by the people!) much is left to be fought for. Merely existing is not satisfying, we are desirous of higher ideals. We strive for a socialist state based on righteousness, truth, and humanity" (*Arbeiter Zeitung* [Chicago] September 23, 1882, 19). This speaker received great applause for this statement. The next speaker reinforced the idea of strong ties between the Turner and socialist movements in Chicago:

The revolutionary socialistic foundation is the origin of the Turner societies. They differ from the Turner of Germany in that they are always ready to take the stand against repression; they once adopted the abolitionist platform fighting for it with their own lives. One of the outstanding accomplishments of the Turners was their separation from political parties. (*Arbeiter Zeitung* [Chicago] September 23, 1882, 19)

The Turner movement was thus affirmed as being independent of the mainstream political parties. Turners supported the socialist demands of many of the German workers in the city and were not satisfied with the reformist pronouncements of the two major parties. As Wittke (1952, 157) has put it, "there was little to distinguish the Turner during this post bellum period from other progressive and radical groups except their specific demand that German traditions be preserved for their children and grandchildren, and that the German language be taught in the schools."

The Defense of German Culture and Revolution

Socialism and anarchism were culturally, not simply politically, German throughout this period in Chicago labor history partly because the highly mobilized defense of German cultural practices against nativist attacks became closely associated with political radicalism. Thus, several German social and cultural organizations—not just the free thought societies and Turner halls—were strongly integrated into German revolutionary politics. As Pierce (1957, 2: 167) describes the often militant German Trades Assembly: "To the union's hall on Sundays, men, women, and children came to enjoy the social festivities of their club. Here they could drink their beer and sing their songs in peaceful obscurity, unreproved by puritanical Americans."

Nearly every major German union had a band associated with it. At the first annual picnic of the German Trades Assembly in 1869, the procession included marshalls on horseback, a wagon with a press printing a German workers paper, many unions and workers societies, five bands, and three German singing societies (*Workingman's Advocate* [Chicago] June 19, 1869). The socialist parties and later the anarchist clubs were social as well as political organizations; there was often singing and dancing after a debate on anarchism or communism.

The socialist and anarchist marches and rallies were themselves colorful cultural events with music, banners, signs, and costumes. They held dances to celebrate almost any occasion, including the Fourth of July, Maifest, Mardi Gras, and such anniversaries as the births of Marx and Lassalle and the founding of the Paris Commune (Nelson 1986a, 76). They were famous for their outdoor summer picnics; several anarchist picnics held at Ogden's Grove on the German Northwest Side during 1885 drew thousands. They included poetry, songs, recitations, speeches, games, Turner gymnastic exhibitions, military drills, and sharpshooting. Processions to the picnic grounds were opportunities to display banners, flags, wagondrawn tableaux, and transparencies (Nelson 1986a, 77). Amateur theater groups also offered working-class plays with blatantly political content at these events (Heiss 1984, 169). As Nelson (1986a, 79) argues:

These kinds of events encompassed a community in which workers could live, dance, sing, picnic and parade after work and outside the workplace. . . . With outdoor events in the summer, and with indoor events throughout the fall, winter and spring, the anarchist movement in late nineteenth century Chicago enjoyed a secular and class culture it had created, adapted, and invented for itself.

German political radicalism and the defense of German culture against nativist attacks were inseparable. The relatively moderate *Staats Zeitung* equated the *German* cause with the *socialist* cause in 1877: "Through nothing else the German cause can be helped as much as through mental stimulation, meetings, and debates. And no one has done more in this direction in late years than the Socialist organizations. May they go on, grow and thrive, then the things German worthy of preservation will not be in danger" (*Staats Zeitung* [Illinois] April 10, 1877, 47).

German workers saw obvious connections between the emancipation of the German working class and the struggle to maintain those German cultural traditions that were threatened by the temperance and nativist campaigns. In fact, the situation was so viewed by both sides; the Anglo-Americans labeled the German worker drunken, atheistic, and communist—all in the same breath. The Turners, so important to the German revolutionary movement, were also directly involved in the defense of German working-class culture. Hofmeister (1976, 55) notes the many skirmishes that took place between the Turners and the nativist Know-Nothing parties, and he documents instances of rock pelting of Turner halls by nativists. The following statement was made about the Turner halls as early as 1867: "I feel at home wherever Turners erect a temple, for I know that they dedicate their churches only to the cause of freedom and progress. Every new Turner that we build . . . is a barricade against narrow-minded ideas, a fortress of progress. Turners are welcomed by all but bigots and fanatics" (*Staats Zeitung* [Illinois] October 11, 1867, 55).

The *Arbeiter Zeitung* was the major German anarchist paper in Chicago. With its strong commitment to class-conscious ideologies, the paper might have been expected to espouse solidarity between German and native-born workers; but, it did *not* support the assimilation of Germans into the "American way of life" as a means of creating a unified working class in the city.

The last few editorials of the Tribune are devoted to the Know-Nothing theme, namely that the English language is predominant and that it is the only language which is used by our Chicago citizens. The editorial contends that the forty thousand persons speaking German at the present time will eventually die out, and with them will cease the German language in Chicago, for their offspring have naturally been Americanized.

Contrary to this statement is the fact that the majority of German parents send their children to German [denominational] schools and that German immigration outnumbers that of various other nationalities. (*Arbeiter Zeitung* [Chicago] May 12, 1883, 14)

The paper went on to point out that many other nationalities in the city spoke German or learned it from German co-workers. The paper felt that German culture would be preserved, and with it German socialism and anarchism.

The German character of the city's revolutionary movement was reinforced by ties between that movement and the antitemperance campaign. These ties appeared as early as the first antitemperance meeting held in the city. The twenty-eight delegates at that meeting in August 1867 included five from the Chicago Arbeiterverein, five from the Socialer Arbeiterverein, and twelve from four Turner societies in the city (*Staats Zeitung* [Illinois] August 13, 1867). In the eighties, August Spies, the prominent anarchist, was concerned with the temperance issue; he tied the movement against prohibition to the larger working-class struggle against the economic system and against church hegemony at an anarchist meeting in 1882. He spoke of the history of the Puritans as the source of the temperance movement and concluded:

It would not be for socialists to decide whether the effects of alcoholic beverages are good or bad. The question is one of principle. If we were to allow the majority to dictate to the minority what they should drink, tomorrow or the day after that they would claim the right to dictate what we should think. Religious fanaticism would have free rein, its initial success would spur it on to greater demands. All religious freedom would be ended; one coercive law would follow after another. (*Arbeiter Zeitung* [Chicago] September 1, 1882, 22)

This particular meeting adopted a resolution in which the reactionary agitation for temperance and bigotry was condemned; vows were made to fight against the enemies of freedom using whatever means were necessary.

Ernst Schmidt, the former socialist candidate for mayor, once suggested that temperance was the "fanaticism of the narrowminded Puritan which has spread throughout the country and is threatening our liberty" (*Arbeiter Zeitung* [Chicago] September 18, 1882, 31). Another speaker at this meeting suggested that the temperance campaign was simply one exhibition of the American hatred for foreigners.

German Revolutionary Havens

The strong German cultural emphasis facilitated rather than hindered the growth of a revolutionary alternative within the Chicago labor movement. Patterns of kinship and neighboring, freethinking societies, Turners, antitemperance societies, and the various political clubs and German trades assemblies created *havens* in the German community for the growth of a political tendency distinct from the politics of the Anglo-American working and middle classes. Attacks on German culture led to a withdrawal into German social networks, which in turn led to the possibility of innovation in labor politics and the maintenance of that political alternative through time.

Social structural havens became places where common problems could be identified, their sources could be named, and trends leading to the loss of status and material success among the Germans could be discussed. Puritan ideas concerning the work ethic, temperance, and antiradicalism were rejected; a radical socialist and later anarchist German working-class culture and politics were formulated in its stead. Differences between the experiences of the skilled and the unskilled could often be transcended in the German community and in the German labor movement because skilled and unskilled faced social and political problems common to all Germans.

Once the normal institutional responses to common problems were tried and had failed, these havens were places where radical programs were formulated, where ideas for the solution of the working class's plight were developed without the routine intrusion of moderate or conservative ideas of the Anglo-American or even the Irish residents of the city. In this case, the language barrier and the barriers of differing cultures and segregated social structures allowed the formulation of a revolutionary alternative within the labor movement. Isolated social networks and cultural differences made radicalism possible and insulated this political alternative from the repressive ideas and actions of those in power, at least for a while. The difficulty was that the German social network and cultural emphasis of the movement made it unlikely that non-Germans would be recruited to the revolutionary cause. This was a fatal flaw. The movement enjoyed short-term success, but without the support of English-speaking workers, it was doomed.

There is a natural experiment that allows a test of this notion of the distinctively German character of the revolutionary movement in Chicago in this period. As reported previously, the Germans established two residence areas. The earlier area, at North Avenue along the lake, was settled largely by skilled workers and was fairly heterogeneous with regard to ethnicity. The later area, on the Northwest Side, was more homogeneously German but included unskilled as well as skilled craftsmen.

Marxists might predict that a multiethnic community of skilled workers would produce radical politics because class solidarity transcending ethnic differences would be possible in such a community. But this was not the case. It was the homogeneously German Northwest Side community that produced the most radical working-class politics. It was the Northwest Side settlement's fourteenth ward where the Socialist Labor party had its greatest successes; the same neighborhood provided the most fruitful organizing ground for the Progressive Cigarmakers (Keil and Jentz 1981, 24). Saloons on the Northwest Side's Milwaukee Avenue were the meeting places for the SLP, and that same community supported the growth of the most revolutionary Turner association and the strongest section of the Lehr und Wehr Verein (Keil and Jentz 1981, 25). In other words, the residence area that was most homogeneously German and heterogeneous in economic status showed the greatest degree of support for revolutionary socialism and anarchism.

The German Role in Local Politics

Certainly the response to nativism and the role of German cultural and social organizations are important reasons why many of the city's revolutionaries were German. But there was another important reason why Germans were socialists and anarchists in Chicago: the inability of German-born citizens to gain significant influence in Chicago politics.

Germans entered the United States and Chicago believing that, unlike Germany, this country was a true democracy, a free republic with universal adult male suffrage. They assumed that the serious economic problems they unexpectedly faced in the Chicago labor market could be addressed through moderate economic and political action.

Thus, their first reaction to their economic deprivation and to nativist attacks was not revolution. They formed unions and the German Trades Assembly, and they participated in the attempts of the General Trades Assembly to pass moderate labor reform legislation. In the 1860s, they elected a number of aldermen to the city council.

When the depression made their economic problems worse and economic organizing difficult, Germans tried political alternatives.

They organized and participated in mass marches to demand relief and city jobs, supported strikes, and attempted to elect sympathetic candidates to office. But their attempts to resolve their problems peacefully were met with violent police repression. As reported previously, during the 1877 strikes, several hundred German cabinetmakers met in a Turner hall to consider the eight-hour day and other questions surrounding the strike. Their peaceful meeting was broken up, the proprietor killed, and many workers injured by the actions of unprovoked special police (see Chapter 1). Both the event itself and the subsequent trial of the perpetrators were covered extensively in the German press (*Staats Zeitung* [Illinois] April 26, 1879).

The facts reported were that the attack was unprovoked, that the police had begun firing their revolvers as soon as they had entered the hall, and that those involved were not punished. This event more than any other moved many Germans to reject moderate means of influencing the economic and political systems. Many Germans began to believe, not without justification, that there were separate standards of justice for German, Anglo-American, and Irish residents in the city. The workers defense associations—the Lehr und Wehr Verein—gained many recruits and much credibility as a result of these events because many Germans believed they needed strong, armed groups to prevent such occurrences in the future.

Still German workers showed patience; they had not yet totally rejected the idea that they might influence the system by electing their representatives to city, county, and state offices. They knew that elected officials, especially the mayor, had authority over the police; so they decided to try to elect officials who might be less likely to turn the police loose on German workers. Germans turned out in great numbers to vote for the Socialist Labor party in the late seventies; but from the beginning of the electoral campaigns, it was obvious that there were dual standards of justice in Chicago with regard to elections as well as the degree of toleration of peaceful gatherings. Election fraud was the rule rather than the exception when it came to the efforts of German socialist candidates; in many cases, the German candidates wound up with fewer votes counted than the party knew had been cast.

The electoral strategy lost all remaining legitimacy it may have had among Germans when Frank Stauber, who had successfully been elected to an aldermanic seat in the fourteenth ward several times, was fraudulently denied his seat in favor of an Irishman in 1880. It took a full year for the Irish election judges involved to be found guilty of altering the ballots, by which time most of those in the German labor movement had decided to withdraw from electoral politics. German workers saw no point in working to elect Germans to the council when these representatives would be denied their seats.

This was not an isolated instance. The Irish were just beginning to dominate the Chicago political machine and, as reported previously, were willing to do whatever was necessary to defend their meal ticket from the encroachment of the more numerous Germans. Early German successes in electing aldermen (they had eleven of thirty-two seats on the council in the late sixties) turned to failure by the seventies (Hofmeister 1976, 95). In 1871, although first- and second-generation Germans represented one-third of the city's population, there were only eight German aldermen on a forty-person council; and Germans chaired only four of twenty council committees. By contrast, the Anglo-Americans had seventeen aldermen on the council and the Irish, thirteen.

By 1881, the number of German aldermen had declined still further, and the Irish were blamed for this. Irish committeemen and precinct captains were accused of intimidating and challenging German voters, of refusing to count German votes, of buying German votes with promises of jobs and favors, and even of falsely boasting of their German ethnic origins (Hofmeister 1976, 97).

These tactics prevented Germans from gaining proportional political representation. In ward after ward, an Irish minority managed to elect Irish aldermen despite a German majority in the ward population. As late as the early 1890s, 830 Irish elected an Irishman in the tenth ward, although 2,285 Germans resided there, and 575 Irish elected two aldermen in the fifteenth ward with its 3,054 Germans. The Irish often managed this by excluding German candidates from the election altogether; in the Westtown area, a ticket of three Irishmen and one Bohemian was fielded in a neighborhood that included 19,737 Germans, 9,993 Irish, and 3,906 Bohemians (Hofmeister 1976, 97).

Unable to influence the system through conducting peaceful

labor meetings or in the electoral arena, the Germans felt few choices were left. To them, it made sense to return to economic organizing, to form workers self-defense associations, and to create an anarchist movement that withdrew from mainstream politics. They rejected capitalism because that economic system was degrading the skills, eliminating the jobs, and decreasing the wages of the average German worker, who had been unable to gain entry to exclusive Anglo-American trade unions. They rejected electoral politics and called for the abolition of the state because they had been denied access to the political arena by political bosses who were using that system to further Irish interests.

The Germans tried to form a class-conscious, multiethnic anarchist movement; they were aware of the impossibility of a successful revolutionary movement without the support of English-speaking workers. But the reformism of the more affluent Anglo-American labor aristocrats and the support of the Irish for the developing political machine made such efforts unsuccessful. Both the Anglo-Americans and the Irish had used their own ethnic networks to gain success, and their ability to do so made it easy for them to reject all class-conscious, revolutionary alternatives. The social and cultural isolation of the revolutionary movement simply reinforced the separation of the German tendency from that of the Anglos and Irish. The failure of the Anglo-American and Irish workers to support the anarchist movement made it easy for the city's economic and political elite to gain consent for the violent repression of the revolutionary labor movement following the Haymarket affair.

Conclusions

Most German workers were products of a German economic system that was threatening their livelihood and social honor. To their surprise, they faced similar problems in the Chicago labor market. They were excluded from many of the highest status, most successful unions by Anglo-American craftsmen; many were badly hurt by skill degradation and the business cycle. Socially, they faced severe nativist attacks on their culture and politics, which forced them to withdraw defensively into the German community and German social and cultural organizations.

Within this German community, revolutionary labor politics

were developed. It was not likely that Germans would accept Puritan values regarding the work ethic, temperance, and antiradicalism; they viewed such ideas as direct attacks on their way of life. Their different language and the high degree of in-group social interaction in the German enclave helped them resist being influenced by those ideas. The revolutionary labor movement was mobilized using social networks in such closely intertwined organizations as the Turners, the antitemperance movement, the free thought societies, and German trade assemblies and political clubs.

Almost alone among Chicago workers, Germans responded to the problems spawned by industrialization with the notion that an entirely new, noncapitalist system ought to be created, a system that would better meet the needs of the entire working class. Proposed solutions vacillated between Marxist-inspired union organizing during business expansions and Lassallean political parties during the recurring, union-destroying slumps.

The Germans' choice of socialism was due in part to their familiarity with such militant politics in Germany. But it would be a mistake to assume, as the Chicago press often did, that Germans imported ideologies that were inappropriate for American conditions. Radical German politics were viable because of the unique economic, social, and political problems Germans faced in the city and because traditional solutions to those problems did not work.

Continued economic deprivation, police repression of peaceful meetings, and the denial of political access to the Irish-controlled political machine forced the Germans to develop an even more revolutionary alternative: anarchism, an ideology that proposed eliminating capitalism in favor of a system of worker cooperatives and abolishing the state. This was a reasonable response to the plight of the German worker, but it could not succeed without the support of Anglo-American and Irish workers. That support never came from the Anglo-Americans because they occupied a privileged economic position and accepted a Puritan-influenced, hegemonic ideology that rationalized the operation of the economic system. The Irish never became anarchists because they accepted an ideology that blamed the British for their poverty, because of their ties to a conservative Catholic church, and because they enjoyed a privileged political position in the city.

Chapter Six

Theories of Urban Political Movements

The preceding chapters have documented the mobilization of a strong labor movement in a rapidly growing, industrializing city—nineteenth-century Chicago. But the nature of the political response of various workers in that movement varied dramatically. Some accepted the economic and political systems as given and tried to work within them to gain benefits for themselves or their trades. Others used moderate means, including collective bargaining and arbitration in the economic sphere and efforts to elect sympathetic candidates to office and lobbying efforts in the political realm, to attempt to reform the system. Still others asserted that the economic and political systems had to be drastically changed and used noninstitutional tactics such as mass strikes, protest marches and rallies, armed workers defense associations, and dynamite bombs to further a revolution.

What theory or theories of social and political movements are best able to account for this mobilization pattern in the nineteenth-century Chicago labor movement? Theorists of many persuasions have recognized the potential of cities to incubate social and political movements. Such diverse thinkers as Marx, Weber, Durkheim, Simmel, Park, and Wirth agree that significant social movements, defined as collective efforts that use noninstitutional means of influence to promote or resist social change, were likely to arise among those forced into new roles as factory workers and residents of ethnically heterogeneous, rapidly growing cities. There is less agreement on which social groups were likely to become involved in those movements.

Marxist *class analysis* perspectives emphasize the importance of the introduction of the industrial mode of capitalist production and predict that movement mobilization will be based on consciousness of objective class interests. Classical *social movement* theory suggests that the increase in the division of labor and urbanization leads to a loss of normative direction and value consensus; recruits to urban political movements will be the socially and culturally marginal seeking social direction. *Resource mobilization* theory argues that movements will be made up of rationally calculating individuals who create social movement organizations to take advantage of the new political opportunities that arise from urbanization and industrialization. The progress of research into urban political mobilization has been based on unraveling the strengths and weaknesses inherent in these three theoretical orientations.

Class Analysis of Urban Political Movements

Marxist explanations of urban political movements depend on an analysis of the economic system. Proponents of class analysis see the worker movement in nineteenth-century Chicago as a response to the economic contradictions of capitalism. Such revolutionary movements mobilize oppressed, exploited factory workers—economically displaced peasants or artisans who have migrated to large industrial cities in search of jobs. These workers attempt to overthrow the capitalist system and substitute socialism because of the unequal distribution of rewards and power in the economic system and because they become conscious of their plight and develop the power to create a new economic system.

Marx and Engels argued that industrial capitalist cities were the most likely locus of revolutionary movements for two basic reasons. First, cities were "hothouse[s] of capitalist contradictions" (Saunders 1981, 22). In other words, the working class experienced the most serious problems created by capitalism in cities, where mechanization displaced workers and the business cycle created increasingly severe depressions. Both trends resulted in severe unemployment and lower wages for factory workers, who formed an increasing proportion of the working class.

As Engels (1958) outlined in his *Condition of the Working Class in England,* low wages and unemployment inevitably created unbearable living conditions in working-class communities. This economic *immiseration* of the working class became a crucial cause of revolutionary mobilization. Revolt was the only alternative for these workers because they could not support themselves by any means other than wage labor.

The other reason cities were expected to be the sites for urban revolution is that they created conditions conducive for the development of *working-class consciousness,* defined as the recognition that one shares common economic interests with other workers, that those interests are opposed to those of the capitalist class, and that capitalists are responsible for the plight of the working class. Prior to the growth of large capitalist cities, the more decentralized settlement patterns—characteristic of the countryside—made it difficult for such consciousness to develop, as Marx noted:

The small holding peasants form a vast mass, the members of which live in similar conditions but without entering into manifold relations with one another. Their mode of production isolates them from one another instead of bringing them into mutual intercourse. In this way, the great mass of the French nation is formed by simple addition of homologous magnitudes, such as potatoes in a sack form a sack of potatoes. (Marx 1972, 515)

In contrast, cities concentrated workers in working-class residence communities and in larger and larger factories, which allowed the development of insights concerning their common economic plight. Comparisons to the relative affluence of the bourgeoisie were also easily made in the industrial city. As Engels put it:

Only the proletariat created by modern large-scale industry, liberated from all inherited fetters including those which chained it to the land, and herded together in the big cities, is in a position to accomplish the great social transformation which will put an end to class exploitation and class rule. The old rural hand weavers with hearth and home would never have been able to do it; they would not have been able to conceive such an idea, not to speak of desiring to carry it out. (Engels 1975, 25)

Economic immiseration and class consciousness facilitated the formation of working-class unions and political parties. Struggles against capitalists would unite the working class as more workers realized that only class-based political action could solve their

severe economic problems. As polarized conflict proceeded, all social divisions other than the one between capitalists and workers
would become irrelevant; conflicts based on different cultural backgrounds, ethnicity, religions, and trade or skill levels would be su-
perseded by the economically based class struggle. Ultimately,
workers' potential to control capitalist production would result in
their winning and establishing socialism (Marx and Engels 1972).

There is a variety of problems with using this perspective to analyze mobilization in the Chicago labor movement. Craig Jackson
Calhoun (1982) has pointed out that the theory does not sufficiently
analyze the *causal connections* between the economic condition of
an abstractly defined working class, the development of working-
class consciousness, and the willingness to act politically as a group.
The problem is due in part to the evolutionary and deterministic
elements of the theory; it assumes that macroeconomic forces will
result in the transformation of capitalism into socialism and that it
will be the *inevitable* historic mission of the working class to create
that revolution. Instead of analysis, there are only assumptions:
that economic forces and concentration in industrial cities result in
common economic interests, immiseration, and the common experience of subjection to authority in the workplace; that because factory employment and urban residence provide a chance to communicate about such exploitation, class consciousness will result;
that such consciousness is a sufficient condition for political action
against the capitalist system (Calhoun 1982, 217).

Because the theory assumes the connections between economic
trends and the political mobilization of a class-conscious class,
Marxists often concentrate their analysis on the macrolevel economic forces but neglect microlevel mobilization issues. As the
subsequent history of the working classes of Europe and the United
States has shown, these relationships cannot be assumed; one must
answer questions that arise at each step in the causal chain—from
the economic situation of workers, to a class-conscious working class, to a fully mobilized working class–based revolutionary
movement.

One result of the failure to analyze such connections is that
Marxist theory ignores the importance of non-class-based discrimination: in-group, out-group social networking, cultural-ideological
elements, and patterns of access to political influence in the politi-

cal mobilization process. Concentration in dense urban neighborhoods provides the opportunity for communication that can lead to non-class-based as well as class-based identifications (among ethnic or racial groups, for example). Urban residence can also intensify cultural differences; and the acceptance of different values, ideologies, and ways of life can lead to a diversity of responses to identical economic circumstances.

Thus, ethnic origin, not economic class position, became the most important determinant of political choice in the Chicago labor movement. Nativist economic, social, and political discrimination created critical problems for workers in subordinate ethnic groups and benefited dominant ethnic group workers. Ethnic community–based social networks and ethnic cultural beliefs and practices determined the political mobilization pattern when workers responded to those problems.

In order to create a viable theory of urban working-class political mobilization, Marxists must address the following questions: Are common economic interests and the means for communicating about them a sufficient basis for class consciousness and political action? What kind of social networks facilitate the development of class consciousness and class-based political mobilization? What is the impact on mobilization of community-based versus workplace-based networks? Does urbanization-industrialization inevitably increase only class consciousness, or can it also intensify other kinds of group identity (such as racial and/or ethnic consciousness), which then affect the political mobilization pattern? What is the effect on such mobilization of different levels of group access to local political influence? Contemporary Marxists have dealt with some of these issues.

Revisionist Marxists

The importance of ethnic identification does not necessarily decline under the impact of industrialization, as Marx and Engels predicted. Job and housing discrimination, as well as residential preferences and ethnically based patterns of occupational recruitment, may make it a more important basis of group formation than class (Olzak and Nagel 1986). Discrimination can result in common problems for members of the same ethnic group at various economic levels. Ethnic and racial groups are often severely segregated by *both* residence community and occupational distribution; this can have dramatic consequences because activists use such social networks in political mobilization efforts.

Because of their obsession with the revolutionary potential of class-based politics, most Marxists who have considered the importance of ethnic identification have suggested only that cultural differences can retard the development of class consciousness. A few Marxists have gone farther by studying patterns of ethnic economic segmentation. Lenin (1966, 251–52) pointed to the importance of an ethnically based *labor aristocracy* in accounting for the reformism of native-born American workers:

> In the United States, immigrants from Eastern and Southern Europe are engaged in the most poorly paid occupations, while American workers provide the highest percentage of overseers or of the better paid workers. Imperialism has the tendency of creating privileged sections even among the workers and detaching them from the main proletarian masses.

Higher and more stable incomes supported a different life-style, fostered identification with the middle class and its reformist values, promoted in-group social interaction during work and leisure time, and reinforced the political conservatism of this labor aristocracy.

Another Marxist, Michael Hechter (1975, 1978), also has considered the impact of ethnically based economic segmentation on working-class political mobilization. He argues that industrialization does not necessarily change an existing system of ethnic stratification by creating a proletarianized, homogeneous class. Elite or core ethnic groups where industrialization occurs first will be allocated to the most desirable jobs, citizenship rights, and social statuses; subordinate groups in peripheral regions will be assigned to less desirable positions. This creates a *cultural division of labor* in which the stratification system assigns individuals to specific roles in the social structure on the basis of objective, readily identifiable cultural or racial distinctions such as skin color, religious differences, language differences, and region of residence. The existence of this cultural division of labor contributes to the development of a distinctive ethnic identity in each of the two or more cultural groups.

However, unlike Lenin, Hechter emphasizes the revolutionary potential of the subordinate ethnic groups rather than the conservatism of those of high status. He argues that ethnic identity is likely to be stronger among members of the subordinate ethnic group in the rural, peripheral regions; ethnic identity becomes a basis of mobilization primarily because it coincides nearly perfectly with subordinate class position.

Contrary to the orthodox Marxist argument, Hechter asserts that this cultural division of labor can be long lasting; neither economic integration nor political incorporation can be assumed. The dominant group's strong interest in economically exploiting the subordinate group guarantees the latter's continued low economic status and often creates an interest in excluding it from political representation as well.

Thus, those groups confined by discrimination or occupational specialization to the lowest status occupational categories will mobilize along ethnic/class lines to fight that status for essentially the same reason that workers are expected to revolt under Marxist urban theory: They are exploited, less privileged, and concentrated in factories and residence communities in such a way that communication about their plight becomes more feasible, and political mobilization becomes easier. Hechter simply extends Marx's class model to the ethnically segmented case, in which economic position is determined by ethnic origins. Ethnic ties are identical to workplace social networks in a cultural division of labor and are the analytical substitute for class ties in explaining political mobilization.

The fact of ethnic residential, as well as workplace, segregation reinforces the development of strong ethnic identity in the periphery. Communication about common problems is facilitated by the social structural isolation of the subordinate ethnic group. Such communication can occur within a wide variety of collectivities (neighborhoods, workplaces, schools, churches, social and recreational clubs, and other voluntary associations). Class and ethnic solidarity reinforce each other in this situation, making each stronger.

The major problem with Hechter's approach is that he views ethnic political mobilization as being most likely among the least privileged, most regionally isolated ethnic groups (in the "Celtic fringe" within Great Britain, for example). This prediction has not withstood testing; in fact, ethnic identity and ethnic political mobilization are more likely in urban settings like Chicago, where ethnic groups are apt to be in contact—and thus in conflict—over scarce political, social, and economic statuses (Olzak and Nagel 1986). His notion of a cultural division of labor is more successfully applied *within* the urban labor market.

But even proposing a city-based cultural division of labor will not make Hechter's theory a particularly useful tool for analyzing mobilization in the Chicago labor movement. Hechter's theory reduces ethnic differences to economic differences; that approach cannot explain why Chicago workers in the same trades often had totally different political responses to the same economic problems. Skilled German printers and cigar makers and unskilled Bohemian lumber shovers all joined the anarchist Central Labor Union in the early 1880s; Anglo-American printers and cigar makers and Irish laborers were likely to be in the reformist Trades and Labor Assembly in the same period.

Hechter does consider the explanatory importance of some social structural factors (patterns of in-group, out-group interaction), but he assumes that economic class and ethnic status coincide. He totally ignores the fact that working-class willingness and capacity to rebel against capitalist industrialization is affected by *cultural* as well as material factors. Culture (knowledge, beliefs, art, morals, laws, customs, tradition, ideas, and values) may affect how workers do or do not respond to the effects of industrialization because cultural values and beliefs affect whether economic and social changes are viewed as unjust. Cultural factors can also affect which responses to economic and social injustices are assumed to be legitimate and effective. Cultural values or traditions may influence workers from different backgrounds to respond to identical economic conditions with various degrees of passivity, reform, or revolutionary action.

The importance of considering culture in accounting for working-class political responses has been recognized by some of the most important twentieth-century Marxists, including Antonio Gramsci (1971, 1977, 1978), and by British and American social historians such as E. P. Thompson (1963, 1978), Eric Hobsbawm (1964, 1984), Herbert Gutman (1977), Alan Dawley (1976), and others (Cantor 1979). Gutman's *Work, Culture, and Society in In-*

dustrializing America (1977) has been one of the most influential works, defining the research agenda of a generation of American social historians.

Gutman (1977, 14) analyzed the impact of industrialization by examining the confrontation between preindustrial cultures and employers' attempts to impose a culture consistent with industrial work discipline. He argued that industrial capitalists viewed a variety of work habits as harmful because they affected the intensity or duration of the work effort; these included such customs and values as consuming beer or liquor, smoking or gambling while at work, having three- to five-day holidays, not working on Mondays, being unwilling to work long hours, preferring small shop to factory employment, and preferring the craft style of work over an extreme division of labor. According to this perspective, some moral reform movements (such as the temperance movement) had less to do with morals per se than with employers' attempts to rationalize outlawing behavior that lowered productivity in a machine-paced workplace.

Gutman examined how the necessity of adapting craft-based community values, norms, and customs to an industrial way of life gave diverse groups of workers a common class experience and a possible source of class consciousness. He also considered the importance of autonomous worker communities and institutions in their challenge to capitalism. Like Hechter, he suggested that the conditions for that challenge arose in villages or towns rather than in large cities.

Gutman argued that the real militants in the industrializing United States were artisans in small industrial towns attempting to preserve traditional values and ways of life. Their power was based on the fact that the working class dominated the smaller industrial towns numerically—as shapers of the town's dominant culture and as consumers of products and services sold by the middle class. The result was that class alliances between the working and middle classes were much more likely in smaller towns than in large industrial cities.

According to Gutman, industrial cities like Chicago were the vanguard settlements of the new order. In cities, ideologies consistent with the capitalist mode of production were successfully imposed on workers who did not have common traditional values and roots to defend. Cities contained a larger, more residentially isolated middle class with less knowledge of and sympathy for workers. Repression of worker movements by upper-class elites was more likely in cities because of working-class failure to dominate urban cultural and economic life.

There are problems in trying to apply Gutman's approach to the Chicago case. The perspective understates the degree to which the cultural and social structural foundations for working-class political mobilization can exist in relatively new urban communities. Dense social bonds, useful in mobilization efforts, often *emerge* within large cities; and revolutionary movements do not necessarily have to defend centuries-old traditions. In fact, the opposite of Gutman's argument may be true. The movements mobilized by urban workers may be more likely to be revolutionary than their small-town counterparts exactly *because* of the greater isolation of city workers from both the middle and upper classes. This was the case within isolated working-class ethnic enclaves in Chicago. A class coalition with a small-town middle class with a real stake in the system is likely to foster a reformist, not a revolutionary, movement.

Another group of Marxists (Katznelson 1981; Katznelson and Zolberg 1986) focuses its attention more specifically on *urban* political mobilization, analyzing especially the political and spatial constraints on unified working-class political action. Their argument, developed primarily within the American Exceptionalism framework to explain the reformism of the American working class, is that U.S. worker moderation is due to a unique feature of the American scene: the separation of the politics of work from the politics of the community. Ira Katznelson argues in *City Trenches* (1981, 18–19) that the failure of attempts to create socialist and labor parties in the United States is due to

sharply divided consciousness about class in American society that finds many Americans acting on the basis of the shared solidarities of class at work, but on that of ethnic and territorial affinities in their residential communities. The links between work and community-based conflicts have been unusually tenuous. Each kind of conflict has had its own separate vocabulary and set of institutions: work, class, and trade unions; community, ethnicity, local parties, churches, and voluntary associations.

Katznelson argues that, prior to the development of industrial capitalism, there was little separation of work and home. In U.S.

commercial capitalist cities such as New York, Boston, Philadelphia, and Baltimore, workers usually worked at home, and most neighborhoods included people of all classes. But as industrial factory employment increased in the mid nineteenth century, many workers began to work outside their homes, and residence areas became increasingly segregated by class, ethnicity, and race.

Workers soon took advantage of the lack of employer control over their home lives by developing autonomous institutions in their neighborhoods: lodges, benefit associations, parish churches, gangs, athletic clubs, fire companies, and political clubs. If they had been closer to work, these institutions might have been the basis for class-based political movements. But given the separation between work and home, community institutions instead became the base for the development of power within the growing urban political machines. Workers developed real political power; politicians had to cater to their needs by giving them patronage jobs and some services in order to garner votes. But the basis for this political mobilization was ethnic and crossed class lines.

Only at work was there class consciousness; workers struggled militantly for better wages and working conditions in multiethnic unions. But their successful fight was for benefits within the system, not for a new system. They did not challenge capitalism itself because the institutions necessary for *accommodating the working class to capitalism*—the franchise and legal unions—were already in place when industrialization began. Katznelson (1981, 71) believes that effective revolutionary movements must involve class-based appeals in workers' home lives as well as at their workplaces. As he concludes:

Over a long period of time, the stark division in people's consciousness, language, and action between the politics of work and the politics of community became a tacit mechanism in the selection of alternatives. . . . The system of city trenches has produced a working class unique in the West: militant as labor, and virtually nonexistent as a collectivity outside the workplace.

This is a very interesting analysis, but it is not of much help in explaining the mobilization pattern in the Chicago labor movement. Katznelson's model does describe the political behavior of Irish workers in the city; the Irish did use the militant mass strike model to gain some benefits at work and created the political machine in their neighborhoods. But separation of work and home cannot explain those political choices because the Irish lived near their workplaces. In fact, it was the Anglo-Americans who had the greatest separation of work and home; but, contrary to Katznelson's predictions, they showed little class consciousness at work and were politically moderate both at work and at home. If not for its inability to account for Irish and Anglo-American politics, the model might work to explain the political behavior of the city's Germans, who had little separation of work and home and were often revolutionary in both workplace and community politics.

The basic problem is that, like the other Marxists, Katznelson does not emphasize the importance of the ethnic factor in explaining choices in both workplace and community politics. In the workplace, he assumes that class-conscious politics prevailed; in fact, however, cultural differences and social structural barriers such as ethnically segregated neighborhoods and segmented labor markets made it difficult to create unified class-conscious worker movements. Katznelson does recognize the importance of ethnicity in the neighborhoods, but he incorrectly assumes that the political machine integrated all ethnic groups equally. In fact, there were significant differences in the degree to which various groups enjoyed political power or received machine jobs and favors. The Irish were in a position of political dominance for much of the history of the machine; the Germans were denied political power and patronage jobs. Thus, Katznelson understates the importance of ethnic divisions in both workplace and community politics.

Consideration of the degree of separation of work and home is an interesting and important addition to Marxist analysis of movement mobilization, but it is not enough. Some Marxists have understood that cultural, social structural, and political factors play a role in that mobilization process, but their analyses of the impact of those factors have not been adequate. Because they have seen class-based movements as inevitable, they have neglected to stress the importance of movements based on ethnic community networks and sentiments of solidarity rather than on the consciousness of objective class interests. Perhaps the sociologists have more to offer than the Marxists on the subject of community and ethnically based political movements.

Classical Social Movement–Collective Behavior Theories of Urban Social Movements

The roots of the sociological perspective on urban social movements lie in the work of the classical sociological theorists St. Simon, Comte, Spencer, Toennies, and Durkheim. Toennies's *Gemeinschaft und Gesellschaft* and Durkheim's *mechanical and organic solidarity* dichotomies suggested that the basis of social integration differed in premodern and modern societies. In traditional societies, value consensus (the internalization of a set of common values by each member of society) was stronger. Social control was easier in traditional societies because of small community size and because individuals interacted with the same people in each of their social roles—in school, at work, at recreation, in church, in the residence community.

The same means of social integration is not possible in modern society, with its large urban communities and its segmented roles. The society's control over individual members is much more tenuous; value consensus is threatened by the decline of traditional values, and the individual interacts with more strangers and with different people in each social role. But system complexity and the extreme division of labor also imply that each member of society must depend on others to survive; thus, integration is accomplished through interdependency, the necessity for cooperation in a system with many specialized roles.

For these theorists, revolutionary movements were a symptom of temporary maladjustment in social control mechanisms, the initial failure of a modernizing society to integrate adequately all its members. The first sociological theories of urban revolution were proposed by the "crowd theorists": Le Bon, Tarde, and Taine. All three saw revolutionary movements as irrational acts by socially marginal troublemakers who were not tied strongly to traditional institutions such as the church and state. Taine (1868) blamed the crowds of revolutionary France for ruining any chance for reasonable compromise because there was no rational goal informing their behavior; the revolution had torn the society apart, and now people had allegiance only to "the mob." Le Bon (1960) suggested that in crowds, the individual's rational faculties came under the influence of *suggestion* by revolutionary leaders.

Tarde (1969) emphasized that ideas are spread through contagion in these irrational crowds, contagion that turns "a moderate desire or uncertain opinion of the originator" into "passion and conviction, hate and fanaticism in the mass" (Oberschall 1973, 13). All assumed that these revolutionary crowds were created from among the disorganized, mentally disturbed, criminal classes of big cities. Thus, revolutionary actions supposedly were based on the irrational, emotional response of rootless masses caught in the grip of contagion.

Robert Park and the Chicago School of Sociology he helped found built on the work of the classical sociologists and the crowd theorists to develop sophisticated theories of *urban social movements*. Park argued that trends associated with urbanization (such as a high rate of change and the rapid occupational and residential mobility of arriving immigrant groups) created unpredictability in social interaction patterns, particularly near the ethnically heterogeneous city center. Value consensus was threatened by the mixing of indigenous with immigrant cultures; because a variety of norms and values was available to be used as standards of proper behavior, no one set of values and norms was firmly in effect. His argument was that the social structural and cultural foundations of social stability were weak in heterogeneous, rapidly changing cities.

The *social disorganization* associated with urbanization led to various urban problems. Park stated that all urban problems were problems of *social control;* they were due to the inability of the city to mold the behavior of its residents through predictable patterns of social interaction and through inducing city residents to follow a consistent set of norms and values (Park 1967, 209). This lack of social control led to increases in individual deviance (crime, suicide, drug abuse) and to group behavior outside the usual institutional channels. Park was the first of many to call such group activities *collective behavior* (Park 1967; Smelser 1962; Turner and Killian 1987).

Park and his frequent collaborator Ernest Burgess (1967) suggested that urban social disorganization resulted in many different kinds of collective behavior in cities:

> Strikes and minor revolutionary movements are endemic in the urban environment. . . . Cities and particularly great cities are in unstable equi-

librium. The result is that the vast causal and mobile aggregations which constitute our urban populations are in a state of perpetual agitation, swept by every new wind of doctrine, subject to constant alarms and in consequence the community is in a chronic condition of crises. (p. 22)

To what extent are mob violence, strikes, and radical political movements the result of the same general conditions that provoke financial panics, real estate booms, and mass movements in the population generally? (p. 27)

Louis Wirth (1964) took the social disorganization view to a greater extreme in "Urbanism as a Way of Life." He asserted that ecological traits of cities (size, density, and heterogeneity) were related to social psychology (anonymity, superficiality, and anomie). Cultural mixing led directly to the disorganization of personality, which was in turn related to the rise in crime rates, suicide, corruption, and madness in the great cities.

On the group level, rootless masses expressed themselves politically through irrational mass movements. Recalling the crowd theorists, Wirth suggested that the masses were easily swayed by propaganda, subject to "manipulation by symbols and stereotypes managed by individuals working from afar or operating invisibly behind the scenes through their control of the instruments of communication" (Wirth 1964, 82). In other words, unintegrated individuals accepted whatever new forms of solidarity were immediately available to them as the old forms lost their force. Mass movements, even revolutionary ones, were created by propagandists exploiting the population's lack of social ties and values.

The Chicago school proposed that social movement participants were drawn from those the city had been unable to integrate socially: the poorest, most recent migrants to the city in central residential areas, especially those from cultures most "alien" to U.S. culture. Questioning of the basic workings of the system came from socially marginal, valueless individuals with little ability to judge right from wrong.

Movements were also viewed as temporary because the system would respond to the demands of the movement and because, as implied in Ernest Burgess's famous zonal model of city growth (Park and Burgess 1967), recent immigrants would soon experience upward occupational and outward residential mobility that would make any demands for basic changes in economic and political institutions irrelevant. Such mobility would occur inevitably because the immigrants' desires for higher social status would compel them to find better jobs and to move out from inner-city ethnic areas to newer housing in more "American" communities and suburbs (Cressey 1930, 174–79). This would enhance the prestige of the family moving to the city's periphery and would be associated with improved living conditions (single-family homes, better recreational opportunities, more space, and better public services).

The Chicago school believed that such residential movement would also have cultural consequences. As each ethnic group moved farther and farther out, it would eventually intermarry and interact socially with "Americans" near the city's periphery. Eventually, the ethnic group would lose its character as a separate entity; assimilation into the American way of life would result from social, occupational, and residential mobility. Social mobility and cultural assimilation would create "good Americans" with a commitment to the U.S. economic and political systems.

The classical social movements perspective is not very helpful in analyzing the nineteenth-century Chicago labor movement. The theory has the same problem as Marxism in one sense. The reliance on a vague contagion concept and the assumption that movement participants are irrational results in an inability to adequately explain the causal processes involved in the mobilization process. It is difficult to give a reasonable explanation of irrational acts; in fact, the Chicago school and other collective behavior theorists felt that one could not predict which type of collective behavior would result from urban social disorganization.

Also, the idea that the use of noninstitutional means for the redress of grievances is necessarily irrational is not useful. Reasonable people often view radical social movements as the only alternative after normal institutional channels fail to solve their problems. In the Chicago case, revolutionary anarchism became viable only after activists had unsuccessfully attempted to utilize the existing political system to redress their serious grievances.

More centrally, the theory's most important premise—that movement participants are drawn from the socially and culturally marginal—is incorrect. All of the various tendencies in the Chicago movement recruited through workplace and community-based social networks; the most likely to participate were in fact the most, not the least, socially integrated. It makes more sense to speak of the recruitment of politically and perhaps economically marginal (but socially integrated) groups rather than socially marginal individuals when trying to explain revolutionary mobilization.

Those movements utilized strongly held cultural values of their constituency in recruitment efforts to maintain participants' commitment and to create a distinctive view of the problems they faced and the best possible solutions. Revolutionary movements in Chicago mobilized residents of socially cohesive ethnic enclaves, using ethnic social organizations for recruitment and ethnic cultural traditions to gain greater commitment to the movement. Many of the revolutionaries were skilled workers, not the poorest unemployed marginal residents. These enclaves were often long lasting, providing a base for political mobilization for decades; they did not immediately dissipate under the impact of occupational and residential mobility.

Although classical collective behavior theory pays more attention to social structure and culture than Marxism, its propositions about those factors' impact on urban political mobilization are not particularly useful. Resource mobilization theory presents propositions that may be more helpful.

Resource Mobilization Theories

Resource mobilization theory (Gamson 1975; McCarthy and Zald 1973, 1977; Oberschall 1973; Tilly 1978) was created to overcome some of these problems with collective behavior theory. According to the resource mobilization theorists, movements do not form because of the participants' needs for normative and value direction in a socially disorganized city. Rather, they have a political basis; they are rational responses to the system's failure to provide equal access to political power for all groups (Gamson 1975).

But movements do not automatically arise due to differential access to power in a society. Political and other conflicts of interest are assumed to be ever present in the system, although political movements protesting this state of affairs are not. Resource mobilization theorists believe that the determinants of movement emergence are trends that result in a decline in the legitimacy of the political institution and/or the creation of new political resources for deprived and powerless groups. Movements emerge if *challenging groups* (Gamson 1975) have available and are able to mobilize resources (such as money, labor power, facilities, and means of communication) to take advantage of political opportunities (such as the decline in governmental legitimacy that results from a serious economic depression or a defeat in war).

Revolutionary mobilization is a special case; it does not take place unless there is a *severe* decline in political legitimacy of the existing regime, which can create *multiple sovereignty* (Tilly 1978), where a parallel government gains the loyalty of a significant proportion of the people. The success or failure of a revolutionary challenge to existing authority would then be determined by strategic political factors: essentially, which side had the more powerful resources and was able to use them effectively against the opponent.

The resource mobilization perspective also has important propositions about the typical organizational form of movements in modern society and the types of incentives that motivate movement participation. Resource mobilization theorists propose that the growth of industrial cities results in a shift from decentralized, informal, communal movements to centralized, formal, bureaucratic *social movement organizations* (Calhoun 1982; Tilly 1978; Zald and Ash 1965). Small traditional groups cannot compete for economic and political power in national and international markets, larger cities, and much more centralized and stronger polities. Movement groups have fewer resources and less internal control over their members than do their targets, who are often corporations or government agencies whose full-time employees will obey commands without question.

The theory asserts that modern movement groups must have a similar apparatus of internal control in order to deal on nearly equal terms with their opponents (Gamson 1975). Movement organizations need to establish both *centralization of power* and a *bureaucratic organizational form* (Gamson 1975). Centralization of power prevents debilitating factional fights for power within the organization and allows for quick decision making in a crisis. Having a bureaucratic organizational form—defined by Gamson as involving such things as written documents that indicate organizational goals and methods, a formal membership list, and at least three levels of internal division—helps the group maintain member commitment; it creates role structures that guarantee members' labor when it is needed (Gamson 1975).

Fortunately for movement groups, urbanization and industrialization facilitate the formation of bureaucratic, centralized, larger, and more powerful movement groups by concentrating and making more readily available both tangible assets such as money, facilities, and means of communication and intangible human assets such as organizing skills and supporters' labor (Freeman 1979).

Craig Jackson Calhoun (1982) elaborated on these resource mobilization themes in his study of the impact of industrialization on the English working class. Recalling Gutman and Hechter, he suggested that the real English revolutionaries were found in traditional communities, not in the emerging industrial cities. He described such revolutionaries as "reactionary radicals," that is, members of traditional craft-based communities who protested their loss of rights, privileges, and status due to the rise of factory production and the mechanization of their trades. Facing the loss of economic control over the crafts—the very basis of their economic, social, and political power—they engaged in relatively spontaneous, decentralized revolt against the violation of traditional values.

The mobilization effort was facilitated by the use of community-based social networks in traditional workplaces and neighborhoods. But their radicalism was not enough; given the decentralized, disorganized nature of the protests, they failed to influence the trend toward increasingly powerful, centralized, capitalist corporations and the state. The real power within the working class was held by factory workers who did not revolt and overthrow capitalism but instead formed strong bureaucratic, centralized unions that used reformist action such as collective bargaining to get what they could out of capitalism.

Thus, Calhoun rejects the collective behavior notion that movements recruit the marginal as well as Marx's notion that the most revolutionary group will be the working class under mature capitalism. Instead, he views revolutionary mobilization as a short-term, ineffective holding action by craft workers attempting to preserve traditional statuses and communities and accepts the resource mobilization view of movement recruitment (McCarthy and Zald 1973, 1977; Oberschall 1973; Olson 1965). Traditional re-

actionary movements base their appeals on solidarity within artisan communities. Modern progressive workers movements recruit
based on the utilitarian cost-benefit calculations of individual industrial workers. Mobilization takes place not because participants
desire social direction, as proposed by the collective behaviorists,
but because the individuals involved believe they will benefit from
their participation.

The resource mobilization view of recruitment to movements focuses on the *free rider* problem. In *The Logic of Collective Action*
(1965), Mancur Olson discusses the difficulty of getting individuals
to join in collective efforts to provide nondivisible *public goods.* A
public good is a product or service that, if it is provided at all, must
be provided to a large group; it bestows benefits from which people
cannot be easily excluded. Nearly pure cases are national defense
and a decrease in air pollution.

Labor movements attempt to provide such goods. Reformist
demands for labor legislation, the eight-hour day, or factory inspection laws and revolutionary demands for new economic and political systems involve providing benefits (or costs) to many individuals. It would be difficult to prevent many members of society from
enjoying those benefits or facing those costs regardless of the extent of their involvement in the attempt to provide them.

According to Olson, most people will free ride when an attempt
is made to provide public goods, letting others bear the costs and
risks of movement participation while the free rider enjoys the
benefits. This is particularly a problem in large groups, where individuals cannot be certain that their contribution to the effort will
make a difference in its success or failure. Under such conditions, a
movement that had as its sole incentive for participation the provision of public goods would never mobilize at all.

Olson suggests that groups form and act for other reasons. One
possibility is for group members to coerce themselves into providing public goods; an example of this is the closed shop, which man-
dates that all employed workers will be union members. Another
possibility, Olson's *by-product* theory, is that participants receive
individual benefits from participating in an organization that also
happens to provide public goods. Thus, participation is based on
furnishing *selective incentives:* divisible benefits that accrue only to

actual participants in the organization's activities. Generally, this economic theory suggests that material and career benefits are the most common and most important selective incentives. A concrete example of the use of selective incentives in the mobilization effort is a union that provides individual benefits such as unemployment insurance in order to convince reluctant workers to join. As a by-product of recruiting workers with such incentives, the union provides public goods such as wage increases through collective bargaining.

Resource mobilization theory can account for some aspects of the political mobilization pattern in the Chicago labor movement. Groups mobilized noninstitutional political movements when they did not believe they were given fair access to higher status economic positions and political power. This lack of access was particularly important in turning movements in a revolutionary direction. Irish nationalists tried to fight a revolution against the British because they perceived they could not gain access to the British political system through "legitimate" means. The Germans in Chicago created a revolutionary movement because they did not believe the Irish-dominated political machine was allowing them the traditional means of influencing political decision making in the city.

There were also aspects of multiple sovereignty in Chicago revolutionary movements. Once the repression of peaceful meetings and election fraud made the existing political system lose legitimacy in their eyes, Germans and Bohemians attempted to create a parallel system of economic organizations, the Central Labor Union, and a parallel political system based on the Social Revolutionary clubs and the anarchist unions. Revolutionary Irish nationalists hoped to create dual governing institutions in Great Britain as well.

Resource mobilization theory's propositions about a "modern" organizing model utilizing selective incentives and a bureaucratic organizational model are less helpful. They do seem to apply to one tendency in the Chicago movement: the Anglo-American reform movement. This tendency became increasingly centralized and bureaucratic as the craft unions and the trades and labor assemblies that were its basis became more powerful. Anglo-American unions utilizing the British new model union scheme recruited and retained members by offering selective incentives such as unemploy-

ment and burial benefits. The *raison d'être* of the Trades and Labor Assembly was to successfully lobby for labor legislation that
would gain material benefits for workers.

Through such tools, the Anglo-American workers were able to
monopolize many of the top trade jobs in the city, and they were
often able to influence the political system. Most Anglo-Americans
accepted the capitalist wage labor system and the Chicago political
system because they worked for them and their children. They remained true to the rational actor model by showing little solidarity
with the unskilled, eventually pulling out of Knights of Labor
Assemblies to return to their centralized, bureaucratic, discriminatory craft unions.

However, there was a variety of other less bureaucratic and centralized, yet effective organizing models in the Chicago labor movement. It is not necessarily helpful to call the more bureaucratic
movement groups "modern" and assume their effectiveness and
the less hierarchical groups "traditional" and ineffective. Like collective behavior theory and Marxism, the resource mobilization
theorists assume a dichotomous model of societal development.
This results in the insistence that there is one modern form of
movement organization and that there is one basic recruitment
strategy. The resource mobilization notion that movement groups
must be increasingly centralized and bureaucratic if they are to
compete for power in urban industrial society is a bit simplistic.

There was nothing "traditional" or backward looking about the
decentralized, nonbureaucratic, German anarchist movement; it
does not make sense to call the anarchists "reactionary radicals."
The movement was built largely within the Northwest Side German enclave, an emergent community that had been established
decades before that movement began. In its recruitment efforts, it
did utilize German ethnic identification. But those ethnic commitments were *not primordial;* rather, they emerged in reaction to
nativism and ethnically based discrimination. Rather than desiring
a return to the old guild way of life, the German anarchists proposed totally transformed economic and political systems based on
the creation of autonomous producer cooperatives.

The movement was not centralized; it was constructed out of decentralized German and Bohemian trade unions and political clubs.
The anarchists went to great lengths to avoid giving the central

committee any real power. It was not bureaucratic; the Progressive Cigarmakers Union, for example, had no full-time officers. It was not built on selective incentives, but rather on ideological commitment and support for the group causes of anarchism and defense of collective German values.

Gerlach and Hine (1970) have argued that this kind of non-hierarchical, decentralized structure is characteristic of many modern movements and is also the type of structure that maximizes mobilization. They suggest that the egalitarian, nonbureaucratic structures do this by providing extensive interpersonal bonds that generate social solidarity and reinforce ideological commitments. Because recruitment to movement groups is generally through face-to-face contact, the most effective mobilization efforts are those that maximize the number of such contacts through a segmented structure of many small movement groups. This lack of formal structure also increases participation by maximizing the ideological and tactical choices available to potential recruits.

They also suggest that decentralized cell structure protects the movement from opponents' attempts to repress or co-opt the movement's leadership because eliminating one group's leaders will not dramatically affect the movement as a whole; other groups will simply continue the fight. Bureaucratic, centralized movements are much more vulnerable to the loss of a few leaders. The argument is echoed by Piven and Cloward (1977), who argue that it is a mistake to organize bureaucratic movement groups because they are likely to be co-opted by those in authority.

Thus, there are serious questions about the validity of resource mobilization propositions about movement organizational form. There are also problems with the theory's use of the rational actor model of utilitarian economics in explaining recruitment. Even within the Trades and Labor Assembly, there were workers who did not seem to follow their "objective economic interests" very carefully. It is not clear that the native-born cigar makers, for example, were receiving enough economic benefits from their union and the Trades and Labor Assembly to justify their continued support of those organizations. Labor reform politics certainly did not prevent the destruction of their union and their trade. Their willingness to remain within the fold of the reform movement may be due more to their identification with upper status Anglo-American workers and their acceptance of conservative Anglo-American ideas about the causes of their plight than to a rational assessment of the individual material costs and benefits of such participation.

Relatively high status German printers and other labor aristocrats joined a risky, militant anarchist movement despite their apparent "objective interest" in labor reform. In fact, it is difficult to use rational actor models to explain why anyone would choose to participate in an urban protest movement like the nineteenth-century Chicago labor movement, where risks included the possibility of losing one's job, being killed or wounded by the police, and being arrested and imprisoned (Salert 1976, 33–35). With few clear individual benefits and a number of high potential costs, recruiting participants into the Chicago socialist and anarchist movements should have been much more difficult than it was (Salert 1976, 35).

Bruce Fireman and William Gamson (1979) have criticized the use of utilitarian models in the analysis of social movement mobilization. They believe that the emergence of a movement, recruitment of participants, and outcome of the challenge are determined "more by changes in group interests than by changes in the provision of 'selective incentives,' more by assessments of collective efficacy than by assessments of individual efficacy, more by solidarity and principle than by individual self-interest" (Fireman and Gamson 1979, 10). They suggest that movement participants assess what their *group* may gain or lose from their participation as well as what they may gain or lose as individuals. They also emphasize the importance of such nonutilitarian human relationships and nonmaterial incentives for participation as reciprocity, altruism, and acting according to group-based norms and values (for example, moral or political principle).

Their argument implies that activists contribute their efforts to a social movement organization because they believe in its goals and methods and understand that *self-sacrifice* is often necessary in working for an important political cause. Self-interest models—particularly those stressing material incentives—cannot explain why ideologically committed movement participants may be willing to sacrifice their time, their welfare, sometimes even their lives, to a cause. This argument seems particularly relevant to the case of revolutionary mobilization, where the risks are extremely high and the potential separable individual benefits are nearly nonexistent.

Resource mobilization theory is an important antidote to Marxist theories, which have no comprehensible analysis of micromobilization, and it is an improvement over collective behavior theory, which wrongly stresses movement participants' social marginality and irrationality. But in reacting to the collective behavior perspective, it may have gone too far in stressing the similarities between movement and bureaucratic organizations with regard to recruitment, participation incentives, and organizational structure.

Solidarity Theory

None of the three theoretical traditions reviewed can adequately account for all the political tendencies in the Chicago labor movement in this period. In particular, none can explain the ethnically based political mobilization pattern in that movement because all three perspectives emphasize the extent to which industrialization and urbanization *break down* communal bonds and ethnic and racial identities. Industrialization, it is assumed, will eventually eliminate "backward, traditional" practices not based on considerations of objective economic interests. Marxists expect class consciousness to develop; collective behaviorists expect short-term disorganization and conflict but long-term cultural and social assimilation; resource mobilization theorists expect eventual dominance of economic and political institutions and movements by bureaucratic organizations that recruit members based on individual cost-benefit calculations.

An alternative perspective, which can be called *solidarity theory,* emphasizes how industrialization and urbanization create new (not necessarily centralized and bureaucratic) forms of solidarity rather than how such processes destroy old traditional forms. Industrialization and urbanization often reinforce or even create ethnic and racial divisions in the labor market and can lead to the formation of close-knit, ethnically homogeneous urban communities.

Labor market segmentation and community ethnic segregation both affect political mobilization. Problems are created for members of subordinate racial or ethnic groups; these problems then may be the basis for the emergence of common grievances and collective political consciousness. Such ethnically based structures also affect the mobilization pattern that results from organizing on common grievances. Each creates routine patterns of in-group, out-group social interaction that are used in recruitment efforts and may help insulate movement activists from their opponent's ideas and repressive and co-optive tactics.

Efforts to recruit and ensure the continuing participation of movement activists often involve the creation of commitments to collective efforts to deal with such grievances; movements mobilize constituents by creating political solidarity—commitments to group goals and tactics—not simply through the use of selective incentives. Various emergent group level factors (patterns of social interaction, cultural and religious beliefs, group political histories) are important in mobilization because they affect the individual's propensity to sacrifice for the sake of group goals. Let us now consider this theory in more detail.

The Ethnically Segmented Labor Market

Contrary to the Marxist view, industrialization does not automatically undermine ethnic ties. *Ethnic competition* theorists (Barth 1969; Deutsch 1953; Hannan 1979; Nielsen 1980; Olzak and Nagel 1986; Van de Berghe 1967), drawing extensively on resource mobilization theory, argue that industrialization and urbanization can create changes that disrupt a previously stable and peaceful ethnic division of labor. Urbanization initiates between ethnic populations contact that leads to competition for scarce resources and political influence (Olzak and Nagel 1986). Far from making ethnic conflict a relic of the past, industrialization results in its *emergence* because it forces previously noncompeting ethnic groups to compete for the same jobs and economic resources (Ragin 1979).

There has been a running debate between advocates of ethnic competition theory and Michael Hechter's cultural division of labor thesis. For the competition theorists, ethnic conflict becomes most likely as a cultural division of labor *breaks down,* as differences in allocation to various jobs are eliminated under the influence of the "rational" forces of supply and demand in a growing city economy. Conflict results from dominant ethnic groups being forced to compete for high-wage jobs with challenging ethnic groups in an urban setting. The conflict is generally based on the willingness of lower status ethnics to accept *lower wages* to perform the same work. But such conflict is short-lived because the market forces of supply and demand will eventually equalize ethnically based wage differentials. Hechter argues that ethnic conflict results from the long-term confinement of lower status ethnic groups living in peripheral areas to *lower ranking jobs.*

As suggested in Chapter 3, it is possible to assume the validity of both the competition theorists' proposal that conflict is more likely in urban settings and Hechter's cultural division of labor concept. There is no reason a cultural division of labor must be based on urban-rural or center-periphery differences; it can exist within a city labor market, as Hechter (1978) has recognized. This idea of long-lasting ethnic occupational specialization is more useful in the Chicago case than the ethnic competition notion of ephemeral ethnic conflict based on wage differentials.

In the initial period of industrialization, employers' hiring decisions may be based on racism or nativism rather than on the belief that discriminatory practices will be economically beneficial. The fallacy lies in assuming that competitive markets will make these discriminatory practices economically detrimental to employers. Once implemented widely, labor market segmentation can benefit employers in a variety of ways.

Confining a readily identifiable group to certain subordinate occupations creates a labor pool whose members facing discrimination are forced to take low-wage, dead-end jobs. Such segmented markets can benefit employers by increasing profits through extreme exploitation of the low-status ethnic or racial group and by preventing the founding of unified, effective, firmwide and industrywide unions. Positive results for employers will be especially likely if all or nearly all employers engage in similar discriminatory hiring and promotion policies; the universality of discrimination makes it necessary for the subordinate group members to accept any job they can get, regardless of the wages and working conditions.

Not necessarily only employers benefit. Higher status ethnic group workers often successfully monopolize desirable jobs through discriminatory practices; the classic means for this is the craft union, which controls access to the trade by restricting entrance to the union's apprenticeship program. The institutionalization of such a segmented labor market creates important economic, social, and cultural divisions within the working class; it can promote a commitment to individual, or at best trade, interests among the labor aristocrats and inhibit the development of a class-conscious labor movement.

The mistake so many analysts make is assuming that capitalist markets are characterized by free competition; in fact, such markets are more commonly dominated by groups able to successfully limit competition. Ethnic, racial, gender, or other social differences are not made irrelevant by the rise of industrial capitalism. Instead, such differences are often utilized by those with power in labor markets (employers and craft unions) to exclude outsiders from the rewards of the system.

Weber gave this idea a somewhat broader sociological cast with his notion of social closure. As Parkin (1979, 44) put it:

By social closure Weber means the process by which social collectivities seek to maximize rewards by restricting access to resources and opportunities to a limited circle of eligibles. This entails the singling out of certain social or physical attributes as the justificatory basis of exclusion. Weber suggests that virtually any group attribute—race, language, social origin, religion—may be seized upon provided it can be used for "the monopolization of specific, usually economic opportunities." "This monopolization is directed against competitors who share some positive or negative characteristic; its purpose is always the closure of social and economic opportunities to outsiders."

Excluded groups often respond in kind by acting collectively to resist their confinement to low-status positions. They will attempt to *usurp* the positions of the dominant group; or they may attempt to monopolize a group of middle level jobs, thus confining groups with even less power than they have to the bottom of the labor market. In this fashion, an *ethnically segmented labor market* is created through the actions of workers themselves, especially in industries where craft workers have a lot of control over entry to their trades.

Far from being automatically eliminated by the forces of free competition, such segmented markets may persist as long as workers can be identified as belonging to some arbitrary category—racial, ethnic, or gender (Hirsch 1980). In the case of readily identifiable racial groups such as black Americans or a gender group such as women, segmented labor markets have persisted for many generations.

In Chicago, Anglo-Americans were able to monopolize jobs in the printing and construction trades by apprenticing their male relatives and friends. Employers' discriminatory acts and use of the craft union model created a segmented labor market that excluded the majority of those in the working class—the less skilled, women, immigrants, the old and the young, and sweatshop workers—from the top trades. Economic divisions within the working class were created with respect to wage levels and job security, working conditions and life-styles between unskilled, low-status skilled, and labor aristocrats.

Worker allocation to each of the three sectors was closely associated with ethnic origin. Most of the city's Irish residents were in unskilled jobs; most British immigrants were labor aristocrats; many Germans were in the lower status trades. The average economic position of each ethnic group's workers was important in affecting each group's view of the labor market. But Chicago's ethnically segmented labor market was not perfect; there was no one-to-one correspondence between ethnic origins and economic status. There were some German and Irish labor aristocrats and a few Anglo-Amercan unskilled laborers.

There was, however, greater differentiation in economic status than political choice within the working classes of each ethnic group. The reform and revolutionary tendencies mobilized workers of diverse economic backgrounds and common ethnic backgrounds. So the tendency for different ethnic groups in the movement to choose different political paths cannot have been based only on the economic position of each ethnic group. There were social, cultural, ideological, and political reasons for strong ethnic identification in the city and for ethnically based political mobilization.

The Emergence of Ethnic Enclaves

The impact of industrialization cannot be easily analyzed through abstract, dichotomous, theoretical models; it must be explained through historical investigation. Likewise, simplistic views of urbanization must be questioned. It is not useful to assume that urbanization is socially disorganizing, that it destroys ethnic and racial identities. Many prominent urban theorists (Fischer 1984; Gans 1962; Janowitz 1952; Suttles 1968; Whyte 1943) argue that the city does not simply *destroy* old communities; it *creates* new ones. Rather than fostering social disorganization, large, dense cities often germinate a variety of distinctive, separate social worlds because they attract *critical masses* of migrants from a great variety of cultural backgrounds (Fischer 1984).

Cultural and political assimilation models (the idea of the melting pot and pluralist political theory) are not any more helpful in understanding the immigrants' social and political experiences than neoclassical economics is in explaining their economic fate. Nineteenth-century immigrants faced an alien environment upon arriving in U.S. cities, experiencing discrimination in social, cultural, and political spheres—not only in the labor market. American society was built on *exclusion*, and that process resulted in ethnic status hierarchies in all institutional spheres. Those of Anglo-Saxon origin attempted to force their culture on immigrants through a variety of nativist laws and practices; cultural conflict was more common than mutual tolerance. Nativist attacks were often based on Puritan religious values such as the assumption that those who were successful in the labor market were the hardest and most sober workers. Acceptance of these values made many Protestant Anglo-American workers more moderate than they might otherwise have been. They often blamed Irish Catholics for urban problems, such as crime and poverty, that may have had their true roots in the nature of the economic and political systems in the city.

Urban political machines did not simply integrate ethnic groups into the polity. Instead, various ethnic groups struggled aggressively for political influence within the machine. The city's Irish workers, and to a degree also the Anglo-Americans, used a variety of legal and illegal tactics, including lobbying, ballot stuffing, vote fraud, kickbacks, and payoffs, to come out on top, usually at the German workers' expense.

The excluded fought back. The experience of economic, social, and political exclusion induced powerless ethnic groups to create tightly knit social and cultural communities as a defensive measure; in such *ethnic enclaves* (Portes and Manning 1986), residents helped each other find jobs, preserved their common culture, and mobilized to gain political influence. The enclaves were nearly self-sufficient—with workplaces, homes, recreation and leisure activities, churches, and ethnic social organizations all within walking distance. Living together was not totally voluntary; poor newly arrived immigrants were generally not welcome in the communities of the native born. The hostile environment created denser, stronger ties (kinship, friendship, and neighboring networks) and more intense ethnic identification than had been characteristic of the country of origin.

Rational actor models are not of much use in accounting for behavior in such settings. Within these ethnic enclaves, relations between residents were built on reciprocity, trust, altruism, and mutual helping (Mollenkopf 1981, 320); they were not governed only by market relationships or by calculations of individual utility. Kinship and neighboring networks and self-help and ethnic social organizations were built, creating dense, strong, mutual support networks. *Community* was not undermined by industrialization and urbanization; it was simply created in a new and different form.

The formation of ethnic enclaves reinforced an ethnically segmented social structure in the city. Those of the same ethnicity were more likely to interact with one another than with those of other ethnic groups. The foreign-born enclaves were to some degree socially isolated from one another and from the communities of the more residentially dispersed Anglo-Americans. So contact between heterogeneous groups did not result in social disorganization; rather, it intensified the values and in-group social bonds within each ethnic group. The cultural and social isolation of ethnic groups in Chicago was commented on by Jane Addams (1910, 110–11) in her book, *Twenty Years at Hull House:*

We were also early impressed with the curious isolation of many of the immigrants; an Italian woman once expressed her pleasure in the red roses that she saw at one of our receptions in surprise that they had been "brought so fresh all the way from Italy." She would not believe for an instant that they had been grown in America. She said that she had lived in Chicago for six years and had never seen any roses, whereas in Italy she had seen them every summer in great profusion. During all that time, of course, the woman had lived within ten blocks of a florist's window;

she had not been more than a five cent ride away from the public parks; but she had never dreamed of faring forth for herself, and no one had taken her.

Many of these ethnic enclaves were preserved through time. This is contrary to the Chicago school notion that fairly rapid assimilation into American life occurred among the immigrants. It is true that immigrants, especially unskilled peasants, often moved into the cheapest housing near the city's center; usually, they moved along the banks of the various branches of the Chicago River to be near their industrial workplaces. The maps in Chapter 3 show that these groups eventually moved toward the city's periphery, and lower status groups, usually newer immigrant groups, did succeed them in the older residence areas. But ethnic groups had some tendency to move *as groups;* they did *not* necessarily disperse into American neighborhoods, forever losing their ethnic identities.

Pioneer ethnic families often moved from the areas of first settlement into areas being deserted by another group; they were then followed by others from the same ethnic group. The ethnics reestablished their community institutions in the new residence area, thus preserving prior social ties, culture, and ethnic political traditions and creating another relatively homogeneous ethnic neighborhood.

So the Irish, Germans, Bohemians, and other immigrant groups created ethnically distinctive communities that lasted for decades. These communities were important to any political mobilization effort in the city because they contained dense social networks that could be used to communicate with potential movement recruits. Abstract, theoretically defined class interests are much less relevant to political recruitment efforts than are actual social networks based on kinship, neighboring, friendship, and membership in social, cultural, and political organizations.

Havens and Urban Revolutionary Mobilization

It is the primary argument of this book that emergent, close-knit urban communities are often the social basis for the mobilization of urban political movements, especially revolutionary ones.

Such movements do not represent mobilization by a unified, class-conscious working class, as predicted by Marxists; they are not manifestations of social disorganization, as suggested by the collective behaviorists; they are not products of the rational calculation of individual interests by participants in bureaucratic movement organizations. Rather, urban revolution is built using structurally isolated workplace and community networks and an oppositional culture.

The Haven and Social Structure

The concept of *haven* can be useful in accounting for urban revolutionary mobilization. The idea depends on the proposition that strong positive horizontal ties and limited positive vertical ones facilitate movement mobilization. The formation of structurally isolated communities is likely to lead to the mobilization of revolutionary movements because it is easier to recruit large numbers for radical politics if there is an organizational base in community, occupational, or religious groups; such groups produce horizontal links of solidarity (Oberschall 1973, 119) so that the recruitment of one leader or several group members can result in the simultaneous recruitment of other members of the group.

This *bloc recruitment* (Oberschall 1973) makes it easier to maintain commitment to the movement because of preexisting identification with group goals. Appeals for participation are effective because *solidarity* (the identification with group rather than individual interests) is already present. As Fireman and Gamson (1979) have pointed out, it is not necessary to use selective incentives in the recruitment process if individuals are already committed to supporting group goals.

Also, the lack of positive vertical ties—the lack of social interaction with upper status groups—makes it more likely that such groups can be successfully defined as the enemy, which makes it easier to sustain commitment to revolutionary goals and tactics and prevents movement participants from developing undue sympathy for the opponent. It also promotes the political effectiveness of revolutionary movements because movement groups are able to develop innovative tactics in a setting that limits their vulnerability to their opponents' repressive and co-optive tactics. It is often possible to use the element of surprise if tactics can be developed in a setting where opponents have limited access to information.

There are three examples of the mobilization of revolutionary movements in ethnic enclaves in Chicago: the German socialist and anarchist movements, the Bohemian anarchist movement, and the Irish nationalist movement. The Germans created an ethnically based revolutionary movement because severe economic and political problems fostered a sense of outrage over the injustices perpetrated against German workers. This facilitated movement mobilization along ethnic lines by increasing ethnic identification and in-group communication and by facilitating identification of the Anglo-Americans and the Irish as the enemy. Appeals to become politically active were spread through dense German community kinship, neighboring, friendship, and organizational networks in the German residential enclave.

The use of dense, in-group social networks that were characteristic of enclave life for political mobilization efforts led to high (but sometimes nearly ethnically homogeneous) turnouts for marches and rallies. The movement was German in terms of membership, language, papers, and the social networks used to mobilize it; it was community oriented, built on the German craft unions but also on community organizations like the Turners, antitemperance groups, cultural organizations, and free thought societies.

This social isolation made it possible to mobilize and strengthen this German movement apart from the political intervention of the movement's opponent. Anglo-American elites, who spoke only English and rarely visited ethnic enclaves, often had little information on the German political movements mobilized in the city and generally intervened only in a crisis, such as during 1877 and immediately following Haymarket.

The Bohemian enclave was another source of revolutionary sentiment and action. Bohemians were only about 2.5 percent of the city population; yet they were mentioned prominently in connection with both the 1877 strikes and the more militant wing of the socialist and anarchist movements. The 1877 mass strikes were based largely in the Bohemian community, with many residents resorting to guerrilla warfare as the conflict neared its conclusion.

Bohemians also formed the Bohemian Sharpshooters, a workers self-defense organization, and a strong union of revolutionary Bohemian lumber shovers who were well known for their militant defense of a precarious economic position.

Bohemians joined the German revolutionary struggle despite different average economic status; most Bohemians had skilled backgrounds, but in the Chicago labor market, they were overwhelmingly in unskilled jobs. What they did have in common with the city's Germans was an inability to gain positions of influence in the Irish-dominated political machine and a strong set of interconnected social organizations that could be utilized to respond to their serious economic and political problems. These included free thought societies, Sokols (the equivalent of the German Turners), bands, singing societies, and protective and benevolent societies (Horak 1928; McCarthy 1950). As in the German movement, there were close and important ties between social, cultural, and revolutionary organizations within the Bohemian community (Schneirov 1984). The Bohemians also spoke German and were able to read the militant German labor papers.

Workers in the Irish enclave did not question the Chicago political system because they were able to use Irish social networks to found a successful nonrevolutionary institution: the political machine. The machine became the road to Irish political power, economic security, and even a measure of social status. Attacking a political institution that was responsible for the small measure of economic security the Chicago Irish did enjoy would have been irrational. Few Irish joined the revolutionary labor movement because it called for eliminating the state, the Irish meal ticket.

Even while the Irish were espousing political moderation in Chicago, revolutionary Irish nationalists were dynamiting London Bridge. Ethnic discrimination reinforced Irish identity, just as it did German, and Irish social bonds became an important means of political mobilization. The most important social institutions in the Irish enclave (the Catholic church, the Irish saloon) were crucial in mobilizing that revolutionary movement.

Again in-group patterns of social interaction meant isolation from the opponent, in this case, English, not Chicago, political and economic elites. Innovative strategies and more revolutionary ideologies could be developed in Bridgeport much more easily than in Dublin because the Chicago Irish were nearly invulnerable to British intervention.

The Haven and Culture

A pattern of in-group, out-group social interaction and its impact on effective political mobilization defines the idea of the haven. But the concept must include a cultural dimension as well. *Havens* insulate the challenging group from the rationalizing ideologies normally disseminated by the society's dominant group. The Marxist Antonio Gramsci (1971) pointed out that dominant groups do not control society through their economic and political power alone. They also use *ideological hegemony* to gain legitimacy for their dominant position in the society.

Hegemonic ideologies present the dominant group's interests as the universal interests of everyone in the society, rationalize the dominant group's privileged position, and suggest reasons why subordinate groups ought to accept their deprived and oppressed condition. The idea that those in top economic and political positions enjoy their privileges due to the will of God or their superior individual merit are examples of hegemonic ideas. The classical economics view of capitalist markets and the pluralist view of the American political system are also concrete examples of legitimating ideologies. Each ideology may convince potential critics of the system that access to economic and political power is based on fair, just, competitive processes. The extent to which hegemonic ideologies describe reality is less important than whether or not subordinate groups believe them. If they do, the ruling class is in a virtually unassailable position; the hegemonic class can weather even severe economic crises because subordinate classes continue to believe in the system.

If diffused from the top down, through such institutions as schools, churches, and the family, hegemonic ideas can become part of *common sense*. Most existing working-class organizations that are well integrated into the existing system (such as trade unions and labor parties) are likely to accept such ideas because they must accept the legitimacy of the system in order to gain advantages within it; compromise and negotiation are possible only after the rules of the game have already been agreed upon. Unions ask for shorter hours and better benefits; parties request narrow reforms designed to gain a few concessions for their constituency. But neither mobilizes for revolution.

People will often accept ideas about their problems and solutions to those problems that they have accepted in the past. A common cultural background reinforced through a pattern of in-group social interaction can facilitate acceptance of a particular ideology by members of a particular group (Fireman and Gamson 1979).

In nineteenth-century Chicago, Anglo-American workers often accepted a hegemonic ideology promoted by the largely Protestant middle and upper classes. Aristocrat, low-status skilled and unskilled Anglo-Americans accepted an ideology that rationalized the way the system worked through the Puritan notion that each individual's economic position was due to educational level, willingness to work hard, and capacity to stay sober. Nativism and antiradicalism were part of the ideology as well. German socialism and anarchism were labeled "foreign" and "heathen," and German revolutionaries were described as being "unable to understand American institutions." These "Red Scares" divided the Anglo-Americans from the more radical Germans and convinced the Americans that the revolutionary Germans were threatening economic and social institutions that were operating in the interests of all Chicago workers.

One reason for their acceptance of this basically individualistic, middle-class ideology may have been the fact that Anglo-Americans generally were able to influence the political system. Even the working class—through political reform unionism—was able to gain a degree of political access, to pass reform legislation (such as factory inspection and contract convict and child labor laws), and to appoint some of their number to political office. So the Anglo-American working class was not disposed to accept revolutionary ideologies that proposed transforming an economic and political system that most felt was meeting their needs.

Another factor was the greater separation of workplace and community in the Anglo-American working class. There were no working-class Anglo-American ethnic enclaves. They had no reason to create defensive communities because they were the attackers, not the attacked. So many of these workers lived in more heterogeneous communities on Chicago's West Side, where many owned homes and interacted socially with the large Anglo Protestant middle class. They were more vulnerable than many immigrants to the arguments of bosses who spoke their language, read the same newspapers, went to the same churches, and shared the same cultural background.

The English-language press generally accepted these hegemonic beliefs, supporting the existing system and capitalism in general. This ideology was also disseminated to the Anglo working class through temperance unions, churches, nativist parties and clubs, and reformist unions and coalitions such as the Trades and Labor Assembly.

Sometimes employers made more specific efforts to indoctrinate their workers. One example was the railroad YMCAs, an Anglo railroad management attempt to deradicalize their largely Anglo and Irish workers. The entire cultural complex—work ethic, temperance, nativism, antiradicalism, and commitment to Protestant religion—was strongly promoted by these organizations, making it difficult for the railroad workers, already divorced from working-class ethnic enclaves by the nature of their work, to be influenced by ideas that might be antithetical to capitalist profit making.

Thus, the importance of havens is due in part to their impact on the acceptance or lack of acceptance of such hegemonic ideologies. They created and preserved a structural isolation from ruling groups that allowed subordinate groups to develop innovative ideas about the nature of the system, to identify those responsible for the subordinate groups' plight, and to discover what action was needed to resolve their common problems.

Such in-group communication patterns can germinate the idea that an oppressive system can be changed. As Piven and Cloward (1977, 3–4) put it, unless people's ideas about the vulnerability of the system of power change, they will not consider challenging that system:

First, the "system"—or those aspects of the system that people experience and perceive—loses legitimacy. Large numbers of men and women who ordinarily accept the authority of their rulers and the legitimacy of institutional arrangements come to believe in some measure that these rulers and these arrangements are unjust and wrong. Second, people who are ordinarily fatalistic, who believe that existing arrangements are inevitable, begin to assert "rights" that imply demands for change. Third, there is a new sense of efficacy; people who ordinarily consider themselves helpless come to believe that they have some capacity to alter their lot.

Effective revolutionary movement mobilization occurs when groups of people begin to question system legitimacy and come to believe that there is a good chance to change it; it is not only the objective economic and political conditions that matter. As McAdam (1982) points out, the development of such *insurgent consciousness*—the sense of collective power to challenge the forces affecting the group—is much more likely and of far greater consequence under conditions of strong rather than weak social integration. In the absence of strong interpersonal links to others, people are likely to feel powerless to change the conditions that affect them. They correctly perceive that they cannot do it alone.

Counterhegemonic ideologies are used to attack privilege; they suggest that the economic and political systems operate in an unfair, unjust manner and must be dramatically changed if they are to serve the interests of subordinate groups. Such challenging systems of ideas are easier to create and promote if a subordinate group has a radical cultural and political tradition. In Chicago, Germans drew on radical traditions of the 1848 revolution and the socialist political clubs that had been created in Germany. Bohemians had a similar political tradition and strong attachments to their atheist free thought societies (Horak 1928; McCarthy 1950). Revolutionary Irish nationalists built on their fights against English landlords and the Crown.

Counterhegemonic ideology was formulated in response to the nativist character of the hegemonic Puritan ideology. Most immigrant groups faced a nativist movement that defined their culture as deficient, their drinking as immoral, their politics as irrational. The anarchist movement rejected temperance and nativism and accepted German and Bohemian cultural and political traditions. Both movements were strengthened when the defense of working-class culture was connected to the revolutionary fight against reformist ideas about the nature of capitalism and representative democracy in Chicago and the United States.

Understanding and using the concept of havens is the key to analyzing urban revolutionary mobilization. Close-knit, structurally isolated, exploited, and institutionally powerless communities are the most likely to mobilize politically. These are often ethnically and class-segregated residence communities where economic and political elites may have little influence. Within these relatively isolated neighborhoods, political mobilization and creative cultural development occur within community groups, bars and pubs, ethnic or racial associations, community-based political clubs, churches, and voluntary organizations of all kinds. Havens are sites where questioning of the sytem is most likely, where recruitment to movements is easiest, where the movement has at least some immunity from the ideological, repressive, and co-optive tactics of the dominant group. All these generalizations apply especially to revolutionary movements, which must make the most complete break with legitimating ideologies. In fact, it may be impossible for revolutionary movements to develop revolutionary ideologies and tactics within institutions that are well integrated into the existing order.

The validity of the haven concept is shown by evidence from both sides of the Chicago movement. Elites eventually saw the importance of havens for mobilizing successful opposition movements. They brutally and violently invaded them, as in breaking up peaceful union meetings in 1877 and invading anarchist meeting places following Haymarket, and managed to limit their tactical usefulness to the challenging group.

Theoretical Convergence on the Haven Concept

Theorists of revolution from each of the theoretical perspectives reviewed (Marxism, collective behavior, and resource mobilization) understand the importance of the use of structurally isolated, close-knit communities in movement mobilization. Resource mobilization theorists (Freeman 1979; Morris 1984; Oberschall 1973; Pinard 1971; Snow, Zurcher, and Ecklund-Olson 1980) point out that movements often utilize existing social networks and sentiments of solidarity in recruitment. Oberschall (1973, 117), a resource mobilization theorist who generally accepts Olson's rational actor view of movement recruitment, recognizes its limitations when considering preexisting group solidarity:

A point at which Olson's theory must be modified and not simply elaborated to make it more applicable to opposition movements is in his assumption that the members of a large collectivity are unorganized individual decision-makers similar to the numerous, small, independent producers in the market of the classical economist. This is but one possibility, and perhaps not even the most frequent one. Discontented groups can be members of a still viable or partially viable community—religious, tribal, ethnic, cultural, and historical—into which they were born and which they accept as a matter of course because it represents the basis of their everyday life, their livelihood, their family life and kinship relations, and their most cherished beliefs.

Also consistent with the haven concept, Oberschall (1973, 119–20) suggests that the likelihood of the mobilization of a group with radical goals using noninstitutional tactics is increased even more if a group with strong *horizontal* bonds of solidarity also has few *vertical* bonds with economic and political elites:

A structural feature facilitating mobilization into protest movements is obtained when the society is not only highly stratified but segmented. Under segmentation the collectivity whose potential for mobilization we are examining has few links and bonds, other than perhaps through exploitative relationships, with the higher classes or other collectivities of the society. . . . On the other hand, if in a stratified society there exist strong vertical, social and political bonds between upper and lower classes, mobilization into protest movements among the lower classes is not likely to take place.

Others working in the resource mobilization perspective have also developed concepts that show the usefulness of the haven idea. Jo Freeman (1975) and Sara Evans (1979) have emphasized the importance of "free social spaces" in the development of the women's movement; consciousness-raising groups, for example, included only women in order to eliminate the negative influence of hegemonic male ideas. It was in such groups that many of the important ideological and tactical challenges to sexism were germinated. Douglas McAdam (1982) and Aldon Morris (1984) have emphasized the importance of black-controlled social and cultural institutions such as colleges and churches in the challenge to segregation and white economic and political supremacy in the South. Craig Jackson Calhoun (1982) emphasizes how craft workers in traditional English communities used existing communal ties to wage a radical fight against industrialism.

Even Mancur Olson—the guru of utilitarian models of movement recruitment—recognizes the importance of social solidarity in certain situations. He suggested that *small groups* might use *social incentives* to induce participation in efforts to provide public goods:

> If a small group of people who had an interest in a collective good happened also to be personal friends, or belonged to the same social club, and some of the group left the burden of providing that collective good on others, they might, even if they gained economically by this course of action, lose socially by it, and the social loss might outweigh the economic gain. Their friends might use "social pressure" to encourage them to do their part toward achieving the group goal, or the social club might exclude them, and such steps might be effective, for everyday observation reveals that most people value the fellowship of their friends and associates, and value social status, personal prestige, and self-esteem. (Olson 1965, 60)

Olson goes on to suggest that a larger movement might be built out of such small groups using a *federal group* model, where small groups motivating their members through social incentives form the basis of a pyramidal coalition structure (Olson 1965, 60–63).

From the Marxist perspective, Antonio Gramsci developed many concepts similar to the haven idea. He defined ideological hegemony to explain how the capitalist class maintained its rule under advanced capitalism. But he expected that such hegemony would eventually end as workers develop alternative beliefs in new protosocialist institutions that would be relatively immune from the damaging influence of ruling-class hegemony. These institutions (such as worker factory councils, collectives, cooperatives, and assemblies) can eventually garner workers' full loyalty and allegiance and become the revolutionary institutions of the new socialist order.

The English Marxist social historian E. P. Thompson also emphasizes the importance of the haven idea. In his analysis of the development of the English working class, he argues that class formation was expressed most clearly in the founding and maintenance of culturally distinctive working-class institutions, including friendly societies, dissenting religious sects, periodicals, and pubs. These institutions were meeting places where the workers associated and discussed politics and strategies for meeting the challenges of their class enemies, where genuine working-class consciousness and culture were germinated.

In the very secretiveness of the friendly society, and in its opaqueness under upper class scrutiny, we have authentic evidence of the growth of independent working-class culture and institutions. This was the subculture out of which the less stable trade unions grew, and in which trade union officers were trained. . . .

In the simplest cellular structure of the friendly society, with its workaday ethics of mutual aid, we can see many features which were reproduced in more sophisticated and complex forms in trade unions, cooperatives, Hampden Clubs, Political Unions, and Chartist lodges. (Thompson 1963, 421–23)

Each Marxist theorist reviewed also recognized the importance of social structural and cultural isolation in the development of challenging movements. In-group social networks created the conditions for radical ethnic movements in Hechter's (1975) theory; Gutman (1977) discussed the ability of workers in isolated industrial towns to mobilize militant strikes; Katznelson (1981) analyzed how the fragmenting of workplace and residence in working-class neighborhoods limited workers' ability to build class-conscious movements.

One would not expect to find within the Chicago School of Sociology theorists who recognize the importance of community-based solidarity in the development of radical movements; after all, they usually argued exactly the reverse: that radical movements are germinated by social disorganization. But some members of the Chicago school did use concepts very much like the notion of the haven. Cressey (1930), for example, stressed the tendency of recent city arrivals to settle in ethnically homogeneous residence communities where they developed autonomous social networks and distinctive cultures and life-styles. Cressey viewed it as natural that individuals would prefer to live in neighborhoods where they could interact with others of their own kind and where they could establish their own churches, stores, and community institutions.

Robert Park (1967) discussed the innovative nature of revolutionary *sects*, which are able to develop radical ideologies due to their structural isolation from other groups. He suggested, "It is in the ferment and fervor of sectarian life that new ideas and new ideals of life take form and make themselves articulate" (Park 1967, 245). Also, recent attempts by Chicago school students to revise the collective behavior view of social movements certainly recognize the importance of existing social networks in movement recruitment. As Turner and Killian (1987, 249, 329) put it in the third edition of *Collective Behavior:*

Prior organization supplies leadership, patterns for decision-making, and an initial supply of indispensable resources. . . . The evidence concerning both religious and political movements seems overwhelming, that unless a movement severs adherents' ties to family, friends, and co-workers by demanding total absorption, recruitment through adherents' personal networks is more productive than other approaches.

Various theorists who are less easy to categorize as Marxist, collective behavior, or resource mobilization theorists have also recognized the importance of havens in the development of revolutionary or insurgent political movements. Sara Evans and Harry Boyte (1986, 17–18) discuss the importance of *free spaces* in movements for democratic change:

Put simply, free spaces are settings between private lives and large-scale institutions where ordinary citizens can act with dignity, independence, and vision. There are, in the main, voluntary forms of association with a relatively open and participatory character—many religious organizations, clubs, self-help and mutual aid societies, reform groups, neighborhood, civic, and ethnic groups and a host of other associations grounded in the fabric of community life. . . . Democratic action depends upon these free spaces, where people experience a schooling in citizenship and learn a vision of the common good in the course of struggling for change.

Barrington Moore (1978, 482) recognized the importance of such social structural factors in movement mobilization in *Injustice: The Social Bases of Obedience and Revolt:*

For any social and moral transformation to get underway there appears to be one prerequisite that underlies all those so far discussed: social and cultural space within the prevailing order. A society with social and cultural space provides more or less protected enclaves within which dissatisfied or oppressed groups have some room to develop distinctive social arrangements, cultural traditions, and explanations of the world around them. Social and cultural space implies room to experiment with making the future.

Conclusions

Industrialization and urbanization created the conditions for revolutionary mobilization in the Chicago labor movement, but not because of the development of class consciousness, social disorganization, or the growth of bureaucratic centers of alternative sovereignty. Industrialization fostered conditions that led to the development *and sustenance* of an ethnically segmented labor market. Urbanization created conditions that led to development *and sustenance* of ethnic enclaves in which immigrants often faced social and political exclusion. The models of free competitive labor markets, pluralist politics, and cultural assimilation—accepted in one way or another by all three dominant theoretical traditions—are not useful descriptions of immigrant working-class experience in nineteenth-century Chicago. Rather, industrialization and urbanization involved processes whereby some groups excluded others from power in economic, political, cultural, and social spheres. Excluded groups fought back using social networks and cultural resources in their relatively isolated communities.

The two major classical approaches to explaining workers' response to industrialization and urbanization cannot explain what happened in the Chicago labor movement. Marxists suggest that ethnic diversity leads to a lesser chance for revolutionary mobilization because it reduces working-class consciousness. But in the Chicago labor movement, ethnic diversity increased the chances for revolutionary mobilization by creating ethnically segmented labor markets, politically excluded ethnic groups, and ethnic residential havens for the development of revolutionary ideology and strategy.

The Chicago school accepts the idea that such ethnic diversity causes revolutionary mobilization but assigns the wrong reasons for that relationship, suggesting that it results from cultural mixing, normative and value ambiguity, and social disorganization. A more reasonable argument is the reverse of the Chicago school hypothesis. Ethnic diversity leads to a greater likelihood of revolutionary mobilization because it results in the economic, political, and social exclusion of subordinate ethnic groups and because it facilitates the use of ethnic community–based resources to fight against such exclusion.

In Chicago, ethnically based status and power differences were created in all major institutional spheres. Employers and an Anglo-American labor aristocracy built an ethnically segmented labor market through discriminatory practices. The creation of an Irish-dominated political machine resulted in differences in access to political power. Anglo-Americans attempted to impose their culture on non-Anglo immigrants.

The political exclusion of Germans and Bohemians was especially important. As is recognized by the best recent theories of revolution (Skocpol 1979; Tilly 1978), revolutionary mobilization does not occur if economic, political, and social grievances can be successfully addressed through "legitimate" existing political institutions. Revolution is a last resort that is attempted on a significant scale only after other forms of action have been tried and have failed to resolve serious grievances. Thus, in Chicago, successful creation of the political collective bargaining model by Anglo-American workers and of the political machine by Irish workers led them down the reformist path; the inability of the city's Germans to find a similar road to political power led them to revolution.

Successful recruitment to a revolutionary movement is more likely if there are social structural–cultural havens available where radical ideas and tactics can be more easily germinated. In Chicago, the fact that different ethnic groups faced different problems intensified ethnic identity and created defensive ethnic enclaves. In these enclaves, hegemonic ideologies were easily rejected, radical critiques of the existing system were created, and innovative political strategies were formulated, all in isolation from the hegemonic ideas and repressive tactics of the Anglo-American and Irish elites.

The resource mobilization approach to movements certainly explains political mobilization in the Chicago labor movement better than the classical approaches. Its emphasis on the use of existing social ties in movement recruitment efforts is especially helpful. But the resource mobilization assumption that the community- or solidarity-based model of organizing is traditional, weak, and backward is much less useful. Different ethnic groups did face different problems and mobilized different responses—some reformist and some revolutionary—using different sets of resources; but it makes no sense to term one organizing model modern and the other traditional. The solidarity model of organizing, as was used in the German and Bohemian anarchist movements, the mass strikes, and the Irish nationalist movement, is just as "modern" as a selective, incentive-based, bureaucratic organizational model.

The social ties used in the solidarity mobilizations were not primordial; they were not left over from some dying traditional past. Rather, they were dynamic products of urbanization and industrialization; they were *emergent* in the ethnically polarized Chicago scene. Ethnic identification and movements based on such identification—such as Irish nationalism, German and Bohemian free thought, Turners and Bohemian Sokols, and the German anarchist movement—were in fact much stronger in Chicago than in Ireland, Bohemia, and Germany. Irish nationalists dynamited targets in London, but the bombers were Irish-Americans, not native Irish. There was no anarchist movement in Germany to compare to the one in Chicago.

The resource mobilization argument concerning the backwardness of such ethnic community–based movements suggests that such decentralized movements cannot compete with the increasingly powerful state and large economic institutions. It is true that community-based movements that recruit members on the basis of solidarity do face the problem that such solidarity is generally built through face-to-face interaction. The key building block of such movements must be a relatively small, relatively powerless group; but the problem can be overcome.

Many movements have used nonbureaucratic, decentralized solidarity models to develop power on a broad, even a national, scale. One means of gaining such power using the solidarity model is to use a *federal group model*. In this model, as even Mancur Olson (1965) recognized, a pyramidal structure of coalitions can be built to tie together a number of small solidary groups. Such a model was used extensively in nineteenth-century Chicago by, for example, the Central Labor Union, the Social Revolutionary clubs, and to an extent also the strike coordinating committee during 1877. They turned out tens of thousands for rallies and showed great political effectiveness, especially in the eight-hour movement in the early 1880s. In fact, even the highly successful Irish-led political machine used important elements of the solidarity organizing model, utilizing decentralized Irish social networks and capitalizing on Irish ethnic identity to build political power in the city. The machine was not a bureaucratic organization; it certainly did not hire employees based on their objective qualifications for the position.*

Perhaps resource mobilization theorists, had they been advising the German anarchists, would have suggested using a more bureaucratic organizing model that included selective incentives—like Anglo new model unionism. But the ability to distribute such incentives was based on control of the labor supply in the elite trades; Anglo-American workers had already reserved such control for themselves and were not predisposed to give up their power to German workers.

The most serious problem for the Chicago revolutionaries was the ethnically segmented nature of the movement, not its organizational structure. The use of ethnic ties, culture, and language to mobilize the revolutionary movement in Chicago proved to be a two-edged sword. It allowed the creation of a strong, highly mobilized, very militant movement; but it confined that movement to a minority of the working class.

Even the less privileged Anglo-American and Irish workers were unwilling to join the German revolutionary movement. German and Bohemian unions, the Socialist Labor party, the Social Revolutionary clubs, and the Central Labor Union were consistently unsuccessful when they attempted to develop long-lasting coalitions with Anglo-American and Irish unions and political groups. The socialists and anarchists were never able to counter the arguments of the Anglo-American middle and upper classes, who managed to convince Anglo and Irish workers of all economic levels that the system worked for them and that German and Bohemian revolutionaries were their enemies.

The problem was reinforced by religious differences between Anglo-American Protestants, Irish Catholics, and German and Bohemian freethinkers. Even those Anglo-American and Irish workers and residents who faced severe economic and political difficulties tended to remain in the reformist fold because they

---

*Of course, a variety of more "modern," contemporary movements have used such an organizing model as well. It is not clear how resource mobilization theorists would explain the success of the solidarity model in the 1960s and 1970s womens, student, peace, and community organizing movements (Evans 1979; Freeman 1975; Hirsch 1986).

identified with their ethnic group. The Anglo-Americans saw that many members of their group had been economically successful; the Irish saw their group develop political power.

The German and Bohemian activists succeeded on one level. They mobilized tens of thousands of Chicago residents into a movement with revolutionary ideals. But those in positions of economic and political power found it relatively easy to repress the movement. A successful urban revolution was impossible because the economic and political systems never lost legitimacy in the minds of the majority of the city's working class. Thus, when the first bomb exploded at Haymarket Square, the Anglo-American and Irish workers defended the system rather than the German anarchists.

References

Abbott, Edith
    1936   *The Tenements of Chicago*. Chicago: University of Chicago Press.
Addams, Jane
    1910   *Twenty Years at Hull House*. New York: Macmillan.
Adelman, William
    1976   *Haymarket Revisited*. Chicago: Illinois Labor History Society.
Alarm (Chicago), 1882–1887
Anderson, Perry
    1976   *Considerations on Western Marxism*. London: New Left Books.
    1977   "The Antimonies of Antonio Gramsci." *New Left Review* 100 (Nov. 1976–Jan. 1977): 5–78.
    1980   *Arguments Within English Marxism*. London: New Left Books.
Andreas, A. T.
    1884   *History of Chicago*, 3 vols. Chicago: Andreas Publishing.
Arbeiter Zeitung (Chicago) [German], 1875–1886
Ashbaugh, Carolyn
    1976   *Lucy Parsons: American Revolutionary*. Chicago: Charles A. Kerr.
Avineri, Schlomo
    1968   *The Social and Political Thought of Karl Marx*. London: Cambridge University Press.
Avrich, Paul
    1984   *The Haymarket Tragedy*. Princeton, N.J.: Princeton University Press.

Baer, Willis N.
1933   *The Economic Development of the Cigar Industry in the United States.* Lancaster, Penn.: Willis N. Baer.

Banfield, Edward C., and James Q. Wilson
1963   *City Politics.* New York: Vintage Books.

Barnett, George E.
1909   "The Printers: A Study in American Trade Unionism." *Economic Association Quarterly* 10 (Oct.): 1–387.

Barth, Fredrik (ed.)
1969   *Ethnic Groups and Boundaries.* Boston: Little, Brown.

Behen, David
1953   "The Chicago Labor Movement: Its Philosophical Basis." Ph.D. dissertation. University of Chicago.

Beijbom, Ulf
1971   *Swedes in Chicago.* Chicago: Chicago Historical Society.

Bizjack, Jack E.
1969   "The Trade and Labor Assembly of Chicago, Illinois." Master's thesis. University of Chicago.

Blumer, Herbert
1946   "Collective Behavior." In Alfred McClung Lee (ed.), *New Outline of the Principles of Sociology.* New York: Barnes and Noble, pp. 167–262.
1957   "Collective Behavior." In Joseph B. Gittler (ed.), *Review of Sociology: Analysis of a Decade.* New York: Wiley, pp. 127–58.

Bogart, Ernest Ludlow, and Charles Manfred Thompson
1920   *The Industrial State: 1870 to 1893.* Springfield: Illinois Centennial Commission.

Boggs, Carl
1976   *Gramsci's Marxism.* London: Pluto Press.

Bottomore, Tom (ed.)
1983   *A Dictionary of Marxist Thought.* Cambridge, Mass.: Harvard University Press.

Boyte, Harry
1980   *The Backyard Revolution.* Philadelphia: Temple University Press.

Bradstreet's, 1886

Brown, Emily Clark
1927   "The Book and Job Printers of Chicago." Ph.D. dissertation. University of Chicago.

Brown, Thomas N.
1976a   "Nationalism and the Irish Peasant." In Lawrence J.

McCaffrey (ed.), *Irish Nationalism and the American Contribution.* New York: Arno Press, pp. 403–45.

1976b　　"The Origins and Character of Irish-American Nationalism." In Lawrence J. McCaffrey (ed.), *Irish Nationalism and the American Contribution.* New York: Arno Press, pp. 327–58.

Browne, Henry J.
1949　　*The Catholic Church and the Knights of Labor.* Washington, D.C.: Catholic University Press.

Bruce, Robert V.
1959　　*1877: Year of Violence.* Chicago: Quadrangle Books.

Bureau of Labor Statistics of Illinois
1880　　Report. Springfield.
1882　　Report. Springfield.
1884　　Report. Springfield.
1886　　Report. Springfield.

Cahill, Marion Cotter
1932　　*Shorter Hours: A Study of the Movement Since the Civil War.* New York: Columbia University Press.

Calhoun, Craig Jackson.
1982　　*The Question of Class Struggle.* Chicago: University of Chicago Press.

Cammett, John M.
1967　　*Antonio Gramsci and the Origins of Italian Communism.* Stanford, Calif.: Stanford University Press.

Cantor, Milton
1979　　*American Working Class Culture: Explorations in American Labor and Social History.* Westport, Conn.: Greenwood Press.

Castells, Manuel
1977　　*The Urban Question.* Cambridge, Mass.: MIT Press.
1983　　*The City and the Grassroots: A Cross-Cultural Theory of Urban Social Movements.* Berkeley and Los Angeles: University of California Press.

Chandler, Alfred
1965　　*The Railroads: The Nation's First Big Business.* New York: Harcourt, Brace, and World.

Chicago Board of Education
1884　　Report on the school census.

Chicago Cigar Makers Union no. 14
1890　　Constitution and bylaws.

Chicago Daily Herald
    1880–1886
Chicago Daily News
    1865–1886
Chicago Times
    1873–1886
Chicago Tribune
    1845–1890
Chicago Typographical Union no. 16
    1880   Constitution and bylaws.
    1864–1887
                Minutes of union meetings.
Cigar Makers Official Journal
    1880–1887
Citizen (Chicago)
    1881–1888
Citizens Association of Chicago
    1884   Report of the Committee on Tenement Houses (Sept.).
Clark, Samuel, and James S. Donnelly, Jr.
    1983   *Irish Peasants: Violence and Political Unrest 1780–1914.*
                Madison: University of Wisconsin Press.
Commons, John, David J. Saposs, Helen L. Sumner, E. B. Mittelman,
    H. E. Hoagland, John B. Andrews, and Selig Perlman
    1918   *History of Labor in the United States*, 2 vols. New York:
                Macmillan.
Cressey, Paul
    1930   "The Succession of Cultural Groups in the City of Chi-
                cago." Ph.D. dissertation. University of Chicago.
Currey, Josiah Seymour
    1912   *Chicago: Its History and Its Builders: A Century of Mar-
                velous Growth.* Chicago: S. J. Clarke Publishing.
David, Henry
    1958   *History of the Haymarket Affair.* New York: Russell and
                Russell.
Dawley, Alan
    1976   *Class and Community.* Cambridge, Mass.: Harvard Uni-
                versity Press.
Department of Development and Planning of Chicago
    1976   *Historic City: The Settlement of Chicago.* Chicago: Depart-
                ment of Development and Planning of Chicago.
Deutsch, Karl W.
    1953   *Nationalism and Social Communication.* Cambridge, Mass.:
                MIT Press.

Duis, Perry
1975   "The Saloon and the Public City: Chicago and Boston, 1880
            to 1920." Ph.D. dissertation. University of Chicago.
Engels, Friedrich
1958   *Condition of the Working Class in England.* Stanford, Calif.:
            Stanford University Press.
1975   *The Housing Question.* Moscow: Progress Publishers.
Erickson, Charlotte
1957   *American Industry and the European Immigrant.* Cam-
            bridge, Mass.: Harvard University Press.
Evans, Sara
1979   *Personal Politics.* New York: Vintage Books.
Evans, Sara, and Harry Boyte
1986   *Free Spaces: The Sources of Democratic Change in Amer-
            ica.* New York: Harper & Row.
Fallows, Marjorie B.
1979   *Irish Americans: Identity and Assimilation.* Englewood
            Cliffs, N.J.: Prentice-Hall.
Fanning, Charles
1978   *Finley Peter Dunne and Mr. Dooley: The Chicago Years.*
            Lexington: University Press of Kentucky.
Fanning, Charles (ed.)
1976   *Mr. Dooley and the Chicago Irish.* New York: Arno Press.
Feldstein, Stanley, and Lawrence Costello (eds.)
1974   *The Ordeal of Assimilation.* New York: Anchor Press.
Ferree, Myra Marx, and Frederick D. Miller
1985   "Mobilization and Meaning: Toward an Integration of Social
            Psychological and Resource Perspectives on Social Move-
            ments." *Sociological Inquiry* 55 (1): 38–61.
Fireman, Bruce, and William Gamson
1979   "Utilitarian Logic in the Resource Mobilization Perspec-
            tive." In Mayer Zald and John McCarthy (eds.), *The Dy-
            namics of Social Movements.* Cambridge, Mass.: Winthrop,
            pp. 8–45.
Fischer, Claude S.
1984   *The Urban Experience,* 2nd ed. New York: Harcourt, Brace,
            Jovanovich.
Fischer, Ernst, and Franz Merek (eds.)
1972   *The Essential Lenin.* New York: Herder and Herder.
Flinn, John Joseph
1973   *History of the Chicago Police.* New York: Macmillan.

Foner, Philip
1955 *History of the Labor Movement in the United States*, vol. 2. New York: International Press.
1977 *The Great Labor Uprising of 1877*. New York: Monad Books.
Foner, Philip (ed.)
1969 *The Autobiographies of the Haymarket Martyrs*. New York: Humanities Press.
1976 *The Formation of the Workingman's Party of the United States*. New York: American Institute for Marxist Studies.
Foster, John
1974 *Class Struggle and the Industrial Revolution: Early Industrial Capitalism in Three English Towns*. New York: St. Martin's Press.
Freeman, Jo
1975 *The Politics of Women's Liberation*. New York: McKay.
1979 "Resource Mobilization and Strategy." In Mayer Zald and John McCarthy (eds.), *The Dynamics of Social Movements*. Cambridge, Mass.: Winthrop, pp. 167–89.
Funchion, Michael F.
1976 *Chicago's Irish Nationalists, 1881–1890*. New York: Arno Press.
Gamson, William
1975 *The Strategy of Social Protest*. Homewood, Ill.: Dorsey Press.
Gans, Herbert
1962 *Urban Villagers*. New York: Free Press.
Garner, Roberta
1977 *Social Movements in America*. Chicago: Norton.
Gerlach, Luther P., and Virginia H. Hine
1970 *People, Power, Change: Movements of Social Transformation*. Indianapolis: Bobbs-Merrill.
Gordon, David
1978 "Capitalist Development and the History of American Cities." In William K. Tabb and Larry Sawers (eds.), *Marxism and the Metropolis*. New York: Oxford University Press, pp. 25–63.
Gramsci, Antonio
1971 *Selections from Prison Notebooks*. New York: International Publishers.
1977 *Selections from Political Writings, 1910–1920*. New York: International Publishers.

1978 *Selections from Political Writings, 1921–1926.* New York: International Publishers.

Griffin, William D.

1973 *The Irish in America, 550 to 1972.* Dobbs Ferry, N.Y.: Oceana Publications.

Grob, Gerald N.

1976 *Workers and Utopia.* New York: Quadrangle Books.

Gutman, Herbert

1977 *Work, Culture, and Society in Industrializing America.* New York: Vintage Books.

Handlin, Oscar

1973 *The Uprooted: The Epic Story of the Great Migrations That Made the American People.* Boston: Little, Brown.

Hannan, Michael

1979 "The Dynamics of Ethnic Boundaries in Modern States." In Michael Hannan and John Meter (eds.), *National Development and the World System.* Chicago: University of Chicago Press, pp. 253–75.

Harzig, Christiane

1983 "Chicago's German North Side, 1880–1900: The Structure of a Gilded Age Ethnic Neighborhood." In Hartmut Keil and John B. Jentz (eds.), *German Workers in Industrial Chicago: A Comparative Perspective.* DeKalb: Northern Illinois University Press, pp. 127–44.

Hechter, Michael

1975 *Internal Colonialism: The Celtic Fringe in British National Development, 1536 to 1966.* Berkeley and Los Angeles: University of California Press.

1978 "Group Formation and the Cultural Division of Labor." *American Journal of Sociology* 84 (2): 293–319.

Heiss, Christine

1984 "Kommerzielle deutsche Volksbuhnen und deutsches Arbeitertheater in Chicago 1870–1910." *Amerikastudien* 29 (2): 169–82.

Higham, John

1977 *Strangers in the Land.* New York: Atheneum.

Hillquit, Morris

1977 *History of Socialism in the United States.* New York: Russell and Russell.

Hirsch, Eric

1980 "Dual Labor Market Theory: A Sociological Critique." *Sociological Inquiry* 50 (2): 133–45.

1986   "The Creation of Political Solidarity in Social Movement
            Organizations." *Sociological Quarterly* 27 (3): 373–87.
Hobsbawm, Eric
1964   *Labouring Men*. London: Weidenfeld and Nicolson.
1984   *Workers: Worlds of Labor*. New York: Pantheon.
Hofmeister, Rudolf A.
1976   *The Germans of Chicago*. Champaign, Ill.: Stipes.
Holt, Glen, and Dominic Pacyga
1979   *Chicago: A Historical Guide to the Neighborhoods*. Chi-
            cago: Chicago Historical Society.
Horak, Jakub
1928   "Assimilation of Czechs in Chicago." Ph.D. dissertation.
            University of Chicago.
Hoyt, Homer
1933   *One Hundred Years of Land Values in Chicago: The Rela-
            tion of the Growth of Chicago to the Rise in Its Land Value*.
            Chicago: University of Chicago Press.
1939   *The Structure and Growth of Residential Neighborhoods in
            American Cities*. Washington, D.C.: U.S. Federal Housing
            Administration.
Hull House Maps and Papers
1970   New York: Arno Press.
Hunter, Robert
1901   Report of the Investigating Committee of the City Homes
            Association. Chicago.
Illinois State House of Representatives
1879   Report of the Special Committee on Labor. Springfield.
Inland Printer
1878–1890
Inter-Ocean (Chicago)
1875–1888
Janowitz, Morris
1952   *The Community Press in an Urban Setting*. Chicago: Uni-
            versity of Chicago Press.
Jenkins, J. Craig
1983   "Resource Mobilization Theory and the Study of Social
            Movements." *Annual Review of Sociology* 9:527–53.
Jerome, Harry
1926   *Migration and Business Cycles*. New York: National Bureau
            of Economic Research.
Johnson, Stanley
1966   *A History of Emigration from the United Kingdom to North
            America, 1763–1912*. London: F. Cass.

Karson, Marc
1958   *American Labor Unions and Politics 1900–1918.* Carbondale: Southern Illinois University Press.
Katznelson, Ira
1981   *City Trenches: Urban Politics and the Patterning of Class in the United States.* New York: Pantheon.
Katznelson, Ira, and Aristide R. Zolberg (eds.)
1986   *Working Class Formation: Nineteenth-Century Patterns in Western Europe and the United States.* Princeton, N.J.: Princeton University Press.
Keil, Hartmut
1986   "The Impact of Haymarket on German-American Radicalism." *International Labor and Working Class History* 29 (1): 16–27.
Keil, Hartmut, and John B. Jentz (eds.)
1981   "German Workers in Industrial Chicago: The Transformation of Industries and Neighborhoods in the Late Nineteenth Century." Paper presented at the convention of the Organization of American Historians. Detroit, April 1–4.
1983   *German Workers in Industrial Chicago, 1850–1910: A Comparative Perspective.* DeKalb: Northern Illinois University Press.
Knights of Labor (Chicago)
1886–1889
Laslett, John, and Seymour Martin Lipset
1974   *Failure of a Dream: Essays in the History of American Socialism.* Garden City, N.Y.: Doubleday.
Laurie, Bruce
1979   "Nothing on Compulsion: Lifestyles of Philadelphia Artisans, 1820–1850." In Milton Cantor (ed.), *American Working Class Culture: Explorations in American Labor and Social History.* Westport, Conn.: Greenwood Press, pp. 91–120.
Le Bon, Gustave
1960   *The Crowd: A Study of the Popular Mind.* Robert K. Merton, ed. New York: Viking Books.
Lenin, Vladimir
1966   *The Essential Works of Lenin.* Henry M. Christman, ed. New York: Bantam Books.
Levine, Edward M.
1966   *The Irish and Irish Politicians.* Notre Dame, Ind.: University of Notre Dame Press.

Lightner, David
　　1977　　　*Labor on the Illinois Central Railroad, 1852 to 1900.* New York: Arno Press.
Long, Clarence D.
　　1960　　　*Wages and Earnings in the United States.* Princeton, N.J.: Princeton University Press.
Marx, Karl
　　1972　　　"The Eighteenth Brumaire of Louis Bonaparte." In Robert C. Tucker (ed.), *The Marx-Engels Reader.* New York: Norton, pp. 436–525.
Marx, Karl, and Friedrich Engels
　　1972　　　"Manifesto of the Communist Party." In Robert C. Tucker (ed.), *The Marx-Engels Reader.* New York: Norton, pp. 331–61.
Matthews, Fred H.
　　1977　　　*Quest for an American Sociology: Robert E. Park and the Chicago School.* Montreal: McGill-Queens University Press.
McAdam, Douglas
　　1982　　　*Political Process and the Development of Black Insurgency 1930–1970.* Chicago: University of Chicago Press.
McCaffrey, Lawrence (ed.)
　　1976　　　*Irish Nationalism and the American Contribution.* New York: Arno Press.
McCarthy, Eugene
　　1950　　　"The Bohemians of Chicago and Their Benevolent Societies: 1875–1946." Master's thesis. University of Chicago.
McCarthy, John, and Mayer N. Zald
　　1973　　　*The Trend of Social Movements in America; Professionalization and Resource Mobilization.* Morristown, N.J.: General Learning Press.
　　1977　　　"Resource Mobilization and Social Movements: A Partial Theory." *American Journal of Sociology* 82 (6): 1212–39.
Merrington, John
　　1977　　　"Theory and Practice in Gramsci's Marxism." In *Western Marxism: A Critical Reader.* London: New Left Books, pp. 140–75.
Mollenkopf, John.
　　1981　　　"Community and Accumulation." In Michael Dear and Allen J. Scott (eds.), *Urbanization and Urban Planning in Capitalist Society.* New York: Methuen, pp. 319–38.

Moore, Barrington
    1978   *Injustice: The Social Bases of Obedience and Revolt.* White Plains, N.Y.: M.E. Sharpe.

Morris, Aldon
    1984   *The Origins of the Civil Rights Movement.* New York: Free Press.

Musson, A. E.
    1976   "Class Struggle and the Labor Aristocracy." *Social History* 12 (3) (Oct.): 335–56.

Myers, Howard Barton
    1929   "The Policing of Labor Disputes in Chicago: A Case Study." Ph.D. dissertation. University of Chicago.

Nelson, Bruce
    1981   "Counting Anarchists: The Numbers and Patterns in Anarchist Organizations in Chicago, 1880–1886." Paper presented to the Labor History Group, Illinois Labor History Society. Chicago, May 22.
    1986a   "Dancing and Picknicking Anarchists?: The Movement Below the Martyred Leadership." In Dave Roediger and Franklin Rosemont (eds.), *Haymarket Scrapbook.* Chicago: Charles Kerr, pp. 76–79.
    1986b   "'We Can't Get Them to Do Aggressive Work': Chicago's Anarchists and the Eight-Hour Movement." *International Labor and Working Class History* 29 (1): 1–13.

Nielsen, Francois
    1980   "The Flemish Movement in Belgium After World War II: A Dynamic Analysis." *American Sociological Review* 45 (1): 76–94.

Noyes, P. H.
    1966   *Organization and Revolution: Working Class Associations in the German Revolution of 1848–1849.* Princeton, N.J.: Princeton University Press.

Oberschall, Anthony
    1973   *Social Conflict and Social Movements.* Englewood Cliffs, N.J.: Prentice-Hall.

O'Brien, David J.
    1975   *Neighborhood Organization and Interest Group Processes.* Princeton, N.J.: Princeton University Press.

O'Ferrall, Fergus
    1985   *Catholic Emancipation: Daniel O'Connell and the Birth of Irish Democracy 1820–30.* Atlantic Highlands, N.J.: Humanities Press International.

Olson, Mancur
    1965   *The Logic of Collective Action.* Cambridge, Mass.: Harvard
                University Press.
Olzak, Susan, and Joane Nagel (eds.)
    1986   *Competitive Ethnic Relations.* Orlando, Fla.: Academic
                Press.
Park, Robert E.
    1967   *Robert E. Park on Social Control and Collective Behavior.*
                Ralph Turner, ed. Chicago: University of Chicago Press.
Park, Robert E., and Ernest Burgess
    1967   *The City.* Chicago: University of Chicago Press.
Parkin, Frank
    1979   *Marxism and Class Theory: A Bourgeois Critique.* London:
                Tavistock.
Parsons, Lucy
    1889   *The Life of Albert Parsons.* Chicago: n.p.
Pennsylvania State Senate and House of Representatives
    1878   Report of the Committee Appointed to Investigate the Rail-
                road Riots in July 1877. Harrisburg, May 23.
Pierce, Bessie Louise
    1957   A *History of Chicago,* 3 vols. Chicago: University of Chi-
                cago Press.
Pinard, Maurice
    1971   *The Rise of a Third Party.* Englewood Cliffs, N.J.: Prentice-
                Hall.
Piper, Ruth
    1936   "The Irish in Chicago." Master's thesis. University of
                Chicago.
Piven, Frances, and Richard Cloward
    1977   *Poor People's Movements.* New York: Pantheon.
Portes, Alejandro, and Robert D. Manning
    1986   "The Immigrant Enclave: Theory and Empirical Examples."
                In Susan Olzak and Joane Nagel (eds.), *Competitive Ethnic
                Relations.* Orlando, Fla.: Academic Press, pp. 47–68.
Ragin, Charles
    1979   "Ethnic Political Mobilization: The Welsh Case." *American
                Sociological Review* 44 (4): 619–35.
Railway Age (Chicago)
    1876–1888
Rakove, Milton
    1975   *Don't Make No Waves, Don't Back No Losers.* Bloom-
                ington: Indiana University Press.

Robinson, Thomas
  1925   "Chicago Typographical Union no. 16: Fifty Years of Devel-
             opment with Emphasis on Its Relations with the Daily
             Newspaper Publishers." Ph.D. dissertation. University of
             Chicago.
Roediger, Dave, and Franklin Rosemont (eds.)
  1986   *Haymarket Scrapbook*. Chicago: Charles H. Kerr Pub-
             lishing.
Rosenblum, Gerald
  1973   *Immigrant Workers: Their Impact on American Labor
             Radicalism*. New York: Basic Books.
Salert, Barbara
  1976   *Revolution and Revolutionaries: Four Theories*. New York:
             Elsevier.
Saunders, Peter
  1981   *Social Theory and the Urban Question*. New York: Holmes
             and Meier.
Schaaf, Barbara
  1977   *Mr. Dooley's Chicago*. Garden City, N.Y.: Anchor Press.
Schneirov, Richard
  1975   "The 1877 Great Upheaval: Life by Labor or Death by
             Fight." Paper. Chicago Historical Society.
  1984   "The Knights of Labor in the Chicago Labor Movement
             and in Municipal Politics: 1877–1887." Ph.D. dissertation.
             Northern Illinois University.
Schoff, S. S.
  1873   *The Glory of Chicago: Her Manufactories*. Chicago: Knight
             and Leonard.
See, Katherine O'Sullivan
  1979   "Toward a Theory of Ethnic Nationalism: A Comparison of
             Northern Ireland and Quebec." Ph.D. dissertation. Uni-
             versity of Chicago.
Sennett, Richard
  1969   "Middle Class Families and Urban Violence: The Experi-
             ence of a Chicago Community in the Nineteenth Century."
             In Stephen Thernstrom and Richard Sennett (eds.), *Nine-
             teenth Century Cities: Essays in Urban History*. New Ha-
             ven, Conn.: Yale University Press, pp. 386–420.
  1974   *Families Against the City: Middle Class Homes of Indus-
             trial Chicago. 1872–1890*. New York: Vintage Books.
Skocpol, Theda
  1979   *States and Social Revolutions*. Cambridge, England: Cam-
             bridge University Press.

Skogan, Wesley
   1976   *Chicago Since 1840: A Time-Series Data Handbook.* Champaign, Ill.: Institute of Government and Public Affairs.
Smelser, Neil
   1962   *A Theory of Collective Behavior.* New York: Free Press.
Snow, David A., Louis A. Zurcher, and Sheldon Ekland-Olson
   1980   "Social Networks and Social Movements: A Microstructural Approach to Differential Recruitment." *American Sociological Review* 45 (5): 787–801.
Staats Zeitung (Illinois) [German]
   1865–1887
Staley, Eugene
   1930   *History of the Illinois State Federation of Labor.* Chicago: University of Chicago Press.
Stead, William T.
   1964   *If Christ Came to Chicago.* New York: Clarion.
Stearns, Peter N., and Daniel Walkowitz
   1974   *Workers in the Industrial Revolution: Recent Studies of Labor in the United States and Europe.* New Brunswick, N.J.: Transaction Books.
Steinberg, Steven
   1981   *The Ethnic Myth.* Boston: Beacon Press.
Suttles, Gerald
   1968   *The Social Order of the Slum.* Chicago: University of Chicago Press.
Taine, Hippolyte
   1868   *The Origins of Contemporary France.* n.p.
Tarde, Gabriel
   1969   *On Communication and Social Influence.* Chicago: Phoenix Books.
Thernstrom, Stephen, and Richard Sennett (eds.)
   1969   *Nineteenth Century Cities: Essays on Urban History.* New Haven, Conn.: Yale University Press.
Thompson, E. P.
   1963   *The Making of the English Working Class.* New York: Vintage Books.
   1978   *The Poverty of Theory and Other Essays.* New York: Monthly Review Press.
Tilly, Charles
   1978   *From Mobilization to Revolution.* Reading, Mass.: Addison-Wesley.

Townsend, Andrew
    1927   "The Germans of Chicago." Ph.D. dissertation. University of Chicago.
Turner, Ralph H., and Lewis Killian
    1987   *Collective Behavior,* 3rd ed. Englewood Cliffs, N.J.: Prentice-Hall.
U.S. Census of Population
    1870, 1880, 1890
U.S. Department of Labor
    1898   Bulletin no. 18, "Wages in the United States and Europe." Washington, D.C., Sept.
U.S. Senate
    1885   Report of the Committee of the Senate Upon the Relations Between Capital and Labor. 4 vols. Washington, D.C.
    1911   Reports of the Immigration Commission. Vol. 4, "Emigration Conditions in Europe." Washington, D.C.
Van den Berghe, Pierre
    1967   *Race and Racism: A Comparative Perspective.* New York: Wiley.
Vorbote (Chicago) [German]
    1881–1886
Walker, Mack
    1964   *Germany and the Emigration, 1816 to 1885.* Cambridge, Mass.: Harvard University Press.
Weeks, Joseph D.
    1880   Report on the Statistics of Wages in the Manufacturing Industries. Tenth Census of the United States, pp. 39–50.
Whyte, William Foote
    1943   *Street Corner Society.* Chicago: University of Chicago Press.
Wirth, Louis
    1964   *Louis Wirth on Cities and Social Life.* Albert J. Reiss, ed. Chicago: University of Chicago Press.
Wittke, Carl
    1952   *Refugees of Revolution: The German Forty-Eighters in America.* Philadelphia: University of Pennsylvania Press.
    1956   *The Irish in America.* Baton Rouge: Louisiana State University Press.
Workingman's Advocate (Chicago)
    1864–1876
Zald, Mayer N., and Roberta Ash
    1965   "Social Movement Organizations: Growth, Decay, and Change." *Social Forces* 44 (3): 327–41.

Index

Immigration (*continued*)
  political assimilation models and, 200;
  German, 12, 149–52, 156; Irish,
  119–23; nativism and, 108–10; social
  movement theory and, 185–86. *See
  also individual nationalities*
Immiseration, of working class, 173, 174
Inclusive strategy, union, 3–4, 5, 54
Income, 95–98; Anglo-American, 95–98,
  124, 151, 153; German, 95, 151; Irish,
  95, 96, 124; of labor aristocracy, 9–10,
  96–98, 176; low-status worker's, 9–10,
  95–98; unskilled worker's, 9–10,
  95–98, 151. *See also* Wages
Industrialization, xiii, xv, 1–10, 84; British and, 88–89, 90; Germans and, 147,
  150, 170; political mobilization theories
  and, 172–81 passim, 189, 195–201 pas-
  sim, 215, 217. *See also* Mechanization
Industrial union organizing model, 3–4, 6
Inflation, 15–16
Injustice (Moore), 214
Inland Printer, 4, 104
Inspectors, reformists and, 57, 114
Insurgent consciousness, 209
Interdependency, social movement the-
  ory and, 183
International (Workingmen's Association):
  and depression, 17–18, 83; Germans and,
  13, 17, 41, 82, 83, 144; Irish and, 117
International Carpenters and Joiners, 68
International economics, and German
  guilds, 147
International Typographical Union, 51
International Union, cigar makers,
  49–51, 52–53
International Workingmen's Association.
  See International
International Working People's Associa-
  tion, 44. *See also* Black International
Inter-Ocean, 29, 30, 74
Investment, in Chicago, xiii
Ireland, 119–20, 129–30, 138
Irish Americans, 117–43; and anarchism,
  117, 129, 134, 135, 143, 158, 169, 170;
  class analysis and, 181–82; and coalitions, 117, 135, 143, 178, 218 (*see also*
  Knights of Labor); and eight-hour day,
  66–67, 68, 69, 70, 84; and Haymarket
  affair, 73, 75, 117, 128, 133–34, 219;
  immigration of, 119–23; income of, 95,
  96, 124; Irish nationalism of, 126, 127,
  129–35, 142–43, 191, 204, 205–6,
  209, 217; and mass strikes, 21, 22,
  41–42, 83, 118, 141, 181–82; occupational status of, 91, 94, 123–24, 142,

199; in politics, 114–18 passim, 127,
  135–41, 142, 143, 152, 168, 169, 170,
  182, 191, 205, 216, 217–18, 219; population of, 87; and railroad and general
  strike (1877), 28, 41–42, 82; reformist,
  83, 114–18 passim, 124–29 passim,
  134–35, 141–43, 178, 216, 218–19;
  and religion, 108, 119–42 passim, 200;
  residence of, 103, 125–26, 127, 182,
  202, 205, 206; unskilled, 14, 83, 118,
  121–22, 135, 136, 137–38, 199; and
  worker resistance groups, 22, 117
Irish Home Rule Bill, 132–33
Irish National Land League, 126,
  131–32, 135
Iron molders: benefit systems of, 91; and
  coalitions, 47, 56; craft union model of,
  3; German, 37, 155; Irish, 114, 118;
  Irish police and, 114; in labor aristocracy, 8; and SLP, 37
Iron Molders Union, 3
Iron workers: craft union model of, 4–5;
  and eight-hour day, 70; Irish, 118, 124;
  mass strikes by, 118. *See also* Iron
  molders
Irrationality, social movement theory
  and, 183–85, 186
Isolation: German, 204; of Irish, 125–26,
  127, 205–6; of revolutionary sects,
  213–14. *See also* Ethnic enclaves;
  Havens
Italians, nativism and, 109

Jaeger Verein, 39, 44, 46
Jahn, Friedrich, 158–59
Jentz, John B., 151, 155
Johnson, Andrew, 130
Joiners: and coalitions, 47, 56, 58; and de-
  pression, 17; and eight-hour day, 63,
  68, 69, 71–72; German, 17, 47, 58,
  71–72, 83
Journeymen, in Germany, 147–48
Judges: election, 114, 141; United Labor
  Party, 79

Katznelson, Ira, 103, 180–82, 213
Keil, Hartmut, 151, 155
Kendrick, Archbishop, 128
Kenna, Michael "Hinky Dink," 140
Kilgubbin settlement, 125
Killian, Lewis, 214
Knights of Labor, 54–62; and anarchism,
  54–62, 75, 78, 128, 134, 158; Anglo-
  Americans and, 192; and eight-hour
  day, 66–67, 70, 84, 143; and Hay-
  market affair, 75, 79–80, 117, 128;

Compositor: G & S Typesetters, Inc.
Text: 11/13 Caledonia
Display: Caledonia
Printer: Braun-Brumfield, Inc.
Binder: Braun-Brumfield, Inc.